Before You Were Born, I Anointed You

Uncovering Scripture's "Hidden" Female Prophets

ANNA BERESFORD

WIPF & STOCK · Eugene, Oregon

BEFORE YOU WERE BORN, I ANOINTED YOU
Uncovering Scripture's "Hidden" Female Prophets

Copyright © 2022 Anna Beresford. All rights reserved. Except for brief quotations in critical publications or reviews, no part of this book may be reproduced in any manner without prior written permission from the publisher. Write: Permissions, Wipf and Stock Publishers, 199 W. 8th Ave., Suite 3, Eugene, OR 97401.

Wipf & Stock
An Imprint of Wipf and Stock Publishers
199 W. 8th Ave., Suite 3
Eugene, OR 97401

www.wipfandstock.com

PAPERBACK ISBN: 978-1-6667-3748-6
HARDCOVER ISBN: 978-1-6667-9697-1
EBOOK ISBN: 978-1-6667-9698-8

"The Visitation" by Malcolm Guite is © Malcolm Guite, 2012. Published by Canterbury Press. Used by permission. rights@hymnsam.co.uk.

The Scripture quotations contained herein, unless otherwise indicated, are from the New Revised Standard Version Bible: Catholic Edition (NRSVCE) copyright © 1993 and 1989 by the Division of Christian Education of the National Council of the Churches of Christ in the United States of America. Used by permission. All rights reserved worldwide.

Scripture texts in this work designated (NABRE) are taken from the New American Bible, revised edition © 2010, 1991, 1986, 1970 Confraternity of Christian Doctrine, Washington, D.C. and are used by permission of the copyright owner. All Rights Reserved. No part of the New American Bible may be reproduced in any form without permission in writing from the copyright owner.

Scripture quotations marked (NLT) are taken from the Holy Bible, New Living Translation, copyright ©1996, 2004, 2015 by Tyndale House Foundation. Used by permission of Tyndale House Publishers, Carol Stream, Illinois 60188. All rights reserved.

Scripture quotations marked (KJV) from The Authorized (King James) Version. Rights in the Authorized Version in the United Kingdom are vested in the Crown. Reproduced by permission of the Crown's patentee, Cambridge University Press.

Scripture quotations marked (NET) are from the NET Bible® https://netbible.com copyright ©1996, 2019 used with permission from Biblical Studies Press, L.L.C. All rights reserved.

Scripture quotations marked (NIV) are taken from the Holy Bible, New International Version®, NIV®. Copyright © 1973, 1978, 1984, 2011 by Biblica, Inc.™ Used by permission of Zondervan. All rights reserved worldwide. www.zondervan.com. The "NIV" and "New International Version" are trademarks registered in the United States Patent and Trademark Office by Biblica, Inc.™

The Visitation

MALCOLM GUITE

Here is a meeting made of hidden joys,
Of lightenings cloistered in a narrow place,
From quiet hearts the sudden flame of praise
And in the womb the quickening kick of grace.
Two women on the very edge of things
Unnoticed and unknown to men of power,
But in their flesh the hidden Spirit sings
And in their lives the buds of blessing flower.
And Mary stands with all we call "too young,"
Elizabeth with all called "past their prime."
They sing today for all the great unsung,
Women who turned eternity to time,
Favored of heaven, outcast on the earth,
Prophets who bring the best in us to birth.

Table of Contents

Acknowledgments .... *ix*
Introduction .... *xi*
1. Prophets 1
2. Parables 16
3. Named Female Prophets 34
4. Unnamed Female Prophets 56
5. What Do You See? 71
6. The Forgiven Woman 78
7. Whose Wife Will She Be? 98
8. The Woman Caught in Adultery 118
9. The Canaanite Woman 135
10. Conclusion—Why Is This Important? 156
Bibliography 163
Subject/Names Index 179
Scripture Index 187

Acknowledgments

Many thanks to the kind and helpful people at Wipf & Stock who helped bring this project to fruition.

A special thank you to my husband, Tom—encourager, proofreader, devil's advocate, and heresy checker. This book is better because of you.

Introduction

> There's no such thing as an uninteresting life, such a thing is an impossibility. Beneath the dullest exterior, there is a drama, a comedy, a tragedy.
> —Mark Twain

I've always been fascinated by people's stories and how our upbringing and the stories we are told about ourselves can mold the people we become. My work as a chaplain in a psychiatric hospital affords me the privilege of being invited into the often secret, broken, and painful parts of someone's life as they share their stories with me. I am constantly amazed and humbled by the courage, strength, and level of trust patients demonstrate when they disclose issues and events that have often had a catastrophic impact on their lives. If I have learned anything, it is that you can't judge a book by its cover, and, as Mark Twain once said, "inside of the dullest exterior, there is a drama, a comedy, and a tragedy."[1]

When I read the stories in the Bible, I tend to look for the drama, comedy, and tragedy in characters often considered to be peripheral to the "real action." It is disappointing that these characters are usually women, but it is also not surprising as, until fairly recently, most theological scholarship and discourse was conducted by white, middle-class, middle-aged men. It was not until the advent of various liberation theologies that an attempt has been made to give a voice to the vulnerable, marginalized, and voiceless.

The Bible does have some stories "starring" women—Deborah features prominently in the book of Judges, while Esther, Judith, and Ruth have books named after them (although Judith and parts of Esther are considered apocryphal by some Christian communities). The vast majority of female characters, however, are either only referred to fleetingly, and are

---

1. "Life," para. 14.

Introduction

therefore considered to be bit players making cameo appearances, or their contributions to the moral of the story are subsumed because the main focus is firmly on whatever the male characters are doing or saying.

However, given the patriarchal context within which these stories are set and the fact that the authors were probably mostly male, that there are so many female characters at all should give us pause. Perhaps the authors' intent was obvious to the audiences for whom the stories were written, but given the distance of thousands of years, not to mention vastly different cultures and traditions, I believe that for modern readers, these women's stories warrant closer scrutiny.

For example, what was the author trying to convey through the story of Lot's daughters? Over the course of two nights, the daughters made Lot drunk in order to have sex with him so they could bear children (Gen 19:30–38). I suspect not too many sermons have been preached on that text!

Of interest, too, is the genealogy found in Matthew's Gospel that lists the names of five women—Tamar, Rahab, Ruth, Bathsheba, and Mary. Apart from the fact that it was most unusual to include women in genealogies of that time, it can be argued that the five women mentioned had very questionable backgrounds. Tamar disguised herself as a prostitute in order to seduce her father-in-law, Rahab was a prostitute, Ruth (on the instructions of her mother-in-law, Naomi) seduced Boaz, Bathsheba allegedly committed adultery with King David, and Mary became pregnant out of wedlock. What were Matthew and, more importantly, the authors of the original stories trying to tell their audiences?

It is the premise of this book that the authors were endeavoring to shine a light on a society that was unwilling to recognize the plight of its most vulnerable, and they chose to use the prophetic "voice" of women to do so.

Over the next few chapters, we'll look in depth at the stories of some of the women mentioned above, as well as some other memorable female characters. A lot of stories are confronting and raise some uncomfortable questions, not least of which are questions surrounding Jesus' own level of compassion, motives, and acceptance of his mission. How, for example, are we to reconcile the image of Jesus as the fulfillment of Isaiah's suffering servant who came to serve all people with the image of a man who treats a woman desperate to find healing for her daughter with disdain, likening

INTRODUCTION

her to a dog? How compassionate is it to carry on a theological discussion when there is a clearly distressed woman weeping at your feet?

These difficult questions arise when the focus is purely on what the perceived main characters are doing or saying. It is the contention of this book that these uncomfortable questions can only be answered adequately when the stories are seen as enacted parables. When viewed through this lens, the women and the situations in which they find themselves highlight the extent to which their respective societies had strayed from their covenantal obligations and become morally bankrupt. It was precisely in these circumstances that prophets were called to bring the authorities to account. As the human "signs" in these enacted parables, the women fulfilled the role of prophet in the same way as Isaiah, Ezekiel, and Jeremiah did in their enacted parables.

The at-times bizarre actions of some of these male prophets were signs through which the original audiences were confronted with the consequences of their hard-heartedness, scrupulousness, and lack of compassion. In the same way, we are invited to look through the situations in which these women found themselves to see the reality of what life in God's kingdom is meant to be.

In order to lay the foundation, the first chapter will deal with the role of the Old Testament prophet, various stereotypes surrounding those called to the office, and the difference between being a prophet and acting in a prophetic manner—a difference which is integral to uncovering Scripture's hidden female prophets. In the second chapter, we will discuss the use of parables in general before turning our attention to how and in what circumstances prophets used enacted parables. The third chapter will look at the stories of those women recognized as being prophets either in Scripture or Jewish tradition. Succeeding chapters will consider the lives and contexts of other female characters I believe fulfill a prophetic ministry when their stories are interpreted through the lens of enacted parables.

The authors of the various biblical texts crafted their stories very carefully—every situation, every character, had a purpose and contributed to the overall point being made. It is important not to be blinded by the action taking place between what seem to be the "main" characters. It is often the one who is silenced that has the most to teach.

It is the aim of this book to give these silenced women their voice and, in so doing, reveal their prophetic ministry.

1

Prophets

We can always be sure of one thing—that the messengers of discomfort and sacrifice will be stoned and pelted by those who wish to preserve at all costs their own contentment. This is not a lesson that is confined to the Testaments.
—CHRISTOPHER HITCHENS

Introduction

For many, the word "prophet" probably conjures up the image of a somewhat-disheveled, wild-eyed male bearing a remarkable likeness to Charlton Heston in the Cecil B. DeMille movie *The Ten Commandments*. This imagined prophet would spend his time railing against the injustices of the day and leading a large, albeit reluctant, group of newly liberated slaves to freedom by parting large bodies of water. This is not surprising given the at-times bizarre behavior attributed to many Old Testament prophets. Ezekiel is said to have lain on his side staring at the city walls for a total of 430 days (Ezek 4:1–8), while Isaiah walked naked and barefoot for three years as a portent against Egypt and Ethiopia (Isa 20:3). This type of behavior led authorities to see them as hostile, abrasive cranks whose speeches were most unwelcome.[1] In the New Testament, John the Baptist is described as

---

1. Brueggemann, "Truth-Telling," 1096.

wearing "clothing of camel's hair with a leather belt around his waist, and his food was locusts and wild honey" (Matt 3:4).

That the image would almost certainly be male is also not surprising given that the prophetic writings are attributed to men and most other named prophets are believed to be men, as are the members of groups, or schools, of prophets. Whether these assumptions are correct will be discussed later.

That the role was considered to be of great importance cannot be argued. Apart from the sixteen prophets who have books named after them (the exploits of whom take up a considerable part of the Old Testament),[2] the Old Testament names a further seventeen men as being prophets. There is also mention of the "400 prophets" (1 Kgs 22:6) and the "company of prophets" (2 Kgs 2:3, 5, 7). Distinctions are usually made between the major prophets (Isaiah, Ezekiel, Jeremiah, and Daniel) and the minor prophets (Hosea, Joel, Amos, Obadiah, Jonah, Micah, Nahum, Habakkuk, Zephaniah, Haggai, Zechariah, and Malachi). This distinction is not a reflection on the importance or accuracy of the prophets or their prophecies—rather, it refers to the length of the book(s) attributed to them.

Another distinction is between the so-called "writing" and "non-writing" prophets. Written prophecy appeared around the eighth century BCE, with the last book (Malachi) being dated at around the fourth century BCE, a time frame of some five hundred years.[3] Morgan suggests that the appearance of written prophecy coincided with the time Israel went from being a theocracy to a monarchy.[4] It was the prophet's role to remind both the king and the people that they were to act as a theocracy amongst other nations in order to reveal what it meant to have God as their king.

Israel's enemies were also prophetically well-endowed, boasting 450 prophets of Baal and 400 prophets of Asherah (1 Kgs 18:19). By contrast, the Old Testament names only five female prophets: Miriam, Deborah, Huldah, Noadiah, and the prophetess of Isa 8:3.[5]

There is far less mention of prophets in the New Testament, with only nine men and five women mentioned. Of these, only John the Baptist is recognized as a prophet in the traditional sense (Matt 11:9–11). Others, while they may have been designated as prophets or teachers (Acts 13:1,

---

2. The Catholic and Orthodox canons include Baruch, making the total seventeen.
3. Lewis, *Minor Prophets*, 10.
4. Morgan, *Voices*, 8.
5. Jewish tradition also considers Sarah, Hannah, Abigail, and Esther to be prophets.

21:9), were seen to be demonstrating various "gifts of the spirit" (1 Cor 12:4–11) rather than fulfilling a true prophetic ministry. Nevertheless, the sheer numbers involved would indicate that the stories contained in the prophetic books and elsewhere in Scripture are only the tip of Israel's prophetic iceberg.

So, what was the role of the prophet? Over the years, there has been a variety of opinions put forth, the main ones of which we will discuss below.

The Role of the Prophet

How many people routinely think of prophets or the place, if any, of prophecy in the world today? While it is not unusual for people to read their stars, I suspect the whole concept of prophets and prophecy is something that many believe belongs in the past and has little or no relevance in a time where reason is valued above all else and where things that are considered overtly "religious" are looked upon with either suspicion or ridicule. Ironically, the practice in many churches of preaching almost exclusively from the Gospels leads to the impression, albeit probably unintentionally, that the Hebrew Scriptures have been superseded by the New Testament and that all we need to know is contained in the Gospels. This is, of course, not the case. The evangelists themselves recognized the importance of the Hebrew Scriptures as the foundation of any kind of understanding of the New Testament. It was common for them to state that something occurred so that a certain prophecy could be fulfilled (e.g., Matt 8:17, Mark 14:49, Luke 4:21, John 12:38).

Indeed, Tucker points out that if the prophets cannot be read as if they were speaking directly to us today, then there is very little point in reading the rest of the Old Testament and most of the New Testament either.[6]

There are three main "offices" described in the Old Testament: prophet, priest, and king. Kreider has summarized the functions of these roles as being the following: a prophet speaks for God, a priest mediates between God and people, and a king reigns over people and territory.[7] The offices of priest and king were mostly hereditary, whereas a prophet was called by God. This meant it was not usual for one individual to fulfill more than one of the offices. Indeed, Tiemeier has suggested that since prophets were charismatic figures, whereas priests were institutional, the two offices were

6. Tucker, "Role of the Prophets," 159.
7. Kreider, "Jesus the Messiah," 176–77.

often in tension.[8] However, Kreider has identified four people whom he believes did exercise both these offices—Adam, Melchizedek, Moses, and David. He considers them as "types" of the coming Messiah.[9] Berkhof identifies Calvin as being the first person to draw attention to the importance of distinguishing the threefold office of Jesus.[10]

Of these three offices, it is arguably that of the prophet that causes the most confusion. Petersen suggests the confusion is due to the fact that the roles of king and priest have survived down the ages, whereas prophets seem to have been relegated to another time and place. This unfamiliarity with the prophetic role has meant that each society has injected its own value structures and models into the discussion when speaking about Israel's prophets.[11] Lessing believes that unlike the roles of priest and king, which carried institutional authority, prophets had to convince audiences of the divine origin of their calling, which, in an increasingly secular society, is yet another hurdle any would-be prophet would face today.[12]

Weber states that the distinguishing feature between prophets and priests was the prophet's personal call. He argues that while the priest's authority was gained through his service in a sacred tradition, the prophet's authority was due to his personal revelation from God and his charisma—his presence drew people to him.[13] Petersen disagrees, stating that the concept of Israel's prophets as charismatic[14] leaders does not fit well with what we know about them, nor is there much evidence they exercised any form of leadership role.[15] In fact, Wolff claims that rather than being charismatic leaders, most of the prophets were outsiders who dwelt on the periphery of society rather than being members of any central group within their society. He also maintains that the appearance of the prophets was purely occasional, triggered when the marginalized in society were being mistreated

---

8. Tiemeier, "Catholic Feminism," 60.
9. Kreider, "Jesus the Messiah," 178–85.
10. Berkhof, *Systematic Theology*, 356.
11. Petersen, "Ways of Thinking," 1.
12. Lessing, "Preaching Like the Prophets," 401.
13. Weber, "Prophet," 99.
14. In this context, the term "charismatic" refers to a person's attractiveness or popularity, rather than the theological usage that suggests the possession of a charism, or "gift of the Spirit."
15. Petersen, *Role of Israel's Prophets*, 15, 11.

as a result of institutional decay.[16] There were, of course, exceptions. For example, Nathan is portrayed as being a kingmaker when, together with Bathsheba, he ensured Solomon was made king instead of Solomon's brother Adonijah (1 Kgs 1:5–31).

What is beyond doubt is that if they were doing their job properly, prophets were very inconvenient people to have around. They condemned the practices of kings (2 Sam 12:4–14), priests (Ezek 22:26), and society's elite (Amos 4:1). Their edgy messages were a counterpoint to the foolishness and hardheadedness of the people they addressed. They were usually unpopular with those in positions of power and privilege and had to deal with victimization, vilification, and even attempted murder (Jer 38:4–6).

So, given the confusion over their role, what have been some of the views regarding the function of Israel's prophets?

Interpreters of the Law

This view is proposed by Stanglin, who believes that the prophet's main responsibility was to interpret the law and call the people back to their covenantal responsibilities.[17] Weber agrees, stating that the core of the prophet's mission was to articulate doctrines based on the commandments and to ensure that Israel adhered to them.[18] Tucker, however, disagrees, suggesting it is a mistake to look to the prophets for any type of doctrinal interpretation because they did not organize their addresses systematically with a view to answering a particular theological question, nor did they write down many of their pronouncements—they addressed a particular problem at a particular time.[19]

Defenders of the Covenant

Another popular view is that the prophet's role was to remind the people of their covenantal responsibilities toward God and toward each other.[20] The Mosaic covenant outlined how God expected the Israelites to order

16. Wolff, "Prophets and Institutions," 7–8.
17. Stanglin, "Spiritus Propheticus," 33.
18. Weber, "Prophet," 100.
19. Tucker, "Role of the Prophets," 162.
20. Oswalt, "Anything Unique," 172.

their lives in response to God's act of delivering them from slavery (Exod 20:2). The covenant was designed to strengthen the Israelites' relationship with God (Exod 20:3–11), each other (Exod 20:12–18), the stranger in their midst (Exod 23:9), and the rest of creation (Exod 23:10–12) and, as such, combined gratitude, awe, and religious observance, and was instrumental in preserving the peace.[21] Covenantal observance would ultimately have a positive impact on the people's moral, political, spiritual, and economic development.[22]

To this end, the prophets often railed against the rulers of the day, both political and religious, accusing them of believing they were fulfilling their obligations by the performance of external rituals based upon the bare letter of the law.[23] This has led to a popular view that prophets were radicals, intent on changing society and introducing new, more compassionate but subversive ideals into society. However, Fretheim argues that this was not the case. He believes the prophets were not radicals but conservatives—they recognized that social justice was a value which was embedded into the very fabric of the covenant but that, unfortunately, it was all too often neglected.[24] What was radical was the way they delivered their messages. They pulled no punches and were not afraid to offend those in power. Their aim, therefore, was not to bring about a social revolution but to defend the social system, which was founded on the covenant, from the unscrupulous behavior of greedy leaders and from the assimilation of other codes or cultural practices.[25]

Repentance and Conversion

Proponents of this view, including Archbishop Oscar Romero, believe there were two foci to prophetic activity. Firstly, the prophet denounced society's sin and called the people to conversion, warning of the disasters that were to come should they not change their ways. Secondly, and of equal importance, was the prophet's assurance that when disasters did strike, it was not the end of the story—God would not forsake them forever; there was

---

21. Mendenhall, "Covenant," 719.
22. Oladejo, "Prophetic Guilds," 115.
23. Tupek, *Torah*, 22.
24. Fretheim, "What Biblical Scholars Wish," 304.
25. Matthews, "Prophecy and Society," 627.

always hope.[26] Morgan agrees, stating that although prophets highlighted the failure to adhere to covenantal obligations and the punishment which was to come, they nonetheless saw a time when the people would repent and they would again know glory and victory.[27]

Political Orators

Commentators including Barton and Lessing believe prophets were a type of political orator, similar to those found in Ancient Greece.[28] They used rhetoric in order to persuade their audience, being well aware of the impact their words, and how they were delivered, would have. As mentioned earlier, the rise of prophetic activity can be traced back to the institution of a monarchy in Israel. That being the case, it would make sense for prophets to take on the responsibilities of political commentators as they endeavored to ensure that the monarchy lived up to the rigorous ethical principles of a theocracy.

God's Messengers

This is possibly the most common view of a prophet's function, which is not surprising given that the prophets often used a specific formula when speaking to the people. This formula (coined by Ludwig Köhler as *Botenspruch*, literally "messenger's speech") is a stereotyped phrase which prefaces the message by indicating the sender and usually the recipient (Jer 4:3).[29] Ross states that the prophets used *Botenspruch* as a way of claiming that their authority had been given to them either by Yahweh or his council, with some going so far as to claim they had stood in the council of Yahweh.[30] An example of this is the prophet Isaiah, who, Petersen says, is given a "conciliar perspective," answering God's question of "Whom shall I send, and who will go for us?" (Isa 6:8a) with "Here am I; send me!" (Isa

---

26. Romero, *Prophetic Bishop Speaks*, 254–55.
27. Morgan, *Voices*, 12.
28. Barton, "Ethics in Isaiah," 94; Lessing, "Preaching Like the Prophets," 400.
29. Schoors, *I Am God*, 11.
30. Ross, "Prophet," 118.

6:8b).³¹ Holladay goes so far as to state that the prophet, because he was called by Yahweh, was actually an officer of the heavenly court.³²

Lessing states that prophets were heralds of God's word. Interestingly, the New American Bible, revised edition, often translates "said the Lord" as "oracle of the Lord" (Jer 1:8, 5:29 NABRE).³³ Therefore, a passage such as "Do not be afraid of them, for I am with you to deliver you, says the Lord" (Jer 1:8 NRSVCE), becomes "Do not be afraid of them, for I am with you to deliver you—oracle of the Lord" (NABRE). Again, at Jer 5:29, the NRSVCE reads: "Shall I not punish them for these things? says the Lord, and shall I not bring retribution on a nation such as this?" whereas the NABRE reads: "Shall I not punish these things?—oracle of the Lord; on a nation such as this shall I not take vengeance?" The Hebrew word translated "says" comes from the root word *nāʾam*, which can mean either "to say" or "to utter" as an oracle.³⁴ This is important, as it means the prophet actually becomes the word (or oracle) of God in his or her own person.

Referring to Jesus' role as prophet in his exercising of the threefold office, Milton commented that "God hath now sent his living oracle into the world to teach his final will."³⁵ As Jesus himself often stated that he only spoke what the Father instructed him to (John 7:16, 8:28, 12:49, 14:10), the concept of someone being, in their person, an "incarnation" of God's word is a reasonable conclusion.

It is also interesting to note that the Hebrew word for angel (*mal'āk*) can also be translated as messenger, deputy, ambassador, or prophet.

Westermann, in his books on angels (from the Greek *angelos*, meaning "messenger"), states variously that angels are messengers from God, servants of God, and heralds of God's possibilities, all roles fulfilled by the prophets.³⁶

Seers

While the term "prophet" is overwhelmingly the most common, there are instances where prophets were identified as "seers." Examples include

31. Petersen, "Introduction to Prophetic Literature," 19.
32. Holladay, "Assyrian Statecraft," 123.
33. Lessing, "Preaching Like the Prophets," 391.
34. Strong, "Hebrew and Chaldee Dictionary," 75.
35. Milton, *Paradise Regained*, lines 460–61.
36. Westermann, *God's Angels*, 16, 94–103, 12.

Samuel (1 Sam 9:19), Gad (2 Sam 24:11), Iddo (2 Chr 9:29), and Heman (1 Chr 25:5). It would seem that "seer" was the title used before "prophet" superseded it (1 Sam 9:9) and that the terms, while not quite synonymous, described similar functions (Isa 30:9–10).[37]

Interestingly, consulting seers was prohibited (Deut 18:9–14), and it is important to keep in mind the differences between Greek seers and Hebrew seers/prophets. Hebrew seers used intuitive divination, relying on divinely inspired visions or messages, which they in turn communicated to the people. Greek seers, on the other hand, used deductive divination, gleaning messages from the entrails of sacrificed birds or analyzing the patterns made by oil thrown into water.[38] It was consulting this type of seer that was prohibited.

Poets

The fact that much of the prophetic literature contains striking imagery and lofty phrases and is laid out in poetic form has led some commentators to suggest that the prophets were inspired poets. However, Tucker does not agree, pointing out that it is doubtful the prophets wrote down their speeches. Their pronouncements were short and sharp, addressing a particular situation at a particular time. It was not until later that their words were written down and collated into the books we know today.[39]

While Brueggemann agrees that the primary role of the prophet was not to be a poet, he does state that the prophets deliberately used language that was lyrical and evocative. Their task was twofold: firstly, they wanted to "touch" the marginalized and mobilize them to claim what was rightly theirs; and secondly, their words were a challenge to those who were actively denying the poor and marginalized their rights. He believes poetic language is able to affect people at a deeper level and can achieve much more than the use of the clinical language of either philosophy or psychology.[40] In his 1983 article published in *Interpretation*, Brueggemann states the following:

---

37. Napier, "Prophet, Prophetism," 919.
38. Lange, "Greek Seers," 463.
39. Tucker, "Role of the Prophets," 161.
40. Brueggemann, *Prophetic Imagination*, 65–70.

The shattering and forming of worlds is not done as a potter molds clay or as a factory makes products. It is done as a poet describes the world, reconfigures public perception, and causes people to re-experience their experience. To do that requires that speech must not be conventional, reasonable or predictable; it must shock sensitivity, call attention to what is not noticed, break the routine, cause people to redescribe things that have long since seemed settled, bear surpluses of power before routine assessments.[41]

A Call for Justice

With the advent of liberation theology, there has been greater emphasis placed on the role of the prophet to call the people back to justice. Many commentators have noted how often the words "justice" and "righteousness" appear in prophetic literature. Laney, for example, sees the prophetic role in legal terms, stating it was the prophet's role to bring a complaint against Israel on behalf of Yahweh, thus progressing God's lawsuit against Israel.[42]

Mays states that the concept of justice calls to mind issues such as fairness, equality, goodness, and equity—all things vital for the well-being of a society. He believes the prophets had such an impact and were, at times, so unpopular because they placed justice before all other political considerations, thus calling into question the machinations of the ruling class and threatening the status quo.[43]

Prophets were called by God when justice was not being done, when the rights of the marginalized were not being upheld, and when restoration was required to reestablish harmony and equity in the community.[44] It was the prophet's role to speak out and demand that the rights of the poor and the marginalized be respected, not just because that was the law but because the well-being of every member of society was of utmost importance.[45]

In his paper "The Role of the Prophets and the Role of the Church," Tucker discusses what he considers to be the six most popular "misconceptions" regarding prophets and their role, most of which have been discussed

---

41. Brueggemann, "Book of Jeremiah," 135.
42. Laney, "God's Case against Israel," 315.
43. Mays, "Justice," 145.
44. Malchow, *Social Justice*, 12–16.
45. Malchow, *Social Justice*, 22.

above. His view is that while there is a grain of truth in each of the images and, indeed, in some more than a grain, each image also misses the mark. He concludes that the role of the prophet was to speak the word of God for the immediate future. As such, they were not predictors of the future but people who spoke on behalf of God for a particular situation at a particular time.[46] As Stanglin points out, they were not foretellers but forth-tellers.[47] Yates likens this activity to that of the Ghost of Christmas Future in Charles Dickens's *A Christmas Carol*—what is being "predicted" is not what will happen but what is likely to happen if behavior is not altered.[48]

Having said that, prophets such as Zechariah, Daniel, and Ezekiel did dedicate much of their writings to eschatological and apocalyptic themes, written during times of persecution but which looked forward to the deliverance and reward that were sure to come. Referring to the writings of Daniel, Morgan states that "out of the midst of historic night, he spoke in the language of prophetic light."[49]

A New Way: Prophetic Imagination

Walter Brueggemann has posited a new way of viewing the role of the prophet—a way which "embraces the very imagination of God" and is able to form a new community that matches God's vision of freedom.[50] He sees the role of the prophet as being "to nurture, nourish, and evoke a consciousness and perception alternative to the consciousness and perception of the dominant culture."[51]

Using the Exodus event as the basis of his argument, Brueggemann argues that the problem with the Egyptian (or, as he calls it, the royal) consciousness was that it maintained the status quo by ensuring that the Egyptians wanted for nothing. This led to a numbness which rendered them not just unwilling to see the suffering of those around them but actually unable to do so. It is, therefore, the aim of the royal consciousness to block out the

---

46. Tucker, "Role of the Prophets," 160, 170.
47. Stanglin, "Spiritus Propheticus," 36.
48. Yates, "Prophetic Sign Acts," para. 3 of subtitle "General Principle: Return and Change the Future."
49. Morgan, *Voices*, 12.
50. Brueggemann, *Prophetic Imagination*, xxi, 7.
51. Brueggemann, *Prophetic Imagination*, 3.

cries of the "denied ones."[52] It was the prophet's task, argues Brueggemann, not to transform the regime but to address the consciousness that undergirded it.[53]

However, that is only the first part of the solution—the prophet must then energize the "denied ones": to provide them with hope that there can be a different way and to inspire them to believe it is they who are the ones who are able to bring this new consciousness to fruition. Brueggemann insists this can only be done by the denied ones. It is only through the example of their lived experience of grief and hardship that the hopes and yearnings that have been denied and suppressed for so long can be brought to light, thus breaking the numbness and inertia of the royal consciousness.[54] This was what Moses achieved. However, over time, the "Moses movement" became too radical for the Israelites, who decided they would be better off with the comfort and stability they believed a king could provide.[55]

A key aspect of the royal consciousness is an abhorrence of compassion for the vulnerable and a denial of its own vulnerability. Doat agrees, stating that from the moment society turns its attention away from the most vulnerable, it begins the process of dehumanizing itself.[56] It is precisely this ability to stand in solidarity with the victims of the royal consciousness from a place of his own vulnerability that enabled Jesus to empower the denied ones with whom he came into contact.

In summary, over the years there has been a variety of opinions as to what the role of the prophet may have been. As noted earlier, the image of the prophet has tended to be of a person who was strong, decisive, argumentative, and, almost without question, male. It is not until Brueggemann posited his theory of the prophetic imagination and the importance of the "denied ones" in bringing that prophetic vision to fruition that the image of a prophet was able to include the vulnerable, the marginalized, and—of most importance for the purposes of this book—women.

The image of a vulnerable, downtrodden prophet is obviously very different from the popular Charlton Heston type, which leads us to the question of whether there is a difference between "being" a prophet and "acting" in a prophetic manner, and why the distinction is of importance.

52. Brueggemann, *Prophetic Imagination*, 35.
53. Brueggemann, *Prophetic Imagination*, 21.
54. Brueggemann, *Prophetic Imagination*, 65.
55. Brueggemann, *Prophetic Imagination*, 115.
56. Doat, "Disability, Theology," 149.

Being a Prophet or Acting in a Prophetic Manner?

As discussed above, over the years there has been a variety of opinions regarding the prophet's role. However, as Scripture reveals, prophets were involved in many areas of day-to-day life. For example, prophets offered intercessory prayers (Jer 42:4), prophesied by playing musical instruments (1 Chr 25:1–3), anointed kings (1 Kgs 1:34), resolved disputes (2 Chr 28:9–15), worked wonders (1 Kgs 17:8–24), mustered troops (Judg 4), and documented history (2 Chr 13:22). Indeed, Sweeney, including wise men and women in his definition of prophet, states they were also consulted on a wide variety of private issues, from locating lost property (1 Sam 9:1–10) to asking whether a child would live or die (1 Kgs 14:1–18).[57]

In his book *The Role of Israel's Prophets*, Petersen discusses whether there was a difference between being a prophet and taking a prophetic role. Citing the work of T. Sarbin and V. Allen on role theory, he states that prophets were taking on a role, much like an actor or actress when playing a part—their conduct adhered to the part they were playing rather than to the person themselves.[58] This is certainly true of two prophets who are portrayed as taking on very specific roles indeed: Jonah, the sulky, recalcitrant prophet, and Hosea, the cuckolded husband.

We will discuss role theory, especially its relevance when considering the importance of enacted parables as a prophetic tool, in the next chapter; however, put briefly, Sarbin and Allen identify four types of roles: ritual acting, where a person acts "on cue"; engrossed acting, whereby a situation is manufactured to achieve a desired end; classical hypnotic role taking, where external stimuli are seen only by one person; and histrionic neurosis, which involves some kind of ecstatic experience.[59]

While there is evidence that some prophets formed "schools" and, therefore, had followers (1 Sam 19:18–24),[60] it should also be noted that several of the prophets were called away from their professions to fulfill the missions God had given them. For example, Amos was a herdsman and a dresser of sycamore trees (Amos 7:14), and Jeremiah was a priest (Jer 1:1). It would appear, therefore, that apart from the handful of "career prophets," the majority of people named as prophets in Scripture were acting in a

---

57. Sweeney, "Prophetic Books," 962.
58. Petersen, *Role of Israel's Prophets*, 16.
59. Petersen, *Role of Israel's Prophets*, 30–33.
60. Tucker, "Isaiah 1–39," 28.

prophetic manner—that is, taking on that role in response to a specific situation. This distinction is, of course, artificial, as prophets who were advisors to kings—like, for example, Nathan—were obviously acting in a prophetic manner. The point is that if the distinction is artificial, then the number of people taking on a prophetic role (and, therefore, being prophets) is much greater than first thought.

This is where it becomes critical to consider the different ways men and women act and relate to others. Cavalcanti has commented that while male prophets used denunciation in an attempt to bring about changes in society, women were more likely to use exhortation to, on the one hand, encourage the oppressed to defend themselves and engage in the struggle for equality and, on the other, awaken the conscience of those who were violating their rights. In other words, these prophetic women were constantly endeavoring to reclaim their oft-violated rights. As examples, she cites Judith, Esther, Ruth, and Tamar as women who were not called prophets but nonetheless acted in a prophetic way. Their ministry impacted significantly the social, political, and religious lives of their people because it reminded those in power of their covenantal obligations to defend and uphold the rights of the weakest in society.[61] As we have seen, this is one of the most important aspects of a prophet's ministry.

It would, therefore, also stand to reason that apart from the few women that are specifically named in Scripture as being prophets (to be discussed in chapter 3), there are many more who acted prophetically and should, therefore, also be considered to have had a prophetic ministry. Kessler agrees, pointing out that if every form of contact that women are said to have had with transcendent powers is included, then the ministry of female prophets becomes much more broad-based.[62] This, too, will be discussed in detail later in the book.

Conclusion

In this chapter, we discussed the overall portrayal of prophets in Scripture and how that has been instrumental in creating the popular archetypal image of prophets as being slightly disheveled, bad-tempered, erratically behaved, and male.

---

61. Cavalcanti, "Prophetic Ministry of Women," 122.
62. Kessler, "Miriam," 77.

The various theories concerning the role of the prophet were summarized, with the conclusion that while each theory had some validity, a more holistic understanding is required. This holistic approach has been provided by Walter Brueggemann, who believes the prophet's task was twofold. The first task was to challenge the prevailing consciousness that undergirded a regime that allowed sections of society to suffer poverty and marginalization. Secondly, a prophet had to energize the "denied ones," inviting them to reimagine a new, just, and equitable society and enabling them to help bring that society to fruition.[63]

We also considered whether there was a difference between being a prophet and acting in a prophetic manner. While we concluded that any such differentiation was artificial, this chapter did highlight the fact that prophets were engaged in a much wider range of day-to-day activities and did not merely stand on their soapboxes, as it were, railing against the political and religious authorities of their day. This meant it was likely that the number of people fulfilling a prophetic ministry was far greater than first assumed and included people not usually considered to be "prophet material."

The fact that women and men act and interact differently was also discussed. While men tended to argue and cajole, women would use gentler methods to bring about change and encourage the oppressed to reclaim their oft-denied rights—aims which encapsulate a prophet's role. This, too, led to the conclusion that women were one of the main groups that has been dismissed when considering who could be a prophet.

We will attempt to go some way in rectifying this situation. In chapter 3, we will discuss the prophetic ministry of those few women either named as prophets or believed to be prophets in Jewish tradition. Then, in chapter 4, we will broaden our vision to consider other women who may have acted in a prophetic manner, thereby earning themselves the title.

Before we do that, however, we need to discuss the nature of parables and their use in Scripture, with a particular emphasis on enacted parables and their use by Old Testament prophets.

---

63. Brueggemann, *Prophetic Imagination*, 65–70.

2

Parables

A parable is one of those stories in the Bible which sounds at first like a pleasant yarn, but keeps something up its sleeve which suddenly pops up and knocks you flat.

—P. G. WODEHOUSE

Introduction

In the last chapter, we discussed the role of the prophet and the various ways that role has been understood. We also considered more recent scholarship, much of which suggests that the prophet's role was twofold: highlighting how far society had strayed from its covenantal obligations, on the one hand, while encouraging and empowering people to be part of bringing about God's vision of a fair and equitable society, on the other. The question of whether there was a difference between being a prophet and acting in a prophetic manner was explored, resulting in the conclusion that any such distinction is largely artificial. On this point, it was noted that men and women have different ways of relating to others, so the traditional image of a prophet is not appropriate when considering the prophetic ministry of women. Given these observations and conclusions, it would then follow that those exercising a prophetic ministry were not only more numerous than first thought but also included people not usually considered to be "prophet material."

But what did acting in a prophetic manner entail? Friebel points out that in order to convey God's message to the people, prophets used a whole range of verbal cues: they ranted, pontificated, cajoled, threatened.[1] However, given that the majority of communication is nonverbal, they also, not surprisingly, employed body movements, gestures, and facial expressions. There are also examples of prophets using other people or items as "props." As we will see below, when this method was employed, the prop "became" the message. This will play an important part in the argument that the prophetic ministry was exercised by a much wider and more diverse group of people than is often assumed.

As we have seen, a prophet's message was often inconvenient and unwelcome and, therefore, ignored. Therefore, when verbal entreaties failed, more extreme measures were called for. In these cases, prophets often used *enacted parables*. At times, enacted parables entailed prophets displaying quite bizarre behavior, sometimes over considerable periods of time, to demonstrate what would happen should people not amend their ways and return to their covenantal obligations.

However, did a prophet's behavior have to be bizarre to qualify as an enacted parable? Might some behaviors or circumstances not usually interpreted as an enacted parable lend itself, on closer inspection, to that definition? This is an issue we will investigate and consider during the course of this chapter. Before we are able to do this, we need to spend some time discussing the nature and function of parables and why they were such an effective means of communication.

What Are Parables?

The word "parable" comes from the Greek *parabolē*—literally, "throwing (*bolē*) alongside (*para*)," an activity that facilitates the comparison of two situations. A parable, therefore, is a story that, by presenting situations side by side and saying things in a slightly different way,[2] is able to encourage the creation of alternate realities.[3]

---

1. Friebel, "Sign Acts," 707.
2. Tasker, "Parable," 932.
3. Stein, "Parables," 567.

It is likely the word "parable" calls to mind the stories Jesus employed to teach his disciples and the crowds. While, in his Gospel, Matthew states that Jesus used parables exclusively when teaching (Matt 13:34), Hunter has, in fact, calculated that roughly one-third of Jesus' recorded teaching was done through parables.[4]

However, Jesus was not the only one who used parables. As Snodgrass points out, parables were a popular form of prophetic discourse which was used quite extensively not only by the Hebrew prophets but also in various cultures both prior to and contemporaneous with Jesus' time, and they would, therefore, have been a familiar didactic tool.[5] However, Snodgrass believes that even though the use of parables was common, Jesus used them with a greater degree of consistency, creativity, and effectiveness.[6]

The stories Jesus told were funny, quirky, and memorable, but they had a sting in the tail that challenged the status quo. This delighted some in his audience (Mark 12:37); however, for those against whom the parables were directed, these stories held disagreeable truths which meant that parables were often spoken at considerable risk to the speaker.[7]

Parables are good at igniting the imagination and helping form mental pictures. As such, they are a perfect basis for sermons, and over the years, these stories have become very familiar to the average churchgoer. Indeed, the titles and/or morals of some of the most well-known parables have made their way into common secular usage. Most people, for example, know what a good Samaritan is and are familiar with the advice to turn the other cheek, regardless of their churchgoing practices. This is not surprising—storytelling has long been a way of getting a message across or highlighting a moral principle. Indeed, people have been using various types of stories—including fables, myths, anecdotes, and allegories—as didactic tools for thousands of years. What, however, differentiates a parable from these other types of stories? Let us briefly examine each genre.

Fable

Put simply, a fable describes relationships in the human world by recasting animals who think, speak, and behave as people as the protagonists in the

---

4. Hunter, *Interpreting the Parables*, 7.
5. Snodgrass, "Prophets, Parables and Theologians," 45, 49.
6. Snodgrass, "Parable," 594.
7. Hunter, *Interpreting the Parables*, 12.

story.[8] Possibly the most famous of these types of stories are Aesop's Fables, which have given us morals such as "slow and steady wins the race" or "beware the wolf in sheep's clothing."

Myth

A myth is a story about gods and other superhuman beings which is told either to account for a custom, institution, or natural phenomenon or to express a sense of the sacred.[9] Included in this category are myths recounting the exploits of the gods of Mount Olympus and Valhalla or epic tales such as those describing the twelve labors of Hercules.

Anecdote

An anecdote is a story which describes an event or sequence of events from a person's past told in such a way as to make the story interesting, amusing, or inspirational.[10] Take, for example, this anecdote about Mark Twain:

> One day during a lecture tour, Mark Twain entered a local barber shop for a shave. This, Twain told the barber, was his first visit to the town.
> "You've chosen a good time to come," he declared.
> "Oh?" Twain replied.
> "Mark Twain is going to lecture here tonight. You'll want to go, I suppose?"
> "I guess so . . ."
> "Have you bought your ticket yet?"
> "No, not yet."
> "Well, it's sold out, so you'll have to stand."
> "Just my luck," said Twain with a sigh. "I always have to stand when that fellow lectures!"[11]

---

8. Coats, "Parable, Fable, and Anecdote," 373; Blank, "Fable," 221.
9. Gaster, "Myth, Mythology," 481; Dunn, "Myth," 566.
10. Coats, "Parable, Fable, and Anecdote," 379.
11. Fadiman, *Little, Brown Book*, 554–55.

Allegories

Finally, allegories are stories that illustrate principles by proposing new, hidden meanings in otherwise familiar stories which had heretofore been defined literally.[12] Dante's *Divine Comedy* can be included in this category, as the story of Dante's journey through the three realms of the dead can be interpreted allegorically as a description of a soul's journey to God.

Parable

The Bible contains examples of each of the above genres: the animals depicted in the book of Tobit and the story of Balaam's donkey in Numbers can be classified as fables; the creation stories in Genesis are Hebrew myth, as are the descriptions of battles between the forces of good and evil in the book of Revelation (it is important to remember that just because something is a myth doesn't mean that it does not contain truths); the Bible is full of anecdotes describing the exploits of various judges, kings, and warriors; and finally, there are any number of biblical stories that have been allegorized to make didactic points. What, then, makes a parable different?

Over the years, there has been a variety of opinions regarding the genre and/or purpose of parables. Schipper, for example, believes parables are not a distinct genre but a type of short story, much like a fable, which prophets "turned into" parables for the purpose of imparting a spiritual or moral lesson.[13] On the other hand, Fohrer and Warren believe parables form a specific literary genre.[14] Simon agrees, adding that there are also categories of parables within the genre. For example, he identifies the stories of the Tekoite woman (2 Sam 14), the captive who escaped from his keeper (1 Kgs 20:35–43), the vineyard (Isa 5:1–7), and the poor man's ewe lamb (2 Sam 12:1–15) as "juridical parables" (pertaining to judicial proceedings and administration of the law).[15] Coats disagrees, stating that stories as diverse as those of the poor man's ewe lamb and the vineyard could not possibly belong to the same literary genre.[16]

---

12. Vine, "Allegory," 39; Mowry, "Allegory," 82.
13. Schipper, *Parables and Conflict*, 43.
14. Warren, "Parables," 39; see Erzberger, "Prophetic Sign Acts," 104.
15. Simon, "Poor Man's Ewe-Lamb," 207–8.
16. Coats, "Parable, Fable, and Anecdote," 370.

Parables

McFague sees parables as being stories which use familiar elements in strange and vivid ways, thereby challenging the listener to reimagine accepted concepts.[17] Warren agrees, stating that while parables were usually based on local custom and described plausible scenarios, they had an unexpected twist in the tail which had the ability to "sting, proclaim, confront, and comfort," thus inviting listeners to ponder what the point might be.[18]

McFague also states that parables have certain characteristics that differentiate them from other genres—namely, the story had to be mundane, extravagant, and indirect. By *mundane*, she does not simply mean that parables used familiar imagery, although they did. Parables also emphasized that God's kingdom is not restricted to "heavenly" matters; it also touches the secular and ordinary in both the personal and public domains—God is just as interested in the profane as he is in the sacred, in human matters as he is in matters pertaining to the rest of creation (Ps 59:10–12).

Parables also highlighted God's *extravagant* nature. When Jesus performed feeding miracles, there was always an extravagant amount of food left over (Matt 14:20, 15:37), and there was room for everyone, from all points of the compass, to come and find rest in God's kingdom (Luke 13:29). Perhaps one of the best-known examples of God's extravagant generosity is illustrated in the parable of the sower (Mark 4:3–9). What would the conventional opinion be of a farmer who repeatedly goes out and scatters seed all over the place—on stones, amongst weeds and brambles, as well as on ground that has been prepared—without taking heed of where it falls? Such a farmer would probably be described as wasteful at best, or stupid at worst. But as we've already seen, God's way is not the way of the world, and it is just that remarkable and, at times, unsettling fact to which the parables point.

And finally, parables are *indirect*—these stories may seem familiar and innocuous enough, but they have a sting in the tail, and their message often comes as a nasty shock to the listener as the true meaning of the parable "snaps the absolutes of conventional society like so many dry twigs."[19] As P. G. Wodehouse has commented, a parable is a story that sounds like a "pleasant yarn, but keeps something up its sleeve which suddenly pops up and knocks you flat."[20]

---

17. McFague, "Parable," 425–26.
18. Warren, "Parables," 38–40.
19. Crossan, *In Parables*, 82.
20. P. G. Wodehouse, qtd. in Hunter, *Parables Then and Now*, 10.

Mowry believes parables were a popular and familiar form of wisdom teaching that used a brief narrative to forcefully illustrate a single idea, making them perfect for didactic purposes.[21] He states that Jesus used parables as a way of contrasting the kingdom of God to the worldview of, amongst others, the Pharisees, whose main emphasis was exposition of the law.[22]

Snodgrass agrees, stating that Jesus used parables as a means of holding up one reality to serve as a mirror to another.[23] Jesus' parables contrasted the world as it was with how it would be in God's kingdom, and encouraged people to see the world through God's eyes, encouraging them to participate in the transformation of their society.[24]

Blomberg likens parables to metaphors which reveal the in-breaking of the kingdom of God and paint a picture of what that kingdom will ultimately look like.[25] The parables, therefore, create a vivid mental image of how countercultural that world might be. Take, for example, the parable of the mustard seed (Matt 13:31–32), which suggests that all God's people, regardless of their origins, will find safety and shelter in the branches of what was a rather insignificant bush. This parable would have been disturbing to the Jews on two levels. Firstly, they believed themselves to be the "chosen people" to the exclusion of other nations. To be told that everyone would be welcome would not have been popular, despite that having been the teaching of several of the prophets (Isa 2:2–4, Mic 4:1–2, Zech 8:20–23). Secondly, the Jewish authorities were expecting the Messiah to come in triumph and glory; therefore, a more suitable image for God's kingdom, as far as they were concerned, would have been the mighty cedar of Lebanon. But as we have seen, the in-breaking of the kingdom was to bring many surprises—some of them unpleasant.

In his book *In Parables: The Challenge of the Historical Jesus*, Crossan has taken up this concept that parables were intended to discomfit rather than comfort. Crossan states that parables can be very disturbing, because not only do they fail to give hard and fast rules or solutions but they actually suggest behaving in a way that would appear, to most people, to be inexplicable. As an example, he uses the story of "turning the other cheek," pointing out that this story could have finished in a variety of ways, but the

---

21. Mowry, "Parable," 649.
22. Mowry, "Parable," 651.
23. Snodgrass, "Parable," 596.
24. Snodgrass, "Parable," 597.
25. Blomberg, "Miracles as Parables," 427, 327, 330.

most unexpected would have been to invite someone who has just struck you to do so again! This, Crossan points out, goes beyond giving moral advice or even suggesting a pacifist stance. Jesus is highlighting the radical challenge of the kingdom, a challenge that overthrows even the strongest ethical principles.[26]

Importantly, Crossan states that the aim of Jesus' parables was not always to show up the Jewish authorities, most of whom, he states, were superb moral guides. The problem that Jesus was addressing was the belief that leading a good life led to reward, including the reward of God's presence. Rather, it was God who chose to be present amongst his people, and it was the recognition of this that empowered people to lead a good life, which included the observation of covenantal obligations.[27]

Therefore, when properly understood, parables suggested ways of behavior that were counterintuitive and threatened the status quo and people's spiritual and religious certainties. While this could be a very uncomfortable place to be, it was also an invitation to join with God to reimagine and recreate a world where people lived in accordance with God's will.

Hunter also links the use of parables to the engaging of people's imaginations. He states that parables spoke of God's future and people's destiny as sharers in that future. Parables, using, as they did, familiar, mundane imagery (like that of the mustard seed), evoked "unimaginable endings" by pointing out the kingdom's "unremarkable beginnings."[28]

Brueggemann agrees, stating that prophets used spoken word and acted word as a way of igniting people's imaginations so they could see the world through God's eyes and recognize the inequities in their society and, hopefully, effect change.[29]

Notwithstanding the above, various commentators have pointed out that while the Hebrew word *māšāl* is often translated as "parable," it can also, depending on the context, be used to describe songs, sayings, proverbs, riddles, oracles, allegories, similitudes, and fables.[30] This has led Schipper to conclude that the term "parable" denotes the *function* of a story rather than a genre in its own right. Accordingly, he argues that any story, regardless of

26. Crossan, *In Parables*, 82.
27. Crossan, *In Parables*, 80.
28. Hunter, *Interpreting the Parables*, 45.
29. Brueggemann, *Prophetic Imagination*, 63–64.
30. Schipper, *Parables and Conflict*, 43; Beavis, "Feminist (and Other) Reflections," 604.

its narrative genre, can be classified as a parable if a biblical character uses it as a point of comparison within his or her immediate context.[31]

It is clear from the above that parables were a popular tool used, variously, to provide memorable mental pictures which dry doctrines could not; teach, comfort, and discomfit; hold a mirror up to society, thus comparing it to God's view of the world; and engage people's imaginations, inviting them to be partners with God in the establishment of the kingdom. Clearly, parables fulfilled an important function and were used extensively by Jesus and the Old Testament prophets. However, there is one type of parable we are yet to discuss.

If we join the views of Snodgrass (that parables are a form of prophetic discourse), Schipper (that a parable is defined by its function rather than its genre), and Brueggemann (who includes the *acted* word in his definition of parable), our focus must logically turn to the issue of enacted parables.

Enacted Parables

As we have seen, there are numerous examples of prophets employing spoken parables as a way of explaining what would happen if people did not alter their behavior (Isa 5:1–6, Ezek 24:3–5, Zech 11:3–10). However, when their messages were discounted or ignored, prophets used *enacted* parables (e.g., Jer 13:1–11, Ezek 4:1–3), which can be defined as being symbolic actions employed to make public theological statements.[32]

In order to get the attention of their intended audience and ensure there could be no misunderstandings regarding the intent of the message or any risk of being ignored, prophets sometimes displayed quite bizarre behavior.[33] For example, Isaiah reputedly walked naked and barefoot for three years as a portent against Egypt and Ethiopia (Isa 20:3), Ezekiel built a model of Jerusalem and placed an iron plate between it and himself to represent the siege of Jerusalem (Ezek 4:1–17), and Jeremiah bought a linen loincloth only to bury it in the ground for "many days" as a symbol of how useless the Israelites had become in their task of being a light to the nations (Jer 13:1–11).

---

31. Schipper, *Parables and Conflict*, 1–2.
32. Harrington, "Enacted Parable," 47.
33. Yates, "Prophetic Sign Acts," para. 2 of subtitle "Function of Prophetic Sign-Acts."

Enacted parables (or "sign acts," as they are also called[34]), have variously been described as pantomimes and staged events,[35] street theater,[36] and artistic performances.[37] For Houston, enacted parables were a logical progression from spoken parables given that, according to him, the very core of prophetic language was performative. He states that the prophets enacted God's message as a means of challenging the status quo and accusing society of unethical behavior. The meanings of these enacted parables were, therefore, analogous to those of spoken parables.[38]

Friebel agrees, stating that enacted parables are "inherently efficacious" in that their effectiveness was an inherent quality contained within the actions themselves, much like the power of the spoken word.[39] He saw enacted parables as being public performances that employed dramatic, unexpected, and unconventional methods to attract people's attention so that they would stop, listen, and, hopefully, accept messages they would normally reject.[40]

Peterson states that because they went beyond mere words and utterances, enacted parables were a good way of getting people's attention, on the one hand, and ensuring that they remembered the message, on the other.[41] Smith agrees, stating that enacted parables were an effective way of imparting God's message to rebellious and hard-hearted people, as they were more likely to take heed of a message that was performed, whereas they frequently ignored the message if it was simply spoken.[42] Indeed, it would be difficult to ignore a prostrate prophet if you had to step over him every time you exited the city gate!

Yates states that enacted parables were used by prophets to stress the importance of a message and that the prophet actually "became" the word of God in his or her own person.[43] Stacey agrees, stating that prophets knew

---

34. While the terms "enacted parables" and "sign acts" are often used interchangeably, I will use the terminology "enacted parable."
35. Matthews, "Prophecy and Society," 629.
36. Friebel, "Sign Acts," 711.
37. Erzberger, "Prophetic Sign Acts," 105.
38. Houston, "What Did the Prophets," 176, 169.
39. Friebel, "Sign Acts," 711.
40. Friebel, "Sign Acts," 712.
41. Peterson, *John's Use of Ezekiel*, 73–74.
42. Smith, *Interpreting the Prophetic Books*, 43.
43. Yates, "Prophetic Sign Acts," para. 1 of subtitle "Function of Prophetic Sign-Acts."

nothing about professional detachment and were totally involved in their work, including, in many instances, becoming the symbol.[44] There are no better examples of this total involvement than the story of the prophet Hosea, a "gut-wrenching real life drama" highlighting Israel's infidelity to her "husband," Yahweh,[45] or the more comedic tale of Jonah, the sulky, recalcitrant prophet. Importantly, in Jonah's case, it is he, the prophet, who is the prop. Jonah is portrayed as a kind of "anti-prophet," unwilling to preach God's word of repentance and forgiveness to the Ninevites, Israel's sworn enemies.

Interestingly, Irwin identifies God's hardening of Pharaoh's heart in the Exodus narratives as an enacted parable, used in order to affirm divine self-identification and justice.[46] He states that God suspended Pharaoh's free will not simply to convince Pharaoh to let the Israelites go but also to demonstrate his deity to Israel. By refusing to let them go, Pharaoh "throws down the gauntlet" and provokes God into showing that it is he who is divine and not Pharaoh.[47] If this is the case, then it is an example of God using Pharaoh as the "prop" in what would be a series of enacted parables which includes the successive plagues and the stubbornness which led to the parting of the Red Sea. While I do not agree with Irwin's conclusion that God intentionally hardened Pharaoh's heart in order to make a point (albeit a good one), it does, however, highlight Jesus' own explanation for why he taught the people using parables (Matt 13:10–17). Some people may have looked and listened, but they were unable to see or understand. This also ties in with Brueggemann's theme of the "royal consciousness," which is not just an unwillingness to see the suffering of others but an inability to do so, grounded in the fear that it may adversely affect wealth or lifestyle.[48]

When it comes to the New Testament, several commentators have identified some of the miracles as enacted parables. For example, Anderson believes miracles were signs pointing to the dawning of the messianic age, and Blomberg states that the feeding miracles were enacted parables which emphasized the growth and blessings inherent in the imminent in-breaking of God's kingdom.[49] Lapsley states that the miracles were also intended to

---

44. Stacey, *Prophetic Drama*, 66, 61.
45. Chisholm, *Handbook of the Prophets*, 336.
46. Irwin, "Suspension of Free Will," 62.
47. Irwin, "Suspension of Free Will," 58.
48. Brueggemann, *Prophetic Imagination*, 35.
49. Anderson, "Signs and Wonders," 350; Blomberg, "Miracles as Parables," 338.

point to who Jesus was and that, through him, people were already able to participate in God's gifts of life and health.[50] Harrington agrees, stating that Jesus' banquets were enacted parables that were intended to make a theological point—that through Jesus we share in God's own abundance.[51]

Stacey believes the banquet symbolized people's ability to experience God's abundance in the present time, not just in some future "heavenly kingdom." As such, enacted parables point to a fairly complex understanding of time. Stacey states that if an event can be encountered in its dramatic representation (that is, as enacted parable), then it can be encountered before it happens just as easily as afterward.[52] Therefore, it is not necessary to wait for the coming of God's kingdom to be fulfilled; the benefits of the kingdom can be experienced in the here and now, because the prophetic act invites people to reimagine society and enables them to take part in the establishment of the kingdom.[53]

Similar to the question of whether or not a tree makes a noise when it falls in a forest if there is no one there to hear it, there is also discussion as to whether or not an audience is required for an enacted parable to be efficacious. John Bright, for example, argues that for an enacted parable to be effective, there needs to be an eyewitness.[54]

Others, however, disagree. For example, Stacey believes that the function and operation of enacted parables is complex. He believes that the purpose of prophetic drama was to supply another level of existence to an important but perhaps hidden reality. Using the enacted parable of Jeremiah and his loincloth as an example (Jer 13:1–11), Stacey states that the purpose is to be sought in the reality of what the enacted parable signifies, not in the perception by spectators of what that reality might be. The drama, therefore, exists for what it expresses, not—or at least not primarily—for communication, and acts to present, focus on, interpret, and mediate the reality.[55] Friebel agrees, stating that as enacted parables express an existing reality rather than create it, there was no need for an audience to have been present when the acts were performed.[56] The benefits of these

50. Lapsley, "Children in Isaiah," 199–200.
51. Harrington, "An Enacted Parable," 47.
52. Stacey, *Prophetic Drama*, 55.
53. Stacey, *Prophetic Drama*, 282.
54. Stacey, *Prophetic Drama*, 133.
55. Stacey, *Prophetic Drama*, 133, 282.
56. Friebel, "Sign Acts," 711.

unwitnessed enacted parables are timeless. Once written down, they would have informed and reassured postexilic generations, as they continue to inform and reassure to this day.

Of course, concomitant with the ability to imagine reality as God sees it is the kindling of hope and a call to action for those who have been silenced. On this point, Brueggemann states that alternative worlds are purposed and exist "because of and in the act of (prophetic) utterance" and that it is "word," both spoken word and acted word, that effects change, shapes consciousness, and defines reality.[57] The reality these enacted parables pointed to was a world in which everyone would be valued and able to share in God's bounty,[58] because the enacted parables were visible evidence of the presence and purpose of God.[59]

Relevantly, Hooker points out that both the Old Testament prophets and Jesus used objects or other people as the symbol in their enacted parables.[60] From the Old Testament, she cites Jer 35. Here, God used the Rechabites (who faithfully kept the commands of their ancestors) as a foil against the Israelites, who regularly broke God's commandments. The Rechabites became the symbol, a living illustration of what it meant to live in accordance with God's covenant.

As examples of Jesus' use of others in his enacted parables, Hooker cites the disciples' failure to fast (Matt 9:14–17), their "breaking" of the Sabbath rule (Luke 6:1–5), and Jesus' condemnation of behavior that is contrary to the tradition of the elders (Mark 7:5–13). Hooker argues that while Jesus did not perform these parables himself, he nevertheless justified them.[61]

Hooker believes Jesus' behavior, and that of the other protagonists in these prophetic dramas, is integral to the message being conveyed—they are dramatic representations of the gifts of the kingdom, which are already "bursting in" in the here and now.[62] This is an important insight, as it highlights that Jesus used other people as part of his enacted parables. In doing so, he enabled them to undertake the task of being (in their bodies) the dramatic representation of the point he was endeavoring to make. This was

---

57. Brueggemann, *Prophetic Imagination*, xii, 63–64.
58. Nogalski, *Interpreting Prophetic Literature*, 70.
59. Lapsley, "Children in Isaiah," 83.
60. Hooker, *Signs of a Prophet*, 35–40.
61. Hooker, *Signs of a Prophet*, 40.
62. Hooker, *Signs of a Prophet*, 41.

exactly what the Old Testament prophets did—by following the "stage directions" they received from God, they *became* God's message to the people.

Interestingly, unlike other commentators, Hooker believes that there is a difference between sign acts and enacted parables. She states that the miracle of the large haul of fish (Luke 5:1–11) was a sign act because, as Jesus explained, it described what would be happening in the not too distant future. On the other hand, she believes the story of the little child (Matt 18:1–5, Mark 9:33–37, Luke 9:46–48), which describes the characteristics of true discipleship, is an enacted parable because Jesus is using the child as a symbol not of what will be (as in the story of the great haul) but of what should be.[63] I doubt such a distinction can be maintained, as it can be argued that the child is also a sign of what will be in the economy of God's kingdom and of what his disciples were called to help bring about.

Clearly, enacted parables are not simply stories of prophets blindly performing rather bizarre acts on command. These stories are much more complex and nuanced than that. Indeed, it is evident from the above discussion that a variety of situations and interactions can indeed be viewed as enacted parables. Therefore, it may be useful to consider some of their more common forms.

Types of Enacted Parables

Using the work of T. R. Sarbin and V. L. Allen on role theory, Peterson discusses four main types of "organismic involvement" used by prophets when enacting a role: ritual acting, engrossed acting, classical hypnotic role taking, and histrionic neurosis.[64] What follows is a brief discussion of these four types of involvements with some examples.

Ritual Acting

A prophet can be said to be involved in ritual acting when he or she follows instructions and carries out certain ritualistic movements "on cue." According to Matthews, this type of "staged event" was used to elicit questions or reactions from the audience.[65] Examples would include Ezekiel lying on

---

63. Hooker, *Signs of a Prophet*, 41–43.
64. Peterson, *Role of Israel's Prophets*, 30–33.
65. Matthews, "Prophecy and Society," 629.

his left side for 390 days, then on his right for forty days to represent the number of years the Israelites would be in exile (Ezek 4:4–8).

The story of Jeremiah's loincloth (Jer 13:1–11) is also an example of ritual acting. The fact that the Israelites worshiped other gods and behaved in ways which were in breach of the covenant meant that as far as their role of being a light the nations was concerned, they were as much use to God as Jeremiah's soiled loincloth was to him. As in the book of the prophet Hosea, where God is portrayed as a wounded, cuckolded husband, this enacted parable contains language which highlights the close, intimate relationship God seeks to have with his people. At verse eleven, we read:

> For as the loincloth clings to one's loins, so I made the whole house of Israel and the whole house of Judah cling to me, says the Lord, in order that they might be for me a people, a name, a praise, and a glory. But they would not listen.

The verb rendered "cling" (*dābaq*) is the same verb used in Gen 2:24, where it is said that "a man leaves his father and his mother and clings to his wife, and they become one flesh."[66]

Interestingly, this is also an example of an enacted parable which had no audience. It was not necessary for someone to witness the enacted parable for God's purposes to be realized, nor was God's faithfulness to his covenantal obligations subject to the faithfulness of the Israelites.

Engrossed Acting

This type of enacted parable is almost like a scene from a play. Similar to a spoken parable, where the story seems innocuous enough until the "knockout punch," the protagonists seem to verbally dance around each other before the aim of the dialogue suddenly comes to light.

Peterson uses the story of the prophet Nathan and David as an example of engrossed acting (2 Sam 12:1–6). To confront David over the murder of Uriah the Hittite, Nathan told David a seemingly innocent story. By not challenging David directly, Nathan observed social protocol and did not antagonize the king. Nathan maneuvered the conversation in such a way that he allowed David to trap himself, to be confronted by the culpability

---

66. Yates, "Prophetic Sign Acts," para. 3 of subtitle "Discussion of the Loincloth (Jer 13)."

of his orders, which he had conveniently ignored,[67] and to feel the full force of his actions.

Classical Hypnotic Role Taking

In classical hypnotic role taking, a person is said to see things or have visions. In prophetic literature, these visions are often prefaced by the question "What do you see?" (e.g., Jer 24:3; Amos 7:8, 8:2; Zech 4:2, 5:2). The significance of the items (for example, a plumb line, a lampstand, a bowl of fruit, or writing on a wall) is then explained to the prophet, and he or she passes that message on to the people. These are also examples of enacted parables that use items as "signs." These signs then become the message. This was a particularly popular device in apocalyptic literature, which describes signs such as flashes of lightning and flaming torches (Rev 4:5), beasts (Dan 7:1–8), locusts (Rev 9:3–11), and the great whore (Rev 17:1–6).

Histrionic Neurosis

Finally, histrionic neurosis refers to a prophet's physical response to the divine presence. For Jeremiah, that presence was sometimes a source of great distress (Jer 15:17–18). J. J. M. Roberts has linked descriptions of histrionic neurosis with the phrase "the hand of the Lord."[68] Experiencing the hand of God could result in physical or emotional distress (Job 19:21, 1 Sam 5:11) or be the precursor to a vision (Ezek 8:1).

Conclusion

As we have seen, parables were a popular form of storytelling employed in the Ancient Near East as a didactic tool. Consequently, and not surprisingly, parables were used extensively by Old Testament prophets and, in a more deliberate and nuanced way, by Jesus. When endeavoring to convince people they had strayed from their covenantal obligations and impress upon them the consequences of their actions or inaction, prophets would employ all manner of verbal tactics: pleading, haranguing, arguing. However, when their messages were discounted or ignored, prophets would then resort to

---

67. Goldsmith, "Prophetic Imagery," 4.
68. J. J. M. Roberts, qtd. in Peterson, *Role of Israel's Prophets*, 32.

enacted parables as an effective way of getting in people's faces, making it more difficult to ignore the message.[69] In many instances, this involved quite bizarre behavior.

However, as we have seen, enacted parables were not confined to people behaving strangely—they are much more nuanced than that. Enacted parables can include stories describing miracles, feeding stories, and descriptions of banquets. For those unwilling to "get the message," they can also sound a warning: tables overturned (Mark 11:15–17), thieves coming in the night (Matt 24:38–44), sacred cows slaughtered (Mark 7:6–16).

All these stories serve to highlight the generosity and abundance of God's kingdom and the fact that there is a place for everyone at the table. As such, the purpose of these parables is twofold. Firstly, the parables hold a mirror up to the dominant structure of society, comparing it (usually unfavorably) to the society God wishes to create. Secondly, it serves as a clarion call to join with God to reimagine a world where everyone is valued and welcome.

We also saw that it was not unusual for what is thought to be the main character in a story to use either an item or another person as the "sign" in the enacted parable. When this happens, the item or person becomes the "oracle" and focus of the story. And as we saw in the last chapter, "oracle" is another term for someone who fulfills a prophetic ministry.

So far, we have discovered that because a distinction between being a prophet and acting in a prophetic manner cannot be maintained, prophetic ministries were both more numerous than may first appear and also undertaken by a wider variety of people than first believed. Additionally, it has been demonstrated that enacted parables need not be confined to outlandish, bizarre behavior. This, too, would indicate that this means of communication was used by a wider, more diverse section of the population than first thought.

Given this wider, more inclusive definition of both "prophet" and "parable," would it not stand to reason that there were far more women exercising prophetic ministries than has traditionally been assumed?

We will tackle that question in chapter 4. However, let us first look at the lives and circumstances of the women who have been recognized as prophets in the Bible, and also those whom Jewish tradition has afforded the same title. We will discuss which aspects of a prophet's role they fulfill,

---

69. Yates, "Prophetic Sign Acts," para. 2 of subtitle "Function of Prophetic Sign-Acts."

focusing on any differences in the manner in which they interact and behave compared to their male counterparts.

3

Named Female Prophets

> I raise up my voice not so I can shout,
> but so that those without a voice can be heard.
> —MALALA YOUSAFZAI

Introduction

At the beginning of the first chapter, we tried to conjure up a mental image of an Old Testament prophet and concluded that this hypothetical prophet would most likely look determined, powerful, slightly disheveled, perhaps a bit wild-eyed, but most definitely male. This is not surprising—while the male prophets have books dedicated to describing their ministry (albeit some not very long), the few female prophets named in the Bible are only given a fleeting mention.

But if we were to try to imagine a female prophet, what image would we end up with? Would we imagine a female version of Moses, holding her staff aloft and leading the Israelites through the Red Sea? Or a woman lying on her side, gazing fixedly at the city walls? Would we be able to imagine a woman railing against the religious and political authorities of the day and telling them to repent, or else? I suspect we would have trouble coming up with an image at all.

One might argue that given the fact that none of the biblical prophetic writings are attributed to women and those given the title of prophet were overwhelmingly male, it is logical to conclude that female prophets were extremely rare. However, is this assumption overly simplistic, and if so, what factors may contribute to this? Before turning our attention to the attributes and work of those women recognized as prophets in Scripture and Jewish tradition, let us firstly consider some grammatical, linguistic, and sociological issues which may contribute to an inaccurate view of who a prophet can be.

Grammatically Correct, but Historically Misleading

Hebrew is a gendered language—nouns are classified as either masculine or feminine. There is also a distinction between "grammatical" gender and "natural" gender. Very broadly speaking, a noun is either masculine or feminine depending on the ending of the word (although there are exceptions). Similarly, in Italian, nouns ending in *a* are usually feminine (*la sedia*, the chair) and nouns ending in *o* are usually masculine (*il libro*, the book).

Natural gender is determined by the gender of the person to whom one is referring. Although fast going out of fashion, an example of these gendered nouns is "actor" and "actress." In Hebrew, the words for a male and female prophet are *nābî* and *nᵉbî'â*, respectively. Interestingly, in the Hebrew Bible, *nābî* is also used when referring to more than one prophet. Therefore, if a passage mentions, say, five hundred prophets consisting of 499 women and one man, the grammatically correct word would still be *nābî*. Readers of the day may have automatically assumed there would be women in a group of prophets, just as we would assume a mixed group if imagining a gathering of teachers. However, does that hold true when talking about prophets, a category which has become quite alien to the modern way of thinking?

Gender Does Sometimes Matter

In recent years, there has been a trend to more gender-inclusive translations of the Bible to rectify what has rightly been seen as a bias toward masculine language. For example, translations including the New Revised Standard Version and the New Living Translation use gender-inclusive language where it does not "do violence" to the original intent of the passage.

Consequently, "mankind" becomes "humankind" and "brethren" becomes "brothers and sisters."

However, making these changes is not as easy as might seem. The change to "like a human being" from "like a son of man" in Daniel's vision may well obscure the fact that "son of man" was a messianic title. Daniel's "human being" was presented to the Ancient of Days, who bestowed on him "dominion and glory and kingship, that all peoples, nations, and languages should serve him. His dominion is an everlasting dominion that shall not pass away, and his kingship is one that shall never be destroyed" (Dan 7:14 NRSVCE). Changing "son of man" to "a human being" obscures the messianic significance of the passage and the important connection being made when Jesus refers to himself as the son of man.

Ironically, the use of gender-inclusive language may, in fact, be rendering women and the extent of their public ministry invisible to modern audiences. For example, in the Second Book of Chronicles, we are told that those conspiring against King Joash were Zabad the son of Shimeath and Jehozabad the son of Shimrith (24:26). In some translations (KJV, RSV, NLT, NASB), Shimeath is identified as an Ammonitess, and Shimrith is identified as a Moabitess. However, in other translations (NRSV, ESV), the demonyms have been changed to "Ammonite" and "Moabite," respectively. This may not seem a significant difference; however, given most people's unfamiliarity with ancient Hebrew names, this seemingly insignificant change may inadvertently be contributing to the "masculinization" of Scripture.

Another example is Ps 68, a psalm celebrating God's faithfulness in leading Israel to victory over their enemies. News of this great victory was celebrated and made known by a "great company" (verse 11). The Hebrew word rendered "great company" is ṣābā, which is a feminine, plural noun. This means the great company consisted solely of women. This makes sense, as it was common for women to go out to meet a victorious army, singing and playing various musical instruments (Exod 15:20–21). Several translations (ESV, NASB, NIV) have replaced "company" with "women" to make this obvious; however, others have opted for a neutral translation (KJV, RSV, NRSV), thus obscuring the fact that the company contained no men. Indeed, the New Living Translation has rendered this verse "the Lord gives the word, and a great army brings the good news" (NLT) (albeit with a footnote that "a host of women" is an alternative rendition). However, for most people, that translation is sure to give the impression the proclaimers were all men.

Named Female Prophets

Not only do these grammatical and linguistic anomalies serve to make the importance and extent of women's ministry in Israel all but invisible, but as Willett points out, inaccurate language also impacts how women are able to exercise their gifts in society and the church today.[1] As was stated in the heading of this section, gender does sometimes matter.

Selective Reporting

It is interesting to reflect on how the pronouncements of various prophets are treated. For the three major prophets (Isaiah, Jeremiah, and Ezekiel), we are made privy to their actual calling by God. For the minor prophets, while there is no record of their call, each book is prefaced with a comment along the lines of "The word of the Lord that came to Micah of Moresheth in the days of Kings Jotham, Ahaz, and Hezekiah of Judah, which he saw concerning Samaria and Jerusalem" (Mic 1:1).

There are no such explanations for any of the female prophets. Apart from mentioning, in passing, that a woman was a prophet, the closest we come to an "official" recognition is when Deborah (Judg 4:6–7) and Huldah (2 Kgs 22:15–20) are recorded as passing on a direct message from God.

Of course, as we saw earlier, there were many more male prophets in Israel, none of whom had their call recorded or their prophecies collected into a book. Logically, the same would apply to women.

Report vs. Rapport

Notwithstanding the above linguistic and grammatical considerations, perhaps the most important aspect contributing to the invisibility of female prophets is sociological—men and women communicate differently. As discussed earlier, all the prophetic literature is attributed to male prophets, and the space given to the exploits of female prophets is minimal, to say the least. We are also given details about the male prophets' lives (e.g., Amos 7:14), whereas this is not the case for female prophets—we are told little or nothing of their *Sitz im Leben*. This is hardly surprising, as these stories are told through the prism of a patriarchal society where women were usually neither seen nor heard. The fact that any women were mentioned at all

---

1. Willett, "Unveiling Old Testament Women," 13.

is of considerable significance and needs to be taken seriously.[2] Even in these supposedly more enlightened times, this may result in biblical female prophets remaining invisible because we have been conditioned to "see" only male prophets, and then only if they behave in a particular way.

So, how do we imagine a female prophet would act? Do we assume that to break through the prophetic glass ceiling, so to speak, women would simply need to adopt male leadership models, or do we recognize the fact that men and women simply act, relate, and speak differently than one another? If debate in our parliaments is anything to go by, it appears women are forced to adopt a male debating model to have any hope of being heard at all.

In her paper "You Just Don't Understand: Women and Men in Conversation," Tannen labels these differences "report-speak" and "rapport-speak." Men, she maintains, tend to use report-speak as a means of relaying information or as a way of preserving independence and their status in a hierarchical social order. In a social situation, men are also more likely to speak more often than women, for longer, and more forcefully.[3]

Women, on the other hand, use rapport-speak as a means of establishing connections, maintaining relationships, and negotiating mutually beneficial outcomes.[4] In mixed public gatherings, women will hesitate to speak, and when they do, they will speak for a shorter period of time, without preamble. However, amongst friends, women will speak freely about relationships, family, and friends.

Therefore, given that women lived in a patriarchal society, were unable to exercise any authoritative roles outside the home, and, even if they were able to, would have gone about it in totally different ways, it is logical to conclude that female prophets would not have behaved like male prophets. This means that given society's conditioning to recognize prophets only if they behave in a particular way, it stands to reason there are several "hidden" female prophets to be found in Scripture.

Admittedly, from time to time, commentators have suggested that certain women have acted in ways that could be described as prophetic.

---

2. Cavalcanti, "Prophetic Ministry of Women," 119–20.
3. Tannen, "You Just Don't Understand," 111–12.
4. Tannen, "You Just Don't Understand," 111.

Named Female Prophets

These women include Rahab,[5] Hagar,[6] Rebecca, and Tamar,[7] some of whose stories we will consider in later chapters.

It is a bit puzzling, however (not to mention disappointing), that an understanding of the issues affecting a reliable portrayal of women's ministry in general, and prophetic ministry in particular, has largely failed to capture the imagination and provoke more academic curiosity. This is something I hope to address in this book.

Later in this chapter, we will consider the ministry of those women recognized as prophets in Scripture and Jewish tradition. Subsequent chapters will focus on the lives and examples of other women, arguing that they, too, should be "counted amongst the prophets."

Before progressing, however, it would be helpful to establish a working definition of what is meant by having a prophetic role in the Old Testament understanding of that term based on the discussion, in earlier chapters, regarding the prophetic office and the use of enacted parables.

Firstly, it has been concluded that it was difficult for women to exercise public leadership roles in a largely patriarchal society and that, generally speaking, women and men naturally behaved differently—men used a "report" method of communication, whereas women were more likely to use a "rapport" method.

Secondly, any difference between "being a prophet" and "acting in a prophetic manner" cannot be sustained given that, apart from the handful of "career prophets," the majority of people named as prophets in Scripture were acting in a prophetic manner—that is, taking on that role in response to a specific situation. These specific situations usually entailed a society that had become so hard-hearted that the needs of the vulnerable were not so much overlooked as actively disregarded.

In these cases, the prophets began by exhorting the people to return to an observance of their covenantal obligations. When exhortation failed, they often resorted to enacted parables as a way of shocking people out of the spiritual lethargy.

There is also the issue of whether "true" prophecy ceased with John the Baptist, becoming instead just one of many gifts of the Spirit available to believers (1 Cor 12:28, Eph 4:11). There is mention of what can be considered to be "traditional" prophetic activity in the New Testament. Agabus's

5. Clement I, *1 Clement 12:1–8*, cited in Wire, *Corinthian Women Prophets*, 242.
6. Brenneman, "Your Daughters Shall Prophesy," 58.
7. Niditch, "Folklore, Feminism," 58.

prediction of a severe famine, which came about in the reign of Claudius (Acts 11:27–28), and the manner in which Paul would die (Acts 21:10–11) are examples of this. Also, given Simon the Pharisee's comment that if Jesus were a prophet, he would have known what type of woman was touching him (Luke 7:39), it is logical to assume that prophets were still a recognized part of society before Pentecost. Indeed, Jesus himself referred to prophets, sages, and scribes that would be sent to the Jewish people, only for them to be flogged and crucified (Matt 23:29–36).

As well as other more general references to prophets (Acts 13:1–3, 15:32), Paul states that the church was built on the dual foundation of the apostles and the prophets (Eph 2:19–22) and that the Spirit discloses to them the mystery that the church, through the work of Christ, is open to Jews and gentiles alike (Eph 3:5–6)—a message that was not uncommon amongst the prophets of the Old Testament.

Interestingly, and perhaps worthy of note, is the fact that when the activities of these men are discussed, they are called prophets, whereas women are described simply as having the "gift of prophecy" (Acts 21:9).

This shift in emphasis on the prophetic role may, of course, be a reflection of the situation in which the fledgling church found itself. In the Old Testament, while not often making themselves popular, prophets were in a position to confront the religious and civil leaders of the day when they strayed from their covenantal obligations. The new Christian communities, however, were literally between a rock and a hard place, facing persecution from both the Roman and Jewish authorities. It is not unreasonable to assume that the communities' prophets were taking on a different role, that of strengthening and building up the church in what they saw as their role of spreading the good news of Christ.

So, where does that leave us with our working definition of what is meant by having a prophetic role in the Old Testament understanding of that term? We have seen that prophets were called when society had lost its way and that one of their tools, when all else had failed, was to resort to enacted parables. It is also the case that in many enacted parables, objects or people were used as the sign, thus making them the "oracle" of that parable. It is therefore logical to argue that when the situations in which these women find themselves hold up a mirror to the injustices, prejudices, and inequities of society, then they are fulfilling a prophetic role in the Old Testament understanding of that term. As such, they are in the same company

Named Female Prophets

as Jonah and Hosea, whose own stories, as we have seen, can be interpreted as extended enacted parables.

Female Prophets in Scripture

There are ten women who are referred to as prophets in Scripture—five in the Old Testament and five in the New Testament (including Philip's four daughters). Most of them only have one or two lines dedicated to describing what would have been a significant role in their society. These are their stories.

Philip's Daughters (Acts 21:7–14)

Describing part of his travels, Paul states that on arriving at Caesarea, he stayed with Philip, who had four unmarried daughters who had the gift of prophecy. Immediately following this statement, Paul goes on to describe a visit from the (male) prophet Agabus, who performs an enacted parable alluding to what Paul's fate would be should he go to Jerusalem. Nothing more is said about Philip's daughters.

As mentioned above, this may (perhaps) be an example of selective reporting; however, in the absence of any further information or context, it is not possible to comment further on the type of prophetic role fulfilled by Philip's daughters.

Anna (Luke 2:36–38)

Although we are not told very much about Anna, what we are told is significant. We are told that she is very old (or, as the King James Version so quaintly puts it, "she was of a great age"). Longevity was seen as a reward for leading a righteous life (Deut 5:33, Prov 16:31, Ps 91:16) and calls to mind the "great ages" recorded for some of the biblical patriarchs.

Her name is coupled with that of Simeon, an indication that Luke intends his readers to recognize Anna's proclamation and ministry as being of equal validity to Simeon's. We are also told that Anna spoke about Jesus to "all who were looking for the redemption of Jerusalem" (Luke 2:38).

Although Anna never left the temple, it is evident that people went to the temple to hear her speak. As such, Anna can be identified as an eschatological preacher.[8] However, she is also the fulcrum between the few women identified as prophets in the Old Testament and the identification and recognition of the female prophets in the New Testament who have, to date, remained silent and invisible.

Isaiah's "Wife" (Isa 8:1–4)

The only mention of this prophetess is in the following pericope:

> Then the Lord said to me, Take a large tablet and write on it in common characters, "Belonging to Maher-shalal-hash-baz," and have it attested for me by reliable witnesses, the priest Uriah and Zechariah son of Jeberechiah. And I went to the prophetess, and she conceived and bore a son. Then the Lord said to me, Name him Maher-shalal-hash-baz; for before the child knows how to call "My father" or "My mother," the wealth of Damascus and the spoil of Samaria will be carried away by the king of Assyria.

This enacted parable foretold the defeat of Judah's enemies (Damascus and Samaria) by the Assyrians before Isaiah's son (whose name means "the spoil speeds, the prey hastens"[9]) was able to speak, around twelve months.

There has been some discussion as to whether the prophetess was a prophet herself, or whether the designation simply indicated that she was the wife of a prophet. Malchow and Ackerman believe she was Isaiah's wife and that the title "prophetess" was an honorific used to reflect *Isaiah's* place in society.[10] Fischer disagrees, stating that in Hebrew, the feminine form of a verb is not used to designate the "wife of." If the text were to refer to a prophet's wife, grammatically, it would have to refer to her as "the prophet's wife." As this is not the case in this passage, Fischer argues that Isaiah's wife was herself a prophet.[11] Marchetti agrees, also suggesting that Isaiah and the prophetess were both performers in the enacted parable and, as such, each was a prophet in his and her own right.[12]

It should also be noted that Ezekiel, when referring to his wife, called her "my wife," not "the prophetess" (Ezek 24:18).

---

8. Harris, "Letting (H)Anna Speak," 61.
9. Tucker, "Isaiah 1–39," 116.
10. Malchow, *Social Justice*, 33; Ackerman, "Why is Miriam," 49.
11. Fischer, *Des femmes messagères*, 268.
12. Marchetti, "Women Prophets," 10.

Named Female Prophets

Huldah (2 Kgs 22:14–20, 2 Chr 34:22–28)

Although Huldah only appears once in the Second Book of Kings and in the parallel story in the Second Book of Chronicles, her role in interpreting the contents of the book of the law was instrumental in Josiah instituting one of the most comprehensive religious reforms in Judah.[13] Hamori suggests that by interpreting the contents of the book and validating their authenticity, she was the first person to have authorized a canonical text—quite an achievement.[14] Indeed, Otwell goes so far as to declare that she was the most reliable prophetic figure in Jerusalem at that time.[15]

It is ironic, and telling, that the book of the law was found by Hilkiah, the priest, who then gave it to Shaphan, the secretary. It would seem that neither of them recognized the import of what they had found, as Shaphan said to King Josiah, "the priest Hilkiah has given me a book" (2 Kgs 22:10). Shaphan read the contents to Josiah, who tore his clothes, then sent Hilkiah, Anikam, Achbor, Shaphan, and Asaiah to "go, inquire of the Lord" concerning the contents of the book (2 Kgs 22:13a). These five went directly to consult Huldah. Harris believes this meant her authority was well established, and Marchetti argues she was the royal court's official prophet.[16] It should be noted here that Huldah wasn't the only prophet working at that time. Jeremiah, Nahum, Habakkuk, and Zephaniah also exercised prophetic ministries; however, the king's delegates sought out Huldah.

Her authority is also evident by the way Huldah felt she could speak to the king's officials. She was certainly no shrinking violet! When responding to the king's delegation, Huldah referred to King Josiah as "the man who sent you to me" (2 Kgs 22:15), which is logical given she was speaking on God's behalf, but is also indicative that she had authority and respect in her own right.

Few prophets held such sway over the royal court, had such a profound impact on the religious and cultic observances of their day, or were instrumental in the renewal of their society's adherence to their covenantal obligations. Why, then, is Huldah and her contribution to the well-being of her people so invisible?

---

13. Willett, "Unveiling Old Testament Women," 16.
14. Hamori, "Prophet and the Necromancer," 838.
15. Otwell, *And Sarah Laughed*, 157.
16. Harris, "Letting (H)Anna Speak," 66; Marchetti, "Women Prophets," 10.

Before You Were Born, I Anointed You

Noadiah (Neh 6:14)

Noadiah appears just once in the book of the prophet Nehemiah. Nehemiah had decided to rebuild the wall surrounding Jerusalem, thus allowing those Israelites who had been exiled to return. This plan was not popular with the local non-Jewish authorities, and Nehemiah was convinced that those opposed to the rebuilding of the walls (Tobiah, Sanballat, and Geshem) were plotting to kill him and had hired the prophet Shemaiah to deliver a false prophecy in order to intimidate him (Neh 6:10–13). Nehemiah prays that God will "remember Tobiah and Sanballat, O my God, according to these things that they did, and also the prophetess Noadiah and the rest of the prophets who wanted to make me afraid" (Neh 6:14). There are no other references to Noadiah either before or after this pericope to shed any light on what it is she may have done.

There has, not surprisingly, been some speculation as to what Noadiah's part in this conspiracy may or may not have been. Some commentators, while resisting the urge to speculate on the details of her behavior, nonetheless have concluded she was a false prophet.[17] Kidner suggests that like Shemaiah, Noadiah was part of a prophecy-for-pay scheme, and Eza believes Noadiah was trying to "block the work of God" and likens her to Thyatira's evil prophetess, Jezebel, who encouraged fornication and idol worship (Rev 2:20–23).[18]

However, there are commentators who see Noadiah in a totally different light. For example, Batten believes that unlike Shemaiah, she and her fellow prophets were sincere in trying to warn Nehemiah.[19] Marchetti has suggested that Noadiah's concern may have been the impact the repaired wall and return of the exiles would have had on foreign wives and their children, as the genealogy of the returning exiles indicates that only Israelites were able to enter the gate.[20]

Gafney agrees, pointing out that as the Persians were sponsoring the rebuilding of the wall, the aim of the repairs could not have been defense but rather exclusion.[21] Indeed, we see in Ezra 9–10 that the people undertook a lengthy process whereby all foreign wives and children were

---

17. E.g., Shepherd, "Prophetaphobia," 249–50; Klein, "Ezra & Nehemiah," 787.
18. Kidner, *Ezra and Nehemiah*, 100; Eza, "How to Tell," 11.
19. Batten, *Ezra and Nehemiah*, 259.
20. Marchetti, "Women Prophets," 11.
21. Gafney, "Prophet-Terrorist(a)," 172.

identified and then expelled from the community. Interestingly, Nehemiah dedicated only three short verses to this whole distressing process, stating that "when the people heard the law, they separated from Israel all those of foreign descent" (Neh 13:3). Those "of foreign descent" would probably have numbered hundreds of women and their children. These people would not only have been homeless but stateless as well, as it was unlikely they would have been able to return to their ancestral families.[22] Nehemiah may have labelled Noadiah a terrorist (Neh 6:14), but it was he who oversaw the expulsion of so many women and children knowing they would have no means of support.

If this is the case, then Noadiah was following God's instructions to care for resident aliens, widows, and orphans (Exod 22:21–24). The expulsion of these women and their children would effectively have resulted in the creation of hundreds of "widows" and "orphans" whose husbands and fathers were still alive, and for this she should be recognized as a true prophet.

Deborah (Judg 4:4–23)

Deborah is described as a prophetess and judge and as the wife of Lappidoth (Judg 4:4). While identifying a woman who exercised some authority as someone's wife usually indicated she was there with her husband's knowledge and permission, some commentators have suggested that since *lappîdôt* can also be translated as "torches," the author is suggesting Deborah was a "woman of torches," or a fiery woman.[23] If that is the case, it is certainly an appropriate name.

Deborah clearly commanded considerable respect and authority, as it was she who summoned Barak, decided the battleground (Mount Tabor), led the army against Sisera, and made any strategic decisions during the battle. Claassens has suggested that as the deliverer of her people, Deborah can rightly be described as God's human representative.[24]

Fischer believes it is significant that the transfiguration also took place on Mount Tabor. She argues that Moses and Elijah did not simply represent the law and the prophets; rather, it was prophecy that explained the spirit of the law. That Jesus is revealed as the one who fulfills the law and the

---

22. Gafney, "Prophet-Terrorist(a)," 171.
23. Jackson, *Comedy*, 101.
24. Claassens, *Mourner, Mother, Midwife*, 4.

prophets on *Mount Tabor* signifies, according to Fischer, that he is aligning himself with the prophetic work of Deborah and this understanding of the purpose of prophecy.[25]

Deborah's area of influence was also considerable. People from all over Israel would consult her as she sat under "the palm of Deborah" between Ramah and Bethel (Judg 4:5a). Significantly, Samuel seemed to have adopted the same circuit as Deborah. He, too, judged Israel, making a circuit to Bethel, Gilgal, and Mizpah before returning to his home at Ramah (1 Sam 7:15–17).

Deborah is also called "mother" of Israel (Judg 5:7), which, like the male equivalent "father" (Judg 17:10, 18:19), identifies the person as a guide or counselor.[26] And finally, like Huldah, Deborah is truly God's spokesperson, speaking as though God himself were speaking (Judg 4:6–7).

Miriam (Exod 2:1–10, Exod 15:20–21, Num 12:1–16, Num 20:1–13)

Scripture relates four stories in which Miriam, the first woman given the designation of prophet, plays a significant part. Firstly, it was Miriam (although she is simply referred to as "his sister") who watched over Moses after his mother had placed him in the river. It was also Miriam who, bypassing the royal attendants, approached Pharaoh's daughter directly, offered to obtain a wet nurse for Moses, and then brought Moses's own mother to fulfill that role. By ignoring the rigid constraints governing royal/subject intercourse and orchestrating the situation in order to fulfil her aim, Miriam prefigures Nathan's behavior when confronting David with Uriah's murder. This is, of course, engrossed acting, one of the examples of organismic involvement used by prophets when enacting parables.

Miriam's second appearance is during the Exodus story. Following the Israelites' escape from the Egyptian army through the Red Sea, Miriam leads a celebratory song of thanksgiving to God. Philo of Alexandria stated that the Israelites formed a choir, the men being led by Moses and the women, by Miriam.[27] Other commentators disagree, arguing that Miriam fulfilled a

---

25. Fischer, *Des femmes messagères*, 380–81.
26. Williams, "Prophetic 'Father,'" 344.
27. Wire, *Corinthian Women Prophets*, 240.

much more important role because it was women who were responsible for singing "victory songs."[28]

Fischer refutes any suggestion that Miriam led only the women. She states that Miriam led the whole company of Israel and sang on their behalf, thus fulfilling *la fonction médiatrice*, which is one of the classic roles of the prophet.[29] Dennis goes so far as to suggest that Miriam wrote the song sung by Moses, thereby making her one of the important minor prophets of the Old Testament.[30] Porter suggests Miriam's dance was not a victory procession but was intended to remind the people of the spiritual nature of their victory, emphasizing their reliance on God.[31]

Kessler agrees that Miriam's role was much more important than a superficial reading of the texts might suggest. After considering why the prophet Micah specifically mentions Miriam when speaking about the Exodus event (Mic 6:4), he has come to the conclusion that Micah was referring to Moses as being the founder and mediator of theocracy (or, as we would say today, the Torah), to Aaron as the representative of priesthood, and to Miriam as the representative of prophecy. Therefore, Micah was not referring to the arrangement of these historical figures but to the relationship between the institutions for which they stood—Torah, cult, and prophecy.[32]

Miriam's next appearance is somewhat more puzzling. Moses had married a Cushite woman. When both Aaron and Miriam confronted him about his marriage and his ability as a prophet, Miriam was punished for speaking against Moses, but Aaron was not.[33] Why was this? Was it because Miriam had overstepped her authority by questioning Moses? Does that mean Aaron had more authority than Miriam? If Kessler is correct in his assertion that Miriam represented the office of prophet, that could not be the case. Indeed, Lederman-Daniely is of the opinion that it was reported that Miriam was punished because she posed a threat to Moses's regime and the considerable influence she had in the community was played down in order to reinforce the notion of Moses's own power and authority.[34]

28. Ackerman, "Why Is Miriam," 48.
29. Fischer, *Des femmes Messagères*, 92.
30. Dennis, *Sarah Laughed*, 110.
31. Porter, *Leading Ladies*, 68.
32. Kessler, "Miriam and the Prophecy," 78.
33. Wray, *Good Girls, Bad Girls*, 115.
34. Lederman-Daniely, "Revealing Miriam's Prophecy," 10.

Finally, we are told that the Israelites went to Kadesh, where Miriam died and was buried. Immediately following the report of Miriam's death, we are informed that the Israelites' source of life-giving water dried up. Harris suggests this is an indication that Miriam was a conduit between God and the people, and Lederman-Daniely believes it was Miriam who maintained the people's vitality and faith.[35]

Miriam mostly worked within the strictures of her society to fulfill her prophetic ministry to the people, being present in three defining moments in Israel's "emancipation narratives."[36] As a child, she tricked Pharaoh's daughter into hiring Moses's own mother as a wet nurse. As such, she is one of a long line of female tricksters to be found in Scripture, some of whom we will encounter in a later chapter. She worked alongside her brothers in order to bring about the Israelites' freedom from the bonds of slavery to the Egyptians. Unfortunately, after she and Aaron both confronted Moses, it was only she who was deemed to have overstepped the mark and was made to pay. However, Miriam continued to minister to God's people, encouraging them to maintain their faith. Indeed, Lederman-Daniely suggests Moses was forbidden from entering the promised land because he had "sinned against" Miriam.[37]

Female Prophets in Jewish Tradition

Jewish tradition only recognizes seven female prophets: Miriam, Deborah, Huldah, Sarah, Hannah, Abigail, and Esther. Noadiah is considered to be a false prophet, and the prophetess in Isaiah is believed to have simply been Isaiah's wife. We have already discussed the stories of Scripture's named female prophets; let us now turn our attention to those women who have been found to have fulfilled a prophetic role.

Sarah

Not surprisingly, there are parts of Sarah's story that are unedifying. Her treatment of Hagar, her handmaid, for example, is cruel and inhumane.

---

35. Harris, "Letting (H)Anna Speak," 64; Lederman-Daniely, "Revealing Miriam's Prophecy," 21.
36. Wray, *Good Girls, Bad Girls*, 115.
37. Lederman-Daniely, "Revealing Miriam's Prophecy," 26–27.

Named Female Prophets

Firstly, she gave Hagar to Abraham to bear a child for him, then insisted that both Hagar and the child, Ishmael, be banished. We will discuss Hagar in more detail in a later chapter. This behavior is particularly difficult to understand given that she herself had been treated merely as property twice, both times when Abraham feared for his life and believed "gifting" Sarah might save him (Gen 12:10–20, Gen 20:1–18). That God chose to intervene on both occasions to save Sarah is an indication of her equal standing in God's eyes.[38]

Of course, Sarah's behavior does not preclude her being a prophet. If perfection were a criterion, the role would have been impossible to fill. So what is it about Sarah's life and example that qualifies her for this task?

That Sarah was equally important and necessary for the fulfillment of God's plan is borne out by the fact that God gave both Abraham and Sarah new names (Gen 17:5, 15). A change of name in the Bible indicates a new phase in that person's cooperation with the divine purpose.[39] Abraham was to be fruitful, the father of many nations. But Sarah would be blessed by God (stated twice in verse 16), would be the mother of nations, and kings of peoples would come from her. As Fretheim points out, Sarah did not benefit from God's promises simply because she was Abraham's wife; she was a participant in the covenant in her own right.[40]

Fretheim also points out that God also adopted a new name at the instigation of this covenant, as it is the first time the name *El Shaddai* (traditionally rendered as "God Almighty") appears in Scripture.[41] This is particularly relevant because in the Ancient Near East, it was believed that knowing someone's name, even that of a god, gave a degree of power over that person. God disclosing his name to Abraham and Sarah implies intimacy and a willingness to make himself available and known to both Abraham and Sarah, equally.[42]

At a subsequent disclosure of the divine name, God identified himself to Moses as "the God of your ancestors, the God of Abraham, the God of Isaac, and the God of Jacob" (Exod 3:13–15). However, as Brueggemann points out, God's self-identification to Moses might well have added:

---

38. Callaghan, "Covenant Partners," 18.
39. Fretheim, "Book of Genesis," 459.
40. Fretheim, "Book of Genesis," 459.
41. Fretheim, "Book of Genesis," 460.
42. Sanders, *God Who Risks*, 55.

> I am the God of Sarah, the God of Rebekah, the God of Rachel. I am the God of the old ancestral stories, the one who came upon the hopeless old people and gave them children and new life, the one who came among wandering sojourners and promised them land, the one who came where life was all closed down and promised them a future they could not imagine or invent for themselves.[43]

And finally, Callaghan suggests that as the final recension of this narrative probably dates from the Babylonian exile, Sarah's seemingly hopeless situation and divine restoration would have provided comfort to an exiled people and hope that God would achieve the seemingly impossible by restoring them to their land.[44] If this is the case, then Sarah is the protagonist in an enacted parable, a clear indication that she exercised a prophetic role.

Hannah (1 Sam 1:1—2:21)

First Samuel takes up where Judges left off, the intervening book of Ruth relating a story that took place "in the days when the judges ruled" (Ruth 1:1). At the end of the book of Judges, we are told that "in those days there was no king in Israel; all the people did what was right in their own eyes" (Judg 21:25). At the beginning of the First Book of Samuel, we are introduced to Elkanah and his two wives, Hannah and Peninnah. Hannah was barren, whereas Peninnah had children, a situation with which Peninnah tormented Hannah mercilessly. After enduring this treatment and shame for many years, Hannah goes to the temple to pray that God may grant her a child and promises to dedicate the child to God as a Nazirite.

Hannah is praying fervently but silently. Her lips are moving, but she makes no sound, leading the priest, Eli, to assume she is drunk. Hannah corrects Eli and explains her reason for being at the temple. Eli realizes his error and sends Hannah on her way with a blessing. Hannah becomes pregnant and, fulfilling her promise to God, takes her son, Samuel, to the temple once he has been weaned. Hannah then offers a prayer of thanksgiving to God for the gift of her child.

There is, of course, a well-known parallel to this story in the New Testament. Another seemingly miraculous birth—this time a young virgin—with both women giving birth to sons who would change the course

---

43. Brueggemann, *Threat of Life*, 19.
44. Callaghan, "Covenant Partners," 18.

of history. Both women then sing their praises to a God who listens to the vulnerable and acts to bring about positive change in their lives.

Smith also sees parallels between Hannah and the Syrophoenician woman in Mark's Gospel (Mark 7:24–30). Both women are on the receiving end of harsh words from a male authority figure, and both women correct the men and are rewarded by receiving what they have asked for.[45]

I believe Hannah and the Syrophoenician woman are also fulcra in their respective stories. Hannah is the fulcrum between the time of the judges and, through Samuel, to the establishment of a monarchy.[46] The Syrophoenician woman is the fulcrum (and sign) that highlights the equal place to which gentiles are entitled in God's kingdom. As Smith points out, both women alter the trajectory of history.[47] The Syrophoenician woman will be the subject of her own chapter later in the book.

Finally, Kirkpatrick is of the view that Hannah's song is an example of true prophecy. He believes she was inspired "to discern in her own individual experience the universal laws of the divine economy, and to recognize its significance for the whole course of the Kingdom of God."[48] Indeed, she seems to have known a monarchy was to be instituted, for she prayed that "the Lord will judge the ends of the earth; he will give strength to his king, and exalt the power of his anointed" (1 Sam 2:10b).

Abigail (1 Sam 25:3–42)

Abigail, like Hannah, is the fulcrum between two prophets—Samuel, who has recently died (1 Sam 25:1), and Nathan, who is yet to make an appearance. She is described as beautiful and wise (25:3), she is clearly in charge of household affairs (25:18–19), and her workers feel confident in approaching her (25:14–17), unlike her husband, Nabal, who is surly and mean (25:3), unapproachable (25:17, 36), and given to indulging in excessive alcohol (25:36). Abigail is much like the capable wife of Prov 31:10–31.

Chapter 25 describes a situation whereby David, who has protected Nabal's shepherds for what would seem a considerable period of time, asks Nabal to provide some food for David's men so they can observe a feast.

---

45. Smith, "Double Portion," 126.
46. Polzin, *Samuel and the Deuteronomist*, 18–30.
47. Smith, "Double Portion," 138.
48. Kirkpatrick, *First Book of Samuel*, 51.

Not only does Nabal refuse this request, but he also insults David. This enrages David so much that he decides to kill Nabal and all his men. News of this gets back to Abigail, who gathers together what amounts to a "peace offering" and rides out to meet David.

What follows is a perfectly orchestrated scene in which Abigail manipulates the situation (and, indeed, David), thereby saving not only Nabal and his men but also David, the future king of Israel, from committing "bloodguilt."[49] Using a ploy the prophet Nathan would replicate later in the story, Abigail plays the part of the obsequious subject, thus maintaining social protocol, but remains in control the whole time.[50] This is an example of engrossed acting, one of the means used by prophets when enacting parables.

By bravely confronting David with the folly of his proposed actions, Abigail is a prophetic figure who speaks on God's behalf, advises the future king, and alters the course of history. Her speech to David reveals she has been given knowledge that God will make for David a "sure house" (25:28) and appoint him "prince over Israel" (25:30). Her words are clearly prophetic, foreshadowing, as they do, Nathan's "dynastic oracle." Declining David's offer of a building in which to house the ark of the covenant, God (through Nathan) instead decrees that he will make David a "house," promising that David's house and kingdom will be made sure forever (2 Sam 7:1–17).[51]

Esther

The book of Esther is pure farce[52]—a tale filled with plots, subplots, and planned dastardly deeds. Esther and her uncle (or cousin) Mordecai find themselves in the court of King Ahasuerus, ruler of the Persian empire. The king is unaware that Esther and Mordecai are Jews. Following a very amusing, albeit unlikely, scenario, Esther becomes queen and discovers a plot (instigated by Haman, the king's vizier) to wipe out the Jewish people.

No one is allowed to approach the king unless they are summoned. In order to save her people from destruction, Esther risks her own life by

---

49. Carman, "Abigail," 51.
50. Bridge, "Desperation to a Desperado," 17; Baldwin, *1 and 2 Samuel*, 151.
51. Bach, "Pleasure of Her Text," 44.
52. Blue, "Book of Esther," 32.

approaching the king (Esth 4:16). However, in a fit of romantic chivalry, instead of having her executed, he grants her permission to speak. Esther invites the king and Haman to a banquet where, she says, she will tell the king what she wants. However, in a ruse reminiscent of Scheherazade, she declines to divulge her wishes but invites the king and his vizier to another banquet. At the second banquet, when the king asks her what she would like him to do for her, Esther declares herself to be Jewish and exposes Haman's plot to destroy the Jews. She pleads with the king on behalf of her people, resulting in the king writing a decree giving the Jews the right to defend themselves against any aggressors, thus saving them from annihilation (8:11–13).

How, then, did Esther act in a prophetic manner? There may well be a hint in the text that we are meant to see Esther as a prophet. Esther is, at first, reluctant to speak with the king, as arriving at the king's court without an invitation was potentially lethal (4:11). However, Mordecai suggests that she had become queen "for just such a time as this" (4:14). As we have seen, prophets were usually called to address a particular issue at a particular time.

Be that as it may, it cannot be denied that Esther used her ingenuity and feminine wiles[53] to advocate for her people and save them from destruction.[54] By behaving in such a way as to not antagonize the king, she was able to manipulate the situation in order to achieve her aim—yet another example of a prophetess using engrossed acting.

Conclusion

So, what have we learned about, and from, these ten women whom Scripture or tradition consider to be prophets? Firstly, of the ten, nine are from the Old Testament, with only Anna coming from the New Testament. Why should this be so? Also, only Deborah, Huldah, and possibly Noadiah can be considered to have exercised a recognized leadership role. The others either used trickery or psychology and manipulation, or exercised the authority they had within their own households, to achieve their aims.

Myers suggests that a major shift occurred with the institution of the monarchy. Prior to the monarchy, societal structures were more tribal and

---

53. Darr, *Far More Precious*, 165.
54. Porter, *Leading Ladies*, 123.

familial. This enabled women to exercise more power and have more influence over day-to-day matters. Once the monarchy was established, the locus of power shifted, thus disenfranchising women to a large degree.[55]

Lederman-Daniely agrees, adding that as it was men who wrote history, any significant role women may have exercised was downplayed, relegating women to bit players whose purpose was to "provide the needs of the patriarchal order."[56] We saw evidence of this earlier in Miriam's story. Jost suggests nothing much has changed in the intervening centuries, stating that the scarcity of female prophets in Scripture is less an indication of the number of women exercising this role and more a reflection of the attitudes of exegetes toward women.[57]

While it cannot be denied that society in general did not afford women the privilege of acting freely and independently, it is also important to remember that men and women behave in different ways, meaning that even if women had had the same rights and freedoms as men, male and female prophets would have still behaved differently.

What each of these women had in common, however, is that regardless of their situation in life, they were no shrinking violets. They were courageous, taking matters into their own hands. And in their own quiet way, usually from a position of vulnerability, they set about saving family, friends, and entire peoples; saving future kings from themselves; authorizing canonical texts; guiding people through wilderness journeys; advocating for people outside their own community; recognizing messiahs—in short, changing the course of history.

It is important to stress that these women exercised a prophetic ministry not despite their vulnerability but very much because of it. This is precisely what Brueggemann means when he talks about prophetic imagination—the necessity of change coming at the instigation and example of the "denied ones." This is why, he argues, it was to outcasts that the good news was first preached—to an old woman who had been unable to conceive (Elizabeth), to a young woman who was prepared to take the risk to be part of the reimagining (Mary), and to society's rejects (the shepherds).[58]

---

55. Myers, *Discovering Eve*, 188.
56. Lederman-Daniely, "Sarah Heard," 26.
57. Jost, "Daughters," 70.
58. Brueggemann, *Prophetic Imagination*, 103.

Named Female Prophets

And that is why these ten women were undoubtedly prophets. We will now expand on this definition and, in subsequent chapters, encounter other female prophets. In the process, we will hone our ability to recognize the traits and situations in which these inspirational women ministered.

4

Unnamed Female Prophets

> Tremendous amounts of talent are being lost to our society just because that talent wears a skirt.
>
> —SHIRLEY CHISHOLM

Introduction

The rest of the book will now be dedicated to considering two "categories" of women encountered in Scripture whom I believe should be recognized as fulfilling a prophetic ministry: the "trickster" and what I will call the "dismissed." As we saw in the last chapter, for the most part, women—for a variety of reasons—conducted themselves differently when engaging in "prophetic behavior." Traditional roles, societal expectations, and psychological considerations conspired to make it almost impossible for female prophets to minister in the same way as their male counterparts.

Some women responded by "tricking" those who were either refusing them what was rightfully theirs or standing in the way of God's plans. Others, through their participation in enacted parables, became oracles—that is, they embodied God's message. The majority of prophets in this latter category can be classified as "dismissed." As we will see, female prophets, while working within the abovementioned restraints, were every bit as effective as their male counterparts.

Unnamed Female Prophets

Let us now turn our attention to our "trickster" prophetesses.

The Scriptural Use of the "Trickster" Theme

Stories of shrewd tricksters were popular in Jewish folklore.[1] For example, Rebekah tricked Isaac into blessing Jacob instead of Jacob's brother, Esau; Laban tricked Jacob into marrying Leah instead of her sister, Rachel; Judah and his brothers (whose father was Jacob) tricked Jacob into believing Joseph had been killed; and Judah was tricked by Tamar in order to conceive a child. And that's just one family!

Jesus himself used the image of the trickster in his parable of the dishonest manager (Luke 16:1–13). These tricksters were often women who were forced to use their "feminine wiles" to ensure they got what they were entitled to, or simply to survive.

Trickery was also a means of exposing society's inequities, injustices, and inconsistencies. In so doing, it performed a prophetic role by highlighting what *was* and offering the opportunity to cooperate in the creation of what *might be*. Tricksters could, therefore, facilitate change, both for themselves and for their communities.[2]

Examples of tricksters include Rahab, who tricked the king of Jericho into believing the Jewish spies had left when she had them hidden in an upstairs room (Josh 2:1–7), and Jael, who tricked Sisera into believing she would hide him in her tent. She proceeded to ply him with alcohol and, when he had fallen asleep, drove a tent peg into his temple (Judg 4:17–22). Then there is the story of Lot's daughters, who, also using alcohol to aid their trickery, got their father drunk and slept with him so they could "preserve offspring" through their father (Gen 19:34). Their sons, Moab and Ben-Ammi, became the founders of the Moabites and the Ammonites. If you think this showed little faith in their father's ability or willingness to provide for and protect his daughters, remember that he was more than prepared to sacrifice them to an angry, male mob in order to protect two (male) strangers (Gen 19:8). Of course, not all tricksters were prophets (although Clement was of the view that Rahab was a prophet[3]); some had to use trickery simply as a means of survival.[4]

1. See Culpepper, "Gospel of Luke," 310.
2. Jackson, *Comedy*, 45.
3. See Prahlow, "Paranetic Women."
4. Patterson, "Trickster," 388.

Niditch singles out Rebecca (Gen 27) and Tamar (Gen 38) as being women who worked within the limitations imposed on them by society to fulfill their prophetic ministry. According to her, these women used trickery to achieve their goals and to ensure that their rights were upheld and, in so doing, reminded men of their covenantal responsibilities.[5] Their clever manipulation of the strictures imposed on them by a patriarchal society allowed them to "dance with chains on."[6]

So, let us now turn our attention to some of these prophetic tricksters.

Tamar

Tamar is arguably one of the most well known examples of the trickster in Scripture. Left a widow when her husband, Er, died, Tamar was then given to Er's brother Onan to produce offspring for his dead brother. As this custom of levirate marriage is important to understanding this and other stories in the book, an excursus explaining levirate marriage might be helpful.

Excursus: Levirate Marriage

The word "levirate" is derived from the Latin word *levir*, which means "brother-in-law." As a noun, it means "husband's brother"; as a verb, it means "to do a brother-in-law's office."[7] The practice was not confined to the Israelites and is known to have been practiced by other peoples, including Greeks, Persians, Hindus, Mongols, and New Caledonians.[8] While Driver posits that the practice may have originated in Tibet, where a commune of brothers lived together with a single wife, all children being legally reckoned as offspring of the eldest brother, he and other commentators concede that it is more likely that a group of related families lived together, and if the eldest male died, his property (including his wife and children) passed on to the new head of the family.[9]

---

5. Niditch, "Folklore, Feminism," 58.
6. Niditch, "Folklore, Feminism," 57.
7. Manor, "Levirate Marriage," 129.
8. Manor, "Levirate Marriage," 131.
9. Driver, *Deuteronomy*, 284; Manor, "Levirate Marriage," 130; Burrows, "Levirate Marriage in Israel," 27.

Unnamed Female Prophets

The institution of levirate marriage for the Jews can be found in Deut 25:5–10, which reads:

> When brothers reside together, and one of them dies and has no son, the wife of the deceased shall not be married outside the family to a stranger. Her husband's brother shall go in to her, taking her in marriage, and performing the duty of a husband's brother to her, and the firstborn whom she bears shall succeed to the name of the deceased brother, so that his name may not be blotted out of Israel. But if the man has no desire to marry his brother's widow, then his brother's widow shall go up to the elders at the gate and say, "My husband's brother refuses to perpetuate his brother's name in Israel; he will not perform the duty of a husband's brother to me." Then the elders of his town shall summon him and speak to him. If he persists, saying, "I have no desire to marry her," then his brother's wife shall go up to him in the presence of the elders, pull his sandal off his foot, spit in his face, and declare, "This is what is done to the man who does not build up his brother's house." Throughout Israel his family shall be known as "the house of him whose sandal was pulled off."

There has been some discussion as to whether levirate marriage transgressed two Levitical laws which stated that a man "shall not uncover the nakedness of [his] brother's wife; it is [his] brother's nakedness" (Lev 18:16), and that "if a man takes his brother's wife, it is impurity; he has uncovered his brother's nakedness; they shall be childless" (Lev 20:21). Were these hard and fast laws, or did the brother's death render them inapplicable?

Morgenstern believes that the law as stated in Deuteronomy was at a developmental stage that allowed the *levir* to marry the widow under very strict conditions, whereas the Levitical law, which he believes forbade the marriage of a man and his sister-in-law under any circumstances, was the final stage.[10] Seidler and Driver disagree, stating that levirate marriage was such an important part of the social structure of the time that an exception was made to allow for it.[11] Faley, on the other hand, believes the death of the husband rendered the Levitical law inapplicable and that there was no barrier to the brother marrying the widow.[12]

Manor states that by the Tannaitic era (10–220 CE), the practice was considered objectionable and was complied with only by way of duty.[13] This

---

10. Morgenstern, *Book of the Covenant*, 164–65.
11. Seidler, "Forced Marriage," 453; Driver, *Deuteronomy*, 285.
12. Faley, "Leviticus," 74.
13. Manor, "Levirate Marriage," 138.

may well have been because it ran counter to the biblical law of marriage in which a man was free to marry or issue his wife a certificate of divorce at will (Deut 24:1–4).[14] Indeed, the provision of an "appeal process" for the widow (Deut 25:7–10) would indicate that this may not have been uncommon. Perhaps the brother-in-law did not wish to marry his sister-in-law, was scrupulous concerning the Levitical law, or did not want to raise a son that wasn't seen as being his. The stories of Onan (Gen 38:8–10), Tamar (Gen 38:12–26), and Ruth (Ruth 3:1–15) are examples of men not wanting to fulfill their obligations as a *levir* (and in Onan's case, the consequences) and the lengths to which some women had to go to ensure their future safety and well-being.

That the widow became the *levir's* property is attested to by the "ceremony" of the widow removing one of the *levir's* sandals. The exchange of sandals was a way of sealing a transaction (see Ruth 4:7[15]); therefore, by removing the *levir's* sandal, the widow is stating that he forfeits any rights he has over her.[16]

The Aim of Levirate Marriage

The aim of levirate marriage was at least threefold. Firstly, it provided a line of inheritance, ensuring that property would remain within the family. Secondly, it ensured that a deceased male's "name" was not "blotted out of Israel" (Deut 25:6). For the Israelite male, the perpetuation of his name was a means of securing his continued personal existence and immortality through the life of his son.[17] As such, a son fathered by a *levir* would be considered to belong to the deceased husband. Lastly, it also provided for the deceased's continuing welfare in the hereafter, as it was a son's responsibility to perform ancestral rites on his father's behalf.[18]

Although levirate marriages were an obligation placed on the dead man's brother, it is evident from the passage quoted above that the man did, in fact, have a choice in the matter.

14. Seidler, "Forced Marriage," 437.

15. While in this passage, the *levir* removes his own sandal as an indication that he wishes to relinquish his "rights" over Ruth, it still illustrates that the idea behind the custom had survived.

16. Manor, "Levirate Marriage," 133.

17. Keil and Delitzsch, "Deuteronomy," 423; Burrows, "Levirate Marriage in Israel," 31.

18. Olanisebe, "Widow's Inheritance," 3.

Unnamed Female Prophets

It should also be acknowledged that levirate marriages did afford the widow a certain degree of comfort. Widows were not able to inherit property, and there was no social security. By remaining in her husband's family, she had a level of security, and the family had an extra pair of hands to look after children, administer and maintain the property, and perform household duties. Notwithstanding this, Weisberg points out the tension between a woman viewing a levirate marriage as a means of gaining security versus the possibility of the man feeling it was a threat to his own financial interests.[19] It is also important to keep in mind the main aims of levirate marriage—any benefit to the widow was of secondary importance.

A levirate marriage could also save the widow from the shame of being seen to be barren. The extent of the social stigma attached to a woman who could not bear a child can be gauged by the practice of the wife supplying her handmaid to her husband in the hope the handmaid would bear him a child,[20] and the provision for a man to have multiple wives in the event that his first wife was barren.[21]

Onan, not wanting to be responsible for his brother's child, while technically fulfilling his responsibility to his brother, "spilled his semen on the ground" in order that Tamar not become pregnant (Gen 38:9a).[22] This displeased God, and Onan died as a consequence, leaving Tamar once again a widow. The only son left to Judah was Shelah, who was underage. Judah sent Tamar back to her family, promising that he would give her to Shelah once he was of age. Judah, however, had no intention of doing this, as he was afraid that Shelah, too, would die. It is interesting that Judah seemed to blame Tamar for the deaths of his two sons when the text makes it clear that their deaths were as a result of their having displeased God (Gen 38:7, 10).

When it became clear to Tamar that Judah had no intention of either honoring his promise to her or of ensuring that Er's name was not blotted out from the pages of history, Tamar took matters into her own hands. By disguising herself as a prostitute, she tricked her father-in-law into sleeping with her. As payment, she accepted his offer of a kid but insisted he supply

---

19. Weisberg, "Widow of our Discontent," 405–6.

20. For example, Sarai gave Hagar to Abram (Gen 16:1–2), Rachel gave Bilhah to Jacob (Gen 30:4), and Leah gave Zilpah to Jacob (Gen 30:9).

21. For example, Elkanah had two wives. Hannah was (seemingly) barren, and his younger wife, Peninnah, was not (1 Sam 1:1–2).

22. LaCocque, *Feminine Unconventional*, 101.

her with a pledge until the animal was delivered to her. As a pledge, she asked Judah for his signet, his cord, and his staff.

In due course, Judah heard that Tamar was pregnant. Notwithstanding it was he who had behaved so badly, Judah was furious, ordering that Tamar be brought before him and burned. When Tamar was brought before Judah, she calmly stated that she was able to identify the father of her child, as she had some of his possessions. When Judah recognized his signet, cord, and staff, he immediately acknowledged his wrongdoing in not giving Tamar to his son Shelah. Tamar eventually delivered two baby boys, Perez and Zerah.

We have here a contrast between Judah and Tamar. Judah was a powerful, influential man whose responsibility it was to ensure the well-being of his daughter-in-law and the perpetuation of his son's name through levirate marriage. Tamar, on the other hand, was a widow who was discarded by the one on whom she relied for protection and forced to use her cunning and sexuality not only to secure her own survival but also to ensure the continuation of her husband's line.

By standing up to Judah and confronting him with his unethical behavior, Tamar brought home how far he (and, by extension, the society that condoned such behavior) had strayed from his covenantal obligations, which is one of a prophet's responsibilities. Not only that, but without Tamar and her cunning, the people of Judah would not have existed.[23]

Ruth/Naomi

In this story, we meet Naomi, a Jew, and her daughter-in-law Ruth, a Moabite. Both are widows and childless. They return to Bethlehem, Naomi's home, and survive from the gleanings Ruth is able to gather from the field in which she works. The field belongs to Boaz, a relative of Naomi's deceased husband. Boaz is happy for this situation to continue, is kind to Ruth, and instructs his male workers not to harass her.

However, he is in no hurry to do what the law requires of him. He is well aware that he is related to these women, just as he is aware there is another, closer male relative whose responsibility it would be to act as "kinsman redeemer," a role which would entail marrying Ruth and fathering a child to carry on her deceased husband's name. So, yet again, to ensure

---

23. Jackson, *Comedy*, 181.

they received the justice to which they were entitled, the women had to take matters into their own hands.

In chapter 3, we see the women's plans unfolding. On Naomi's instructions, Ruth prepared herself, went to the threshing floor, and waited for Boaz to fall asleep after having consumed a quantity of wine, then she "uncovered his feet" and lay on the threshing floor with him (Ruth 3:7b). This passage is full of double entendres and sexual innuendos.[24] It would have been a shocking story for its time. "Uncover" can refer to something which is revealed (Deut 29:29, Isa 40:5, 53:1) or to something which has been removed, such as the exiles (2 Kgs 25:21, Jer 52:27). It can also have sexual overtones. The book of Leviticus has a whole chapter (18) dedicated to specifications about whose nakedness one can or cannot "uncover."

"Feet" are often used as a euphemism for relieving oneself ("He came to the sheepcotes by the way, where was a cave; and Saul went in to cover his feet: and David and his men remained in the sides of the cave" [1 Sam 24:3 KJV]) or for genitals ("Thou hast built thy high place at every head of the way, and hast made thy beauty to be abhorred, and hast opened thy feet to every one that passed by, and multiplied thy whoredoms" [Ezek 15:25 KJV]).

To "lie down" or "lie with" can also be a euphemism for having sex (Gen 19:33–35, 30:15–16, 38:26, Deut 27:20).

It is important to note that Ruth was not just a puppet in Naomi's hands. Although she did follow her mother-in-law's instructions, she also took the initiative by telling Boaz, after he had discovered her, what he should do in light of the situation in which they found themselves, instead of the other way around (Ruth 3:8).

Did Naomi and Ruth want to "shame" Boaz into doing his duty toward them? If so, it seemed to have worked. He first checked with their nearest relative and—having maintained this man did not wish to exercise his "rights" over the women—Boaz decided to marry Ruth. Had they confronted him directly, he may well have responded by withdrawing the assistance he was already giving them. Instead, they resorted to their feminine wiles to ensure that the levirate law was honored and justice was done.[25]

Clearly, these women were resourceful and feisty. Rather than being passive instruments in a patriarchal society, Naomi and Ruth were women who should be ranked not only among the "matriarchs of the [Jewish]

---

24. Darr, *Far More Precious*, 65.
25. LaCocque, *Feminine Unconventional*, 102.

nation," as LaCocque calls them,[26] but also amongst its prophets. Through their actions, the levirate laws were upheld and the laws ostracizing the Moabites were invalidated.[27] If without Tamar there would have been no people of Judah, then without Ruth and Naomi there would have been no King David[28] and no Judahite royal dynasty.[29]

The Midwives—Shiphrah and Puah

In Exod 1:15–20, we read that Pharaoh, fearful the Israelites were becoming too numerous and powerful, ordered the Hebrew midwives to kill all male babies at birth. While only two midwives are named (Shiphrah and Puah), Porter has suggested there was a network of women who embarked on a campaign of "quiet resistance and strategic waiting" in order to save the lives of the Hebrew boys.[30] Fischer has compared the response of the women with that of the soldiers when Herod gave the order to kill all male children under the age of two to eliminate the threat he believed the new "king" posed to his leadership—the soldiers simply followed orders, whereas the women reflected, decided, then deliberately disobeyed.[31]

Janssen believes Shiphrah and Puah were the overseers of a company of midwives who worked in the royal harem. Consequently, she states that they would have enjoyed considerable power and would have been in a position to challenge Pharaoh's orders. Interestingly, she states that they were both tricksters and prophetesses, claiming that as part of prophecy entails speaking out against injustice, they fulfilled this by standing up to Pharaoh, who considered himself to be a god.[32]

While I agree that Shiphrah and Puah were both tricksters and prophetesses, I don't believe that the claim they were powerful and able to stand up to Pharaoh can be maintained. If they were powerful, there would have been no need for them to be tricksters. Women had to use trickery because they were powerless and vulnerable. The fact is, these women risked

---

26. LaCocque, *Feminine Unconventional*, 89.
27. LaCocque, *Feminine Unconventional*, 102.
28. Van Wolde, *Ruth and Naomi*, 129.
29. Fischer, *Women Who Wrestled*, 129.
30. Porter, *Leading Ladies*, 39; Kalmanofsky, *Dangerous Sisters*, 7.
31. Fischer, *Women Who Wrestled*, 117.
32. Janssen, "Shiphrah and Puah," 15–16, 19.

their own lives in order to save the lives of countless male Hebrew babies, amongst which was Moses.

Shiphrah and Puah, along with all the Hebrew midwives, held up what was—a world of tyranny and death—and promoted what could be—"the power and courage to imagine a different future without slavery and tyranny, transforming the birth of the oppressed into an event of national significance."[33] And that is one of the marks of a true prophet.

Judith

Like Esther, Judith's story is a rollicking yarn of villains, heroines, subterfuge, humor, and its fair share of raunchiness. The story begins with a description of the military might of King Nebuchadnezzar and his successful assaults on various nations (Jdt 1). After resting from his exploits, he decided to take revenge on the nations who had refused to assist him and assigned Holofernes, the chief general of his army, to gather a force and "march out against all the land to the west, because they disobeyed my orders" (Jdt 2:6). This Holofernes does, leaving a trail of death and destruction in his wake (Jdt 2–3). The Israelites, learning of Holofernes's campaigns, became "greatly terrified" for the safety of the newly rededicated temple in Jerusalem, as Bethulia was, strategically speaking, the gateway to Jerusalem (Jdt 4:2). Putting sackcloth on all men, women, children, and cattle (3:5–9), they pleaded with God to save them and Jerusalem from Holofernes's nefarious intentions (Jdt 4:8–15).

In preparation, Holofernes asked for a report on how large the Israelite army was. Achior, the leader of the Ammonites, advised Holofernes not to attack, giving the strength of Israel's God as the main reason (Jdt 5). For his troubles, Achior is tied up, taken to Bethulia, and left for the Israelites to deal with. When Achior explained what had happened, he was feted as a hero (Jdt 6).

Holofernes, deciding to starve the Israelites out, took possession of the springs on which Bethulia relied for its water. Soon, the water ran out and the Bethulians turned on the elders, blaming them for the situation in which they found themselves. Uzziah, one of the magistrates, decided they should continue praying for five more days to see what God would do (Jdt 7).

---

33. Lederman-Daniely, "Revealing Miriam's Prophecy," 13.

Finally, our heroine enters the story. In a speech reminiscent of God's dialogue with Job (Job 40), Judith upbraids the elders for their lack of faith and announces she has a plan that will not only save Bethulia but Israel as well. Judith prepares herself, and then she and her maid leave Bethulia and are soon captured by Assyrian soldiers who take her to Holofernes's tent (Jdt 8–10). Holofernes, totally bewitched by her beauty, believes Judith when she tells him she has a plan for him to capture Bethulia. After three days in the Assyrian camp, Holofernes invites Judith to be a guest at his banquet with the aim of seducing her afterward. She agrees, Holofernes drinks himself into a stupor, and Judith beheads him with his own sword. Judith gives the head to her maid, who, showing considerable sangfroid, places it in a bag. The two women leave the camp and return to Bethulia (Jdt 11–13).

On discovering their dead (and headless) general, the Assyrian army loses heart, flees in panic, and is routed by the Israelites. Judith thanks God for saving the Israelites and returns to her estate, where she lives a long and happy life. Her exploits become well known, and, not surprisingly, no one dares attack Bethulia for a very long time (Jdt 14–16).

So, here we have another woman who, taking matters into her own hands, tricks the seemingly powerful character in the story and achieves literally life-saving outcomes. However, Judith's achievements were greater than simply saving the lives of the Israelites. We were told near the beginning of the story that part of Holofernes's duties on behalf of King Nebuchadnezzar was to "destroy all the gods of the land" and enforce worship of the king (3:8). That means Judith almost single-handedly saved her people, the newly rebuilt temple, and the Jewish cult.[34]

She also chose to go against Deuteronomic law (Deut 23:3–6) by accepting Achior the Ammonite into the assembly in recognition of his assistance (Jdt 14:10). There can be no doubt Judith should be counted amongst the prophets: she stood up to the high priest, protected lives, saved the cult, accepted people from other nations into the assembly, and finally, by way of celebration, she—like Miriam before her—led *all the people* in a dance of celebration and thanksgiving.

---

34. LaCocque, *Feminine Unconventional*, 34.

Unnamed Female Prophets

The "Dismissed"

We now turn to a group of women whom I have called the "dismissed." I hope by now our socially conditioned image of what a prophet should be is changing as we realize prophets can, and do, come in all shapes and sizes. In subsequent chapters, we will meet prophets who are widows, frantic mothers, foreigners, sinners, and servants, and one who is the hypothetical subject of a theological conundrum. Some of these women's stories are so astonishing, I have given them their own chapters. I hope you enjoy getting to know them as much as I have.

Hagar

As discussed briefly in the previous chapter, Hagar was Sarah's Egyptian slave girl. When Sarah was unable to conceive, she gave Hagar to Abraham so that she could bear a child for him. After conceiving, it seems Hagar felt superior to Sarah, a situation Sarah could not abide. Sarah began to mistreat Hagar, resulting in Hagar fleeing into the wilderness. It is here that Hagar had an encounter with the "angel of the Lord," who convinced her to return to Sarah. She did so and delivered a son named Ishmael. Sarah eventually became pregnant, giving birth to Isaac. Sarah did not want Ishmael to have any part in Abraham's inheritance, so she convinced Abraham to have both Hagar and Ishmael driven away. Abraham reluctantly agreed, providing Hagar with bread and water. When the water ran out, Hagar is said to have cast the "child" under a bush because she didn't want to hear its cries. This is slightly confusing, as it seems Ishmael had been circumcised at the age of thirteen (Gen 17:25). Nevertheless, Hagar had another encounter with an angel who reassured her that Ishmael would be the founder of a great nation and who provided water for her and her son.

There are several interesting aspects of this story, as well as important parallels to other Old Testament characters. Firstly, Hagar, an Egyptian, had two lengthy conversations with God, which Brenneman believes cements Hagar's prophetic credentials.[35] While in the second discourse, the angel is identified as God, in the first conversation, the angel's identity does not become clear until he declares that "*I* will so greatly multiply your offspring that they cannot be counted for multitude" (Gen 16:10, my emphasis). This is not unusual, as there are a number of instances in Scripture where the

---

35. Brenneman, "Your Daughters Shall Prophesy," 58.

angel of the Lord is later discovered to have been God himself (Gen 18:1–15, 32:22–32). Hagar realizes to whom she is speaking and then goes on to name God "El-roi," which means "the God who sees me." This is remarkable, as Hagar is the only character in Scripture who gives God a name.[36]

God is also the only one who calls Hagar by her name in this entire narrative. Sarah and Abraham, for whom she had done so much, merely referred to her as a slave girl (Gen 16:2, 5, 6) or "this slave woman" (Gen 21:13). God saw Hagar as a person in her own right, whereas Sarah and Abraham viewed her as a commodity. Hagar's motive for naming God becomes clear—it was not an act of presumption on her part but a response of gratitude and relief at finally being seen as a person.

And as a way of recognizing the importance of this encounter in her life, Hagar immortalizes the place at which she met God by setting up a shrine[37] and naming it $b^e\bar{e}r$ $laḥay$ $r\bar{o}$'$\hat{i}$, which means "the well of Him who lives and sees me."[38]

Hagar's story also has some interesting parallels with the stories of two other prophets, Abraham and Elijah. Like Abraham, although for quite different reasons, Hagar saw no alternative but to allow her son to die (Gen 22:9–10, 21:15–16). However, God intervened, providing what was required to enable both children to live (Gen 22:11–14, 21:19).

The similarities between Hagar's story and that of Elijah are also telling. After running away in an attempt to escape Jezebel, a despondent Elijah sat under a broom tree and asked God that he might die (1 Kgs 19:4). Hagar, too, sat waiting to die after her skin of water had run out (Gen 21:15–16). Again, God provided what was needed: a well of water for Hagar and her son (Gen 21:19), and a cake and jar of water for Elijah (1 Kgs 19:6).

Although Hagar's story has aspects and experiences shared with other well-known prophets, only Hagar can claim to have been the first recipient of a visit from an angel (Gen 16:7), the first annunciation (Gen 16:11–12), the only woman to be promised innumerable descendants (Gen 16:10), the only person who bestows a name on God, and the first person and only woman to have named the place of her encounter with God. Not bad for an Egyptian slave girl.

---

36. Dennis, *Sarah Laughed*, 63; Thompson, *Writing the Wrongs*, 18.
37. Fischer, *Women who Wrestled with*, 18.
38. Hamilton, *Book of Genesis*, 457.

Unnamed Female Prophets

The "Wailing Women"

As we have seen, one aspect of the role of the prophetess was to lead the people in dances and songs of praise and thanksgiving. It would, therefore, stand to reason they would also lead the people in lamentation. Claassens has suggested that the wailing women in Ezekiel (32:16) and Jeremiah (9:17–20) can be classified as prophets.[39] Miller, however, disagrees, stating that the women in Jeremiah were only professional mourners and were not undertaking "prophetic or divine lament."[40]

What was the role of the wailing women? Just as Miriam and Judith led their people in a dance, the purpose of which was to emphasize the spiritual importance of their deliverance, wailing women led their people in a communal expression of the grief and trauma they had endured at the hands of their enemies and continued to endure as exiles. This act of communal lamentation also served as an expression of repentance for having strayed from God's ways (Jer 9:1–16) and as an entreaty for God to look favorably on them again.

Interestingly, in the Ezekiel passage, it is Ezekiel who is instructed to begin the lamentation over Egypt (Ezek 32:1), and the wailing women to finish it (Ezek 32:16). It is also noteworthy that it is not just the Jewish women who are to raise the lament; "women of all nations shall chant it" (Ezek 32:16). This "partnership" between Ezekiel and the wailing women served three purposes. Firstly, it provided the contrast between judgment and mercy. Yes, God was a God of judgment, but there was always the promise that God would never renege on his side of the covenant, regardless of how many times the Israelites did. This also served to put a "feminine" face on God—God loved, forgave, nurtured, and lamented over the plight of the people. And finally, it reinforced one of the main messages of the prophets—God was the God of all nations, the fates of which were entirely in God's hands. The wailing women were in a perfect position to fulfill this prophetic task because, as Claassens states, they were able to bring the community together precisely because they stood outside the traditional expressions of political leadership.[41]

In the Jeremiah passage, God asked who was wise enough to understand how dire things had become and who would declare the things God

---

39. Claassens, *Mourner, Mother, Midwife*, 27.
40. Miller, "Jeremiah," 655.
41. Claassens, "Calling the Keeners," 66.

had explained to them. He then instructed that the "mourning women," the "skilled women," be called (Jer 9:17). These women, therefore, were God's oracles—God instructed them in what to say for the benefit of their community and, as we see in Ezekiel, the benefit of the other nations.

We also see wailing women at work in the New Testament when Jesus encounters them on the way to the cross. Evidently, while the wheels of (male) politics and intrigue grind inexorably toward death, it is left to one of the most marginalized groups in society, the women, to lead the lament, the purpose of which is to bring the people back to their covenantal obligations and to fullness of life and relationship.

Conclusion

In subsequent chapters, we will meet some remarkable dismissed prophetesses. However, in concluding this chapter, let's reflect for a moment on what type of image is emerging of a female prophet.

Not surprisingly, the image is complex and multifaceted. We have encountered women who, despite being vulnerable, are not victims. They are feisty women who are courageous enough to flout the conventions of their respective societies to ensure that those in power fulfill their obligations and adhere to the law. Although seemingly powerless, they used trickery, their feminine wiles, and their sexuality to defeat armies, bamboozle Pharaohs, secure dynasties, and protect monarchs from themselves. They led their people in songs and dances celebrating not political but spiritual victories and emphasizing God's deliverance of the people. They also encouraged the people to reflect on the behavior which led them into exile, composing and passing down to the next generation of wailing women laments of trauma, repentance, and hope.

Such a rich tapestry, such remarkable prophetesses.

5

What Do You See?

> To look at a thing is very different from seeing a thing.
> One does not see anything until one sees its beauty.
>
> —OSCAR WILDE

Introduction

Before going on to our next category of prophetess, we need to consider a particular type of enacted parable—one where an object or person becomes the embodiment of the prophecy. As we saw in chapter 2, it was not unusual for objects to be used to impart a prophetic message. This form of enacted parable is known as classical hypnotic role taking and usually entails the prophet having a vision. This scenario is often (but not always) introduced by God asking the prophet, "What do you see?" Once the prophet has identified the object, God then goes on to explain its significance.

An example of this type of enacted parable is Jeremiah seeing baskets containing good figs and figs so bad they could not be eaten, which signified those who obeyed God and those who did not (Jer 24:3). Other objects used as oracles include plumb lines (Amos 7:8), a lampstand (Zech 4:2), and a flying scroll (Zech 5:2). This was a particularly popular device in apocalyptic literature, where we encounter signs such as flashes of lightning and flaming torches (Rev 4:5), beasts (Dan 7:1–8), and locusts (Rev 9:3–11).

Again, as we saw in chapter 2, there were also instances where people were used as the oracle in these parables. The significance of the Rechabites and the child to whom Jesus referred (Matt 18:1–5, Mark 9:33–37, Luke 9:46–48) have already been discussed.

In the New Testament, these types of enacted parables are often found after a lesson or pronouncement by Jesus. It is very important, therefore, to know the context of these often-short, seemingly insignificant stories to enable us to grasp their full import. While the section headings furnished in many Bibles may make it easier to find particular pericopes, they can, at times, inadvertently raise mental barriers stopping us from seeing the continuity between a story, what has gone before, and what comes after.

A good example of this is the story of the widow's offering.

Our "Generous" Widow

This very short story is found in the Gospels of Mark (12:41–44) and Luke (21:1–4). In both gospels and in most translations of the Bible, the story is separated from previous text by a heading. Most commonly, the heading is "The Widow's Offering," "The Widow's Gift," or "The Widow's Mite." This tends to steer the focus to what the widow is doing rather than what she signifies. Indeed, in Luke, the story actually begins chapter 21. All this may have the effect of erecting false barriers between the stories and obscuring their continuity. In both gospels, the story is preceded by Jesus' criticism of the scribes and followed by his prediction of the destruction of the temple.

The story is short and seemingly simple—Jesus is sitting opposite the treasury watching people depositing money. Those who are rich are depositing large sums; however, a widow comes along and deposits "two small copper coins" (Mark 12:42, Luke 21:2). Jesus then comments that the widow has given, proportionately, more than the rich people, because she has given all that she has. Before taking a closer look at the story within its context, let us firstly consider some of the more traditional interpretations.

Various interpretations

Over the years, the various interpretations of this story have been fairly straightforward. Culpepper believes it to be another example of Luke's praise of pious widows and does not see it as a criticism of either the wealthy people who were contributing to the treasury or the authorities in the preceding pericope.[1] Karris disagrees, stating that Jesus does laud the woman for her generosity; however, he does so in contrast to the authorities who are forcing her to give all she has in order to help preserve a "decaying religious institution."[2] Karris also believes Luke is using the woman as a way of preparing his readers for the generosity of Jesus' own sacrificial giving of himself.[3]

Perkins and Barclay see the widow as an example of sacrificial giving. This interpretation sees Luke contrasting the widow, who gave all she had, with the rich, who contributed only out of their abundance.[4] Morris agrees, pointing out that a literal translation of the phrase "more than all of them" suggests that the widow's contribution was more valuable than all the other contributions combined.[5]

Other interpretations see the widow as an example of authentic discipleship, as she is willing to give up everything in order to follow Jesus,[6] or as displaying complete trust in God, as she gave all she had, confident God would provide for her.[7] If this be the case, she would then be in the same league as the widow of Zarephath, who gave all she had in order to feed the prophet Elijah. She was rewarded with an endless supply of meal and oil, thus saving both herself and her son from starvation (1 Kgs 17:16).

Fallon takes a slightly different approach. He believes people were called to do all they could to build up the community of prayer which was symbolized by the temple. The widow, he says, emphasized that regardless of how little she had, she was still able to serve God. God did not expect her to give what she did not have, what she used to have, or what she may have

---

1. Culpepper, "Luke," 396.
2. Karris, "Luke," 713.
3. Karris, "Luke," 713.
4. Barclay, *Luke*, 266; Perkins, "Mark," 683.
5. Morris, *Luke*, 295.
6. DiCicco, "What Can One Give," 442; Anderson, *Mark*, 287.
7. Geldenhuys, *Luke*, 520; Lane, *Mark*, 443.

in the future but only what she had here and now.[8] Of course, the question arises of whether it was God who expected her to do this or the religious authorities.

As we see from the above, most commentators have focused on the widow's generosity, her trust in God, and/or her example of true discipleship. However, I believe there is much more to this story than that. When considering an enacted parable, particularly one employing a person as the oracle, it is vital to take into account what goes before the story as well as what comes after. It may, therefore, be helpful to read the "extended" story as told by Luke (20:45—21:6) without the benefit of subheadings or chapter divisions:

> In the hearing of all the people he said to the disciples, "Beware of the scribes, who like to walk around in long robes, and love to be greeted with respect in the market-places, and to have the best seats in the synagogues and places of honor at banquets. They devour widows' houses and for the sake of appearance say long prayers. They will receive the greater condemnation." He looked up and saw rich people putting their gifts into the treasury; he also saw a poor widow put in two small copper coins. He said, "Truly I tell you, this poor widow has put in more than all of them; for all of them have contributed out of their abundance, but she out of her poverty has put in all she had to live on." When some were speaking about the temple, how it was adorned with beautiful stones and gifts dedicated to God, he said, "As for these things that you see, the days will come when not one stone will be left upon another; all will be thrown down."

The Parable in Context

As we see from the extended pericope above, immediately before the widow's story, Jesus denounces the scribes, accusing them of swanning around in long robes, expecting to be treated with the utmost respect and enjoying pride of place at banquets. Jesus' diatribe culminates in the image of one of the most vulnerable people in society at that time, the widow. Jesus accuses the scribes of devouring widows' houses, and for this, he proclaims, they will receive the greatest condemnation.

Widows, especially those who were childless, endured a very precarious existence in Hebrew society. If devoid of any (male) relatives on which

---

8. Fallon, *Saint Luke*, 304.

What Do You See?

to rely and in a society where there was no social security, widows had to fend for themselves. In a largely agricultural society, this was sometimes very difficult if they were old or infirm. Consequently, the law contained specific provisions to ensure their survival. For example, every third year, the whole annual tithe would be stored in the towns instead of being given to the temple so that the poor could "come and eat their fill" (Deut 14:28–29); at harvest time, landowners were forbidden from collecting forgotten sheafs, completely stripping the olive trees (Deut 24:19–21), or taking all the gleanings (Lev 19:9–10, 23:22; Ruth 2:3)—these were to be left to ensure widows and the poor had enough to eat.

Indeed, the rights of widows were so important to God that it was unlawful to abuse a widow or orphan. Were this to happen, they had the right to appeal directly to God for justice. If found guilty, the accused would be sentenced to death, and it would be God himself who would be the executioner (Exod 22:22–24). Smith goes so far as to describe the widow in this story as an "exhibit of evidence" in God's lawsuit against Israel.[9]

As is common in an enacted parable, in order to reinforce the oral teaching, a symbol is provided to ensure the message cannot be misunderstood or ignored. Therefore, within this context, our oracle enters the scene—not just a widow but a poor widow who proceeds to deposit into the treasury all that she had, as opposed to the rich, who contributed out of their abundance.

Jesus calls his disciples to make sure that they truly "see" the widow and understand what it is she signifies—the bankrupt state of the temple system.[10] As Smith says, the widow was the image of the "wreckage" left behind by the greediness of the scribes.[11] Seen through the lens of the widow's prophetic enactment, Jesus' next words can be seen for what they are. He is not commending the widow for her generosity or trust, he is uttering a lament for the situation in which she finds herself.

The point of the story, therefore, is not the generosity of the widow or her trust that God would provide for her. Nor is it an indication of the strength of character she displays when she does not stay in the background but joins the rich people in the temple despite the meagerness of her

---

9. Smith, "A Closer Look," 35.

10. While this is the intention in both Luke and Mark, the Markan version makes it more explicit as Jesus is said to "call his disciples" (Mk 12:43) - an invitation to consider what it was they were seeing.

11. Smith, "A Closer Look," 30.

offering.¹² The point of the story is that the scribes and the rich people who are in the temple with her seem to be not just unconcerned with her plight but unable to even see her and the situation in which she finds herself. This, as we have seen, is a symptom of Brueggemann's royal consciousness.¹³ The rich give out of their abundance, believe that is all that is required of them, and are unwilling to countenance anything that would threaten the status quo.

The widow has become God's oracle—in her own being, she epitomizes all that was wrong with society and the attitude of the religious authorities as embodied by the temple. The silent widow had "spoken," and God heard, passed judgment, and would carry out the sentence—the destruction of the temple and all it had come to signify.

Far from being a bit player in the story, the widow is the fulcrum which highlights the difference between society as it had become and the world God was working to create. By bringing the widow to the disciples' attention, Jesus was inviting them to be a part of this re-creation. And by using her as the oracle in the enacted parable, he also identified the widow as a prophet.

Conclusion

Firstly, our consideration of the story of the "generous" widow has highlighted the importance of placing any part of Scripture firmly within its context, regardless of what headings or chapter endings may suggest. This, of course, is not a new lesson, but perhaps it is a lesson of which we need to be reminded from time to time. It also serves to remind us that rigorous exegesis takes time and effort, and any attempt at arriving at an authentic hermeneutic relies on that work being done. We, as Paul points out, have been entrusted with the oracles (Rom 3:2), and we have a responsibility to interpret them as faithfully as we are able.

As we have also seen, the story of the widow's offering is an example of classic hypnotic role taking—a device used in enacted parables. This type of parable uses objects or people as the "oracles" in the story. The most obvious examples are usually found in the prophetic literature of the Old Testament, where God asks the prophet what he or she sees, the prophet identifies the object, and then God explains its significance.

12. DiCicco, "What Can One Give," 445.
13. Brueggemann, *Prophetic Imagination*, 35.

What Do You See?

In our focus story, it is the widow who was the "oracle." Because of her situation in life, she was able to "embody" how far society and the temple system had strayed from their covenantal obligations to the poor and vulnerable. Jesus' invitation to his disciples to "see" the widow only served to uncover the fact that the rich and comfortable had been rendered not only unable but unwilling to see her plight. Not only that, but the system was actually exacerbating her woes.

This nameless, silent woman pleaded her case against Israel in God's court and won. As a result, God would carry out the sentence—the temple and all it had come to embody would be destroyed. However, out of the destruction, a new temple would be erected—a temple around which a more just and equitable society would form, a society built on the lessons embodied by God's oracles. As a prophet, the widow joined with Jesus in inviting the disciples to take their part in creating this new society.

In our next chapter, we encounter another nameless, voiceless woman who firmly and successfully puts a Pharisee in his place.

6

The Forgiven Woman

The eye sees all, but the mind shows us what we want to see.
—WILLIAM SHAKESPEARE

Introduction

The story of the forgiven woman has given rise to a variety of interpretations over the years.[1] Unfortunately, most of these interpretations fail to consider the sheer impact the entrance of this woman would have had, choosing to focus instead on the conversation between Jesus and Simon. Nor do these interpretations take into account the importance of some of the rather curious elements Luke included in this radical story. The arrival of an uninvited guest at a dinner party who proceeds to behave in such an unseemly way would still cause shock and discomfort today. Imagine what the effect would have been were a woman to enter a male-only dinner in first-century Palestine and proceed to act in such a scandalous manner.

The social taboos broken by both the woman and Jesus would have made this a very shocking story for Luke's audience. To make matters worse, the woman's outrageous behavior would also have rendered Jesus ritually

---

1. While this story is more commonly referred to as "A Sinful Woman Forgiven" or "The Story of the Sinful Woman," for the purposes of this book, she will be referred to as "the forgiven woman."

unclean because he came in contact with her tears.[2] The fact that Jesus calmly accepted the woman's actions was a situation which Simon found unacceptable and which led him to question Jesus' reputation as a prophet (Luke 7:39).[3] Finally, Jesus' criticism of Simon's hospitality in comparison to that of the "sinful" woman—in Simon's own home—was a considerable loss of face for Simon, was highly embarrassing, and would have caused considerable offense.[4]

What, then, was Luke's purpose in telling this story as he did, and why did he craft his characters in such a stark way? There are aspects of this story which are quite disorienting—there is much that goes unsaid, and many questions go unanswered. Why, for example, did Simon invite Jesus to dinner in the first place only to treat him so poorly? Who was this woman? She appears from nowhere and does not utter a word but is arguably one of the most memorable and powerful characters depicted in the Bible. Also, Simon's comment regarding Jesus' status as a prophet was internal dialogue only. What did the guests think when Jesus started telling a story which seemingly had absolutely nothing to do with what was going on? And finally, did Simon (or his guests) eventually "see" the woman in a different light?

Given Luke's silence on these matters, it is reasonable to conclude that he had other reasons for telling the story as he did. What, then, was his purpose? Do we approach the story with the wrong set of questions, and if so, what important lessons are we missing? I believe that in endeavoring to answer these questions, we will come to the conclusion that this story can be interpreted as an *enacted parable*, and it is the forgiven woman who fulfills the role of the prophet.

The Story

There are four stories in the Gospels that describe Jesus being anointed by a woman: Matt 26:6–12, Mark 14:3–8, Luke 7:36–50, and John 12:1–8. However, there are significant differences between the Markan, Matthean, and Johannine versions and the story found in Luke. Firstly, Luke is the only evangelist who states that the woman was a *sinner*, and it is only in Luke that the apostles are not with Jesus. Consequently, there is no complaint

---

2. Saunders, *She Has Washed*, 49.
3. Esposito, *Jesus' Meals*, 183.
4. Fallon, *Saint Luke*, 153.

about wasting the perfume or the money which could have been made by selling it (John 12:1–5). Also, the Markan and Matthean versions take place at the home of Simon the leper at Bethany, and the woman anoints Jesus' head, not his feet. In the Johannine version, the dinner is held at the home of Lazarus, Martha, and Mary, and it is Mary who anoints Jesus' feet. This has led many commentators to conclude that while Mark, Matthew, and John are recounting the same story, Luke is describing a different event.[5]

Van Til agrees, adding that in the Lucan account, the woman's intent is different. He maintains that her actions were not an anointing but an offering. The woman's act of pouring out the ointment was an indication of her gratitude after having been forgiven and was, therefore, symbolically the same as pouring out the blood at the foot of the altar during a sin offering.[6]

For the purpose of this discussion, therefore, we will deal only with the story as described in Luke's Gospel, which, for convenience, is printed below:

> One of the Pharisees asked Jesus to eat with him, and he went into the Pharisee's house and took his place at the table. And a woman in the city, who was a sinner, having learned that he was eating in the Pharisee's house, brought an alabaster jar of ointment. She stood behind him at his feet, weeping, and began to bathe his feet with her tears and to dry them with her hair. Then she continued kissing his feet and anointing them with the ointment. Now when the Pharisee who had invited him saw it, he said to himself, "If this man were a prophet, he would have known who and what kind of woman this is who is touching him—that she is a sinner." Jesus spoke up and said to him, "Simon, I have something to say to you." "Teacher," he replied, "Speak." "A certain creditor had two debtors; one owed five hundred denarii, and the other fifty. When they could not pay, he canceled the debts for both of them. Now which of them will love him more?" Simon answered, "I suppose the one for whom he canceled the greater debt." And Jesus said to him, "'You have judged rightly." Then turning towards the woman, he said to Simon, "Do you see this woman? I entered your house; you gave me no water for my feet, but she has bathed my feet with her tears and dried them with her hair. You gave me no kiss, but from the time I came in she has not stopped kissing my feet. You did not anoint my head with oil, but she has anointed my feet with ointment. Therefore, I tell you, her sins, which were many,

---

5. E.g., Karris, *Eating*, 35; Reid, *Choosing the Better Part?*, 108.
6. Van Til, "Three Anointings," 80.

have been forgiven; hence she has shown great love. But the one to whom little is forgiven, loves little." Then he said to her, "Your sins are forgiven." But those who were at the table with him began to say among themselves, "Who is this who even forgives sins?" And he said to the woman, "Your faith has saved you; go in peace."

As mentioned above, this story has been interpreted in a variety of ways over the years. This is a brief summary of the main interpretations. We will then consider whether the story can best be described as an enacted parable.

Allegory of Divine Love

Origen interpreted the story as an allegory, with the woman representing the human soul. In his sermon on the Song of Songs, he used the forgiven woman as an example of the highest possible spiritual connection between the soul and the perfect love of the divine.[7]

An Example of Love and Gratitude

For many commentators, the story is an example of God's boundless forgiveness, and the woman's behavior is an expression of the love and gratitude she feels after having been forgiven in a prior episode not recounted by Luke.[8] Not all commentators agree, however, that the woman's actions were as a consequence of Jesus' forgiveness. Van Til, for example, suggests that Jesus forgave the woman's sins in response to the love she showed him.[9]

Ritchie believes the woman offered Jesus all she had and anointed him with her life. Her love and commitment were unconditional, and she was not afraid to demonstrate to others the depths of her gratitude and love, despite what others thought of her.[10]

---

7. See Hornsby, "Woman is a Sinner," 124.
8. E.g., Culpepper, "Luke," 170; Morris, *Luke*, 147.
9. Van Til, "Three Anointings," 80.
10. Ritchie, "Women and Christology," 88.

Self-Awareness versus Self-Sufficiency

This view sees the woman as a foil for Simon the Pharisee.[11] The woman realized her need for forgiveness and then, despite what anyone thought of her or her actions, lavishly expressed her gratitude to the one whom she believed was her Redeemer.[12] In contrast, Simon believed himself to be "righteous" simply because of his heritage.[13] Not only that, but given that Simon failed to extend to Jesus even the basic rites of hospitality due to a guest, it would seem Simon believed himself to be superior to Jesus as well.[14] The aim of the story, therefore, is didactic, with the emphasis being not on the woman but on Simon and how he responds as the action unfolds.

An Example of Service and Humility

Cassidy argues that the story illustrates that Jesus is instituting a new social order based on service and humilty.[15] This, as Powell argues, challenged traditional power structures.[16] Interestingly, when Jesus chose to use an enacted parable to emphasize that the kingdom of God was based on service and humility and not power, he did so by washing his disciples' feet (John 13:1–17).

The Nature of Forgiveness

Van Til suggests that the story contrasts the woman, who acknowledged her need for forgiveness, and Simon, who felt that his adherence to the law and reliance on the sacrificial system meant he had little for which he needed to be forgiven.[17] Reid, taking this one step further, notes that the story points out the difference in the responses of the woman (who recognizes her need for forgiveness) and Simon (who does not). As a consequence of being "forgiven much," the woman loves much.[18] Neale concurs, stating that this

---

11. Sanders, *Jews in Luke-Acts*, 106.
12. Geldenhuys, *Luke*, 233.
13. Culpepper, "Luke," 172.
14. Saunders, *She Has Washed*, 47–48.
15. Cassidy, *Jesus, Politics and Society*, 34.
16. Powell, *What Are They Saying*, 85.
17. Van Til, "Three Anointings," 76, 82.
18. Reid, *Choosing the Better Part?*, 111.

story, like others in Luke's Gospel (e.g., Luke 5:27–32) compares various "categories" of sinners and discusses their responses to God's invitation to take part in the fruits of the kingdom.[19]

Del Prado also recognizes an intrinsic relationship between love, forgiveness, and freedom. She sees Jesus' message to Simon as being that whoever forgives much, loves much, and whoever loves much, fears little.[20] The woman's fearless behavior teaches Simon (if he is open to learning) that it is love, not adherence to the strictures of the law, that brings true freedom.

Song states that this story goes to the heart of what he calls "the theology of forgiveness."[21] Simon believes that as the woman is known to be a sinner, she is not worthy of God's forgiveness, and Jesus, who seemingly does not know what type of woman she is, cannot possibly be a prophet. Simon's conclusion that Jesus could not be a prophet is a result of his inability to imagine that Jesus would have anything to do with the woman were he aware of her reputation.[22]

Restoration

For Dyck, Luke's Gospel is a description of management theory and practice in first-century Palestine.[23] He believes the story of the forgiven woman is a call for authorities to reject acquisitive economics in favor of sustenance economics with a view to restoring the vulnerable back into the community.[24]

A Feminist Perspective

With the advent of feminist theology, there has been a definite shift in focus away from the male protagonists (Jesus and Simon) and toward the woman. While this has encouraged some biblical scholars to see the woman as the hero of the story, they are yet to identify her role as being prophetic. Below is a brief summary of some of the more relevant interpretations.

19. Neale, *None but the Sinners*, 140.
20. del Prado, "I Sense God," 144.
21. Song, *In the Beginning*, 61.
22. Buckland, *Thoughts of Many Hearts*, 106.
23. Dyck, *Management*, 3.
24. Dyck, *Management*, 72.

An Example of True Discipleship

Reid and Stanford believe the woman is one of Jesus' disciples because she takes up the traditional stance and position of a disciple, which is at a teacher's feet, with Stanford also stating she expressed her discipleship by witnessing to Jesus' status and power.[25]

Reid draws thematic parallels between this story and the story of Jesus' crucifixion and death. These include the pouring out of the perfume and Jesus pouring out his blood; Jesus' assurance of salvation for the woman and the repentant criminal (Luke 23:41–42); her tears of gratitude and Peter's tears of shame after having denied Jesus; and finally, her kisses of adoration and Judas's kiss of betrayal.[26]

Justice for the Marginalized

Swartley argues that Jesus' actions highlighted his acceptance of and care for the marginalized in society.[27] More specifically, Cassidy believes the story highlights Jesus' concern for the plight of women, while Schüssler Fiorenza states that Jesus' actions were an indication that he and his movement invited into their table community not only women but notorious sinners.[28]

A New Identity

Swartley sees this story as being socially revolutionary, as the woman is not only the central character but is seen to be given a new personal and social identity—an identity which would flow onto other women, thus fighting against structural oppression.[29]

Cassidy agrees, stating that Jesus often acted in ways which would promote the possibility of new personal identity and social standing for the marginalized.[30] This new social standing not only benefited the person him- or herself but had a flow-on effect within the community.

25. Reid, "Liberative Look," 117; Stanford, *Luke's People*, 265.
26. Reid, "Paradigm for Feminist Hermeneutics," 48.
27. Swartley, "Politics and Peace," 32.
28. Cassidy, *Jesus, Politics, and Society*, 24; Schüssler Fiorenza, *In Memory of Her*, 129.
29. Swartley, "Politics and Peace, 20–21.
30. Cassidy, *Jesus, Politics, and Society*, 37.

The Forgiven Woman

Women's Equality

Saunders believes this story is significant on two levels. Firstly, he states that as the woman's actions were an example of humility and service, Jesus' interaction with her was an indication of his approval of women serving in their own right, as opposed to through a male.[31] Secondly, he points out that Jesus did not withhold forgiveness from Simon (in the parable, he was the one who was forgiven little)—both Simon and the woman were given the opportunity of a new start. This meant that in God's eyes, Simon and the woman were equal, which was a reality Simon could not accept.[32]

"Embodiment"

Many Latin American, female liberation theologians see this story as an indication of Jesus' preferment of women and an endorsement of their ministry. Aquino, for example, believes the story makes clear that women are recipients not only of the benefits of God's kingdom but also of its power, which is at work in them and through them.[33] Notably, she asserts that as women were considered inferior because of their bodies (they could not be circumcised, and they menstruated), it was precisely in their bodies where Jesus' divine activity often began (e.g., Matt 9:20–22). Bingemer agrees, stating that by accepting women as they were, including their bodies, Jesus tore down the prevailing body/soul dualism, thus declaring not only the integrated nature of the human person but that women should not be deemed unclean and discriminated against simply because of their bodies.[34]

It is interesting (and somewhat alarming) to note that menstruating women were regarded in the same way as lepers and corpses—ritually unclean and untouchable.[35] Coming into any contact with them rendered that person ritually unclean. By allowing this woman to touch him, Jesus restored the dignity of her body and signaled that women and other marginalized people had an equal right to the benefits inaugurated by the kingdom

---

31. Saunders, *She Has Washed*, 42–43.
32. Saunders, *She Has Washed*, 51.
33. Aquino, *Our Cry for Life*, 145.
34. Bingemer, "Reflections on the Trinity," 72.
35. Hubbard, "Woman," 8.

of God.³⁶ This enabled the marginalized to become what Aquino calls "the current of life-giving power of the Spirit."³⁷

The Story as Enacted Parable

As we saw with the story of the poor widow, a narrative is sometimes specifically positioned in order for it to be the "practical representation" of one of Jesus' discourses, thus fulfilling the function of an enacted parable. Therefore, in order to ascertain, firstly, whether the story of the forgiven woman is an enacted parable and, secondly, whether it can be maintained that it is she who fulfills the role of prophet, we need to set the scene for our story.

Context

Immediately preceding our pericope, Jesus accused the Pharisees of being like a group of petulant children who could not decide which game to play or whose side they were on:³⁸

> To what then will I compare the people of this generation, and what are they like? They are like children sitting in the marketplace and calling to one another,
> "We played the flute for you, and you did not dance;
> we wailed, and you did not weep."
> For John the Baptist has come eating no bread and drinking no wine, and you say, "He has a demon"; the Son of Man has come eating and drinking, and you say, "Look, a glutton and a drunkard, a friend of tax collectors and sinners!" Nevertheless, wisdom is vindicated by all her children. (Luke 7:31–35)

The Pharisees had rejected John's baptism, ostensibly because he ate no bread and drank no wine. On the other hand, they rejected Jesus' teachings because he ate and drank with sinners and tax collectors. Tragically, their unwillingness to see that the world could, and should, be different amounted to a self-exclusion from God's kingdom. In contrast, the poor

---

36. Aquino, *Our Cry for Life*, 145.
37. Aquino, *Our Cry for Life*, 147–48.
38. Neale, *None but the Sinners*, 138.

flocked to Jesus, thereby accepting the invitation to become the kingdom's co-creators.

Of particular interest is Jesus' comment that "wisdom is vindicated by all her children" (Luke 7:35). What does this mean, and why is it relevant to the story of the forgiven woman which follows this pericope?

In the Old Testament, we are told that "the fear of the Lord is the beginning of wisdom" (Ps 111:10a). However, this fear does not mean being afraid of God; on the contrary, fear of the Lord is "glory and exultation, and gladness and a crown of rejoicing . . . [it] delights the heart, and gives gladness and joy and long life" (Sir 1:11–12). The first four of the ten commandments relate to right relationship with God, while the remaining six deal with relationships with family, neighbors, and society in general (Exod 20:1–17). The implication is that when right relationship with God is maintained, the rest will follow on.

In the book of Proverbs (3:27–31), wisdom's fruit (or children) include being honest, generous, and trustworthy and not being quarrelsome, perverse, or envious. Of note in Matthew's description of Jesus' interaction with the Pharisees is that he rendered the phrase as "yet wisdom is vindicated by her deeds" (Matt 11:19b). James, one of whose main themes is that faith without works is dead (Jas 2:14–17), states that "the wisdom from above is first pure, then peaceable, gentle, willing to yield, full of mercy and good fruits, without a trace of partiality or hypocrisy" (Jas 3:17).

As one of Jesus' main allegations against the Pharisees was that they adhered to the letter of the law at the expense of justice and mercy and they believed they were justified simply because Abraham was their ancestor, it is evident Luke placed Jesus' interaction with the Pharisees before the story of the forgiven woman as a way of setting the scene for a physical example of what Jesus' teaching highlighted.

Also of note is the statement in the book of the Wisdom of Solomon that "although [Wisdom] is but one, she can do all things, and while remaining in herself, she renews all things; in every generation she passes into holy souls and makes them friends of God, and prophets; for God loves nothing so much as the person who lives with wisdom" (Wis 27–28). Not only is the scene set for the woman to be the embodiment of Jesus' teaching, but the ground has also been laid for her identification as a prophet.

The Characters

In this story, we have three main characters: Simon, Jesus, and the woman. It is probably fair to say that in any Gospel story, it is usually Jesus who is regarded as the main player. Unfortunately, it is also the case that the words and actions of male characters are given more gravitas than those of any female protagonists. This is very much the case in this story. While the woman is no doubt a dramatic character, she is often relegated to the role of a bit player compared to the interaction between Jesus and Simon. However, strong evidence can be assembled to assert that in this enacted parable, it is *the woman* who is given center stage and who enacts the prophetic "word."

The Meal

Jesus is invited to share a meal at the home of Simon the Pharisee. As mentioned earlier, there are many questions left unanswered in this story. Why, for example, was Jesus invited to the meal? Was Jesus a "visiting sage" who had been invited to eat with local dignitaries?[39] If so, did Jesus' scandalous behavior lead Simon to doubt the wisdom of his invitation? This does not explain, however, the disrespectful way in which Jesus was treated when he arrived at Simon's house. Given it was no secret that Jesus enjoyed the company of "sinners," perhaps the invitation was extended as a way of embarrassing Jesus and discrediting him in the eyes of the local dignitaries.

However, regardless of Simon's motives, the placement of this meal scene immediately following Jesus' criticism of the Pharisees' unwillingness to include the poor and vulnerable should alert readers to the fact that the scene has been set for an enacted parable.

The *meal* is a common Lucan motif which illustrates God's inclusion of the marginalized (Luke 5:29–31, 19:1–10), and Jesus often used the image of a meal or banquet to emphasize that everyone is welcome to share in God's bounty (Luke 14:12–14). This has led Harrington to propose that all Jesus' banquets were enacted parables, meant to convey that through Jesus, everyone was able to share in God's abundance.[40] Although Crabbe identifies meal scenes as being very important for interpreting Luke's Gospel,

---

39. Bailey, *Poet & Peasant*, 4.
40. Harrington, "An Enacted Parable," 47.

going so far as to state they embody Jesus' proclamations, she does not actually identify them as enacted parables.[41]

A Dramatic Entrance

Suddenly, a nameless, voiceless woman enters into this male-only event. Mullins sees this as a *fait divers*—an extraordinary occurrence which is often the catalyst for a teaching opportunity.[42] We know nothing about this woman, except that she is a "sinner." Over the years, there has been considerable speculation regarding what type of sin she may have been guilty of, with several commentators concluding she was a prostitute.[43] There is scant scriptural basis for this. Indeed, the passage gives no indication of the woman's age—she could just as easily have been an older woman who was a vicious gossip or who cheated her customers in the marketplace,[44] or whose employment may simply have necessitated her being in close contact with gentiles.[45]

Reid has argued this speculation is purely gender based, as there is little, if any, speculation as to the nature of Simon Peter's sinfulness when he labels himself "a sinful man" in the story of his call (Luke 5:8).[46] Hornsby sees a sinister motive at play in this speculation. For her, the woman is one of the most memorable and powerful characters in the Bible, and as such, it was deemed necessary for her to be neutralized, hence the branding of her as a prostitute.[47] Thurston agrees, stating that labeling this woman (and, indeed, all female biblical characters) as either a sinner or a lover, a good woman or a bad woman, a whore or a virgin, serves to stereotype them and make them manageable and safe.[48] Hornsby also believes the woman's intense femininity is used as a way to highlight Jesus' masculinity in an effort to neutralize the power which is inherent in her character.[49]

---

41. Crabbe, "Sinner and a Pharisee," 247, 250.

42. Mullins, *Luke*, 242.

43. E.g., Culpepper, "Luke," 169; Morris, *Luke*, 146; Higgs, "Forgiven Woman," 30; Saunders, *She Has Washed*, 45.

44. Mullen, *Dining with Pharisees*, 110.

45. Getty-Sullivan, *Women*, 109.

46. Reid, *Choosing the Better Part?*, 115.

47. Hornsby, "Woman Is a Sinner," 131.

48. Thurston, *Knowing Her Place*, 63.

49. Hornsby, "Woman Is a Sinner," 131.

On a more positive note, the woman is lauded for her bravery in coming, uninvited, into a male-only environment (albeit one commentator speculates the men were probably her former clients).[50]

All speculation aside, while it is unfortunate that there is a tendency to jump to the conclusion the woman was a prostitute—and this may indeed be gender based—the important point is that the woman was forgiven regardless of what her particular sin was—in Christ, there is nothing that can separate us from the love of God (Rom 8:31–39).

Scandalous Behavior

The woman stood at Jesus' feet, weeping. She knelt, untied her hair, and proceeded to wash Jesus' feet with her tears and dry them with her hair. She then kissed his feet and poured an alabaster jar of ointment over them. As mentioned, this shameful behavior was not only scandalous in itself, but it would also have brought shame on Jesus and rendered him ritually unclean.[51]

Much has been made of the woman's unbound hair, with suggestions that Simon and his guests would have construed this act as sexually provocative.[52] Indeed, Bailey suggests it was akin to a woman uncovering her breasts.[53] However, Barclay believes the loosening of the woman's hair was an indication of the depth of her gratitude and love, the extent of which was evident in the fact that she had forgotten anyone else was present except for Jesus.[54]

Interestingly, Cosgrove also lists a number of circumstances where it was acceptable, and even expected, for women to have their hair unbound. These included women praying at shrines to implore a god for help or as a sign of thanksgiving, to denote grief, or as a sign they were unmarried. Consequently, Cosgrove argues the diners would likely have assumed the woman's behavior was an expression of grief, gratefulness, propitiation, or pleading.[55]

---

50. Higgs, "Forgiven Woman," 30.
51. York, *Last Shall Be First*, 125; Buckland, *Thoughts of Many Hearts*, 123.
52. Cosgrove, "Unbound Hair," 677.
53. Bailey, *Poet & Peasant*, 9.
54. Barclay, *Luke*, 94.
55. Cosgrove, "Unbound Hair," 688.

The Forgiven Woman

Nevertheless, the end result was that Jesus' acceptance of the woman's behavior led Simon to question Jesus' credentials as a prophet. Jesus responded by telling Simon a story.

A Parable within a Parable

In this story, there are two debtors—one owing a considerable amount of money, the other a much smaller amount. Neither could pay, so the creditor decides to "forgive" both debts. Jesus asks Simon which debtor he thinks would love the creditor more. Simon, somewhat begrudgingly, nominates the debtor who was forgiven the greater amount.

Bailey sees the story of the forgiven woman as a chiasm, with the parable being the pivotal point, thus:

> Introduction (the Pharisee, Jesus, the woman)
> The Outpouring of the Woman's Love (in action)
> A Dialogue (Simon judges wrongly)
> A Parable
> A Dialogue (Simon judges rightly)
> The Outpouring of the Woman's Love (in retrospect)
> Conclusion (the Pharisee, Jesus, the Woman).[56]

While I disagree that the parable is the pivotal point of the story, it is important to note that neither debtor was in a position to repay the debt—the forgiveness of the debts was an act of unmerited grace on the part of the creditor. This means the creditor cared for both debtors, and once their debts had been forgiven, they were equal in the eyes of the creditor. No wonder Simon's response was so unenthusiastic!

What Do You See?

In my opinion, the pivotal moment in this story is Jesus' question to Simon: "Do you see this woman?" (Luke 7:44). Many commentators agree.[57] Getty-Sullivan believes Jesus' question contained a twofold challenge: firstly, for Simon to really see the woman, thereby understanding the motivation for her unorthodox actions, and secondly, to see Jesus and the kingdom in a

---

56. Bailey, *Poet & Peasant*, 1–2. This chiasm is taken verbatim from Bailey.

57. E.g., Reid, *Choosing the Better Part?*, 110; Witherington, *Ministry of Jesus*, 56; Buckland, *Thoughts of Many Hearts*, 107; Johnson, *Luke*, 129.

different light.⁵⁸ Siker believes Simon's "sin" (of which he is ignorant) is that of failing to recognize the woman as someone worthy of respect and consideration, and Worthington states that Jesus tells the parable to encourage Simon to see the woman as Jesus sees her.⁵⁹

While Tannehill considers Jesus to be the pivotal character in the story, both he and Mullen state that Jesus is encouraging Simon to see the woman as someone who can teach him about love and forgiveness.⁶⁰ This, of course, is a matter not of sight but of perception. Both Jesus and Simon have "seen" the same thing—a weeping woman who anoints Jesus' feet—but they perceive the situation very differently. Jesus sees a woman of faith (verse 50) who loved much (verse 47). Simon sees only the sinner (verse 39). For Simon, the woman is not a person but a theological category who cannot change.⁶¹ The real question posed by this story is whether Simon can change, as it is he who is "excluded" from God's table—an exclusion he has brought on himself. This parable has many similarities to that of the prodigal son (Luke 15:11–32), and, like with that parable, we are left to ponder the outcome.

Liberation theologian Paul Farmer believes the basic steps of liberation theology are "observe, judge, act."⁶² How we "see" something will determine what action, if any, we will take. The task of observation implies analysis—the willingness to go beyond what is merely seen to try to get to the heart of a situation. To judge, one must ensure that any preconceptions are laid aside. Simon, in an attempt to uphold the law as he saw it, could not do this—he could only see the woman as a sinner, as being beneath him; therefore, he felt justified in dismissing her.⁶³

A Lesson in Hospitality

Jesus then goes on to describe to Simon what it is that he sees when he looks at the woman. Jesus sees a woman who is aware of her need for forgiveness, trusts in God's mercy, and responds with love and gratitude. Simon, on the other hand, does not believe he is in need of forgiveness; therefore, he

58. Getty-Sullivan, *Women*, 105, 117.
59. Siker, *Jesus, Sin, and Perfection*, 162; Witherington, *Ministry of Jesus*, 56.
60. Tannehill, "Should We Love," 432; Mullen, *Dining with Pharisees*, 122.
61. Card, *Luke*, 103–4.
62. Farmer, "Health, Healing," 201–6.
63. Card, *Luke*, 103–4.

sees little for which he should be grateful. It is likely Simon also believes he is superior to Jesus given Jesus' reputation of fraternizing with the wrong sort of people. This, coupled with Simon's air of self-righteousness, results in Simon's lack of hospitality, which Jesus compares unfavorably with the woman's selfless adoration.

This would have been extremely embarrassing for Simon, as it was culturally unacceptable to criticize a host, regardless of how inadequate his hospitality had been.[64] It would seem from Jesus' comments that Simon did not even offer Jesus the most basic forms of hospitality any guest would have expected: water for his feet, a kiss of welcome, and oil for his head. As Bovan and Mullins point out, the woman did not do only what was required (i.e., what Simon should have done); she did more than Simon should have done—her service went above and beyond what was expected by convention.[65] Consequently, the woman herself became an example of the extravagance of God's love and forgiveness and the instrument through which God's kingdom was being advanced—a task Simon was meant to be fulfilling.[66]

Forgiven

Jesus now confirms the woman's new status and invites her to "go in peace" (Luke 7:50b), a peace based on God's forgiveness and grace. She who showed hospitality to Jesus is now able to enjoy the hospitality of God.[67]

Thurston believes the point here is that Simon was the real "sinner" and not the woman, and thus, the woman can be seen as the catalyst for shattering boundaries.[68] This being the case, it can also be argued she embodies the fact that the work of bringing about God's kingdom is an endeavor in which both God and humans are actively engaged.[69]

However, we are again left with an important unanswered question: What did Simon ultimately make of all this? Would he continue to shut himself off from experiencing the fullness of God's love because of his

---

64. Bailey, *Poet & Peasant*, 15.
65. Bovan, *Luke 1*, 291; Mullins, *Luke*, 243.
66. Tew, *Luke*, 105.
67. Byrne, *Hospitality of God*, 75.
68. Thurston, *Knowing Her Place*, 64, 67.
69. Bovan, *Luke 1*, 297.

attitude of self-sufficiency[70] and self-justification,[71] or would he heed the woman's message, realizing his faults and weaknesses, thereby opening himself to forgiveness, wholeness, and freedom?

Luke chooses not to tell us. What we do know is that the woman was able to begin her new life forgiven, validated, empowered, and free. Although she is not mentioned specifically, it may have been Luke's intention to allude to the woman's newfound status by placing the pericope of the women who supported Jesus' ministry immediately after the enacted parable.

Role Reversal and Loss of "Place"

In this story, there is a strong theme of reversal, as we are invited to see the woman's actions in comparison with those of Simon and then consider how these actions result in a staggering reversal of roles.[72] There is also an emphasis on "place" and who exactly belongs, or is (or chooses to be) in "place" or out of "place."

To begin with, for whatever reason, Simon has invited Jesus to dine with him, to enter Simon's place. The woman, uninvited, invades Simon's place: as far as Simon is concerned, she does not (and, arguably, will never) belong. However, by the end of the story, we find that several reversals have taken place. Firstly, the woman (a sinner) enters the home of a Pharisee (an upholder of the law). However, the woman leaves as a heroine, with Simon cast in the role of the "villain."[73] The actions of one who is an outcast in society are praised by Jesus at the expense of the actions of a pious Jewish man—a pillar of his society.[74] In his own home, Simon has become the sinner and the woman has emerged as the "holy one"[75]—the one through whom Wisdom is acting.

Of particular note, however, is the reversal that sees Jesus and the woman becoming joint hosts at the expense of Simon, in whose "place" the dinner was held. Jesus takes over the role of host by welcoming the woman as a guest to the meal and then blessing the woman by wishing her to go in

---

70. Barclay, *Luke*, 94.
71. Weyermann, "Christ-Centred Preaching," 597.
72. Thurston, *Knowing Her Place*, 62.
73. Neale, *None but the Sinners*, 144.
74. Witherington, *Genesis of Christianity*, 68; Witherington, *Ministry of Jesus*, 56.
75. Grassi, *God Makes Me Laugh*, 127.

peace as she leaves, both the responsibility of the host.[76] Jesus' actions seem to indicate that the woman has more claim to be at the table than Simon, in whose house the meal is being served.[77] The woman herself takes over the role of host by her actions in "welcoming" Jesus into Simon's house, something Simon did not do.[78]

Interestingly, Cosgrove is of the view that the forgiven woman became Jesus' host because he believes that she was indeed one of the women who provided for Jesus and his apostles.[79]

Sadly, having attempted to put both Jesus and this woman in their respective places, it was Simon who was shown to be out of place in the economics of God's kingdom.[80]

Forbes and Harrower suggest that the difference between the woman and Simon was the woman's openness to Jesus' message as opposed to Simon's inner attitudes which made it almost impossible for him to respond to Jesus in a positive way.[81] It is only fair to remember that we should not demonize Simon, who, as a Pharisee, was trying to protect his faith from someone whom he saw to be a danger to it. Despite his "blindness," he was not excluded—in God's kingdom there are to be no outsiders.[82] Like the elder son in the parable of the prodigal son, the door is always to be left open.

Embodiment

As we have seen, Jesus' actions (and, at times, inaction) were scandalous and broke several social taboos. Not only did he criticize Simon's level of hospitality, but he seemed to suggest Simon could learn something important from the behavior of a "sinful" woman. However, I believe Jesus' actions are much more significant than this. In "allowing" the woman to behave in the way she did, it enabled her to embody God's message and thus "speak" the prophetic word.

Tamez believes that when a woman's life "tells" or reveals something similar to the liberating story of God, then her body can be viewed as

76. Thurston, *Knowing Her Place*, 66; Grassi, *Peace on Earth*, 61.
77. Siker, *Jesus, Sin, and Perfection*, 162.
78. York, *Last Shall be First*, 125; Buckland, *Thoughts of Many Hearts*, 104.
79. Cosgrove, "Unbound Hair," 691.
80. Thurston, *Knowing Her Place*, 67.
81. Forbes and Harrower, *Raised from Obscurity*, 81.
82. Crabbe, "Sinner and a Pharisee," 247; Tannehill, "Should We Love," 433.

"sacred text."[83] While the woman's actions are, no doubt, shocking, it is what is done in silence that is most powerful. The woman does not speak a word, and Jesus accepts her actions in silence as well. Luke has described what almost amounts to a ritual, the profundity of which leaves the other guests speechless. This, in itself, is notable, as Dinkler believes that Simon's dinner was a type of symposium where witty and erudite conversation was to take place.[84] In this setting, such an interruption should have been an impetus for further (outraged) discussion. However, the diners were struck dumb by the power of the extraordinary event being played out before them.[85]

Viewed in this light, the forgiven woman's actions, done in silence but achieving maximum impact, may legitimately be viewed as "sacred text"; and that being the case, the story is an enacted parable, and the woman is a prophet.

Conclusion

The story of the forgiven woman is a combination of two organismic involvements—engrossed acting and classical hypnotic role taking. Firstly, Jesus tells Simon a story about "a certain creditor who had two debtors" (Luke 7:41–43). Like David before him, Simon is "tricked" into seeing the error of his ways. This is a classic example of engrossed acting. Secondly, Jesus then looks at Simon and asks, "Do you see this woman?" (Luke 7:44). This is an example of classical hypnotic role taking. Again, in the footsteps of the Old Testament prophets, the woman herself has become the sign. As Stacey points out, this is an important point when considering prophetic enacted parables—the prophet him- or herself was the symbol.[86]

This woman is a liminal character—she embodies and opens the door to a new way of being which has not yet fully dawned but which will bring with it the power of transformation.[87]

As we have acknowledged, by freeing her from the constrictions of only being able to be either a sinner or a lover, we are enabled to see her

---

83. Tamez, "Sacred Text," 63.
84. Dinkler, *Silent Statements*, 122.
85. Karris, *Eating*, 43.
86. Stacey, *Prophetic Drama*, 61.
87. Crabbe, "Sinner and a Pharisee," 250.

as she really is—the character through whose actions boundaries are shattered and God's bounty is recognized as being available to all people.[88]

D. A. S. Ravens believes that the fact that Luke has Jesus embarking on his ministry immediately following his bestowal of peace on the forgiven woman is an indication that she had played a part in preparing Jesus for his own prophetic mission.[89] If this is the case, it can be argued she is fulfilling a similar role to that of John the Baptist.

The woman's actions embody the repentance John the Baptist advocated and prepared the way for God's coming kingdom not only for herself but for other marginalized groups. Her behavior also illustrated the desired response to the teachings of Jesus, which was a stark contrast to the mindset of the Pharisees (Luke 7:28–35).[90]

Therefore, the woman, the embodiment of those who responded positively to Jesus' message,[91] is acknowledged by Jesus as the one through whose actions Wisdom is seen to be vindicated.[92]

---

88. Thurston, *Knowing Her Place*, 67.

89. Esposito, *Jesus' Meals*, 180.

90. E.g., Reid, *Choosing the Better Part?*, 109; Buckland, *Thoughts of Many Hearts*, 104–5; Neale, *None but the Sinners*, 137; Thurston, *Knowing Her Place*, 60; Esposito, *Jesus' Meals*, 178–9.

91. Fallon, *Saint Luke*, 152.

92. Esposito, *Jesus' Meals*, 179.

7

Whose Wife Will She Be?[1]

Women themselves have the right to live in dignity, in freedom from want and freedom from fear . . . Let us rededicate ourselves to making that a reality.

—KOFI ANNAN

Introduction

The story of the woman who had had seven husbands has traditionally been interpreted by only focusing on the thoughts, words, and intentions of the male protagonists—namely, the Sadducees and Jesus. Commentators have debated what the motivation may have been that led the Sadducees to bring this problem to Jesus, and Jesus' response has been seen as merely a defense of bodily resurrection and a correction of the Sadducees' limited understanding of the Scriptures.

The question itself ("Whose wife shall she be?") has been discounted as being irrelevant to the meaning of the story—a *reductio ad absurdum*, much like the question of how many angels can dance on the head of a pin. Taken at face value, the story is a rather mundane, two-dimensional interaction between Jesus and his opponents which ignores the important

---

1. A version of this chapter first appeared as an article in the Autumn 2021 issue of *Priscilla Papers* (Beresford, "Whose Wife").

questions "hidden" in the text: What is life like for this woman? What does it mean to be like an angel? What will life be like in the resurrection? When does resurrection life begin?

As we shall see, it is only by viewing the interaction as an enacted parable, with the woman as the prophet, that these questions can be answered adequately, allowing the real message of the story to be understood.

The Story

This story appears in all three Synoptic Gospels, with the only material difference being that Matthew and Mark include Jesus' teaching regarding the greatest commandment, whereas Luke relates that interaction earlier in his Gospel (10:25–28). Each evangelist also places the story within the same general context.

Luke describes the scene as follows (20:27–44):

> Some Sadducees, those who say there is no resurrection, came to him and asked him a question, "Teacher, Moses wrote for us that if a man's brother dies, leaving a wife but no children, the man shall marry the widow and raise up children for his brother. Now there were seven brothers; the first married, and died childless; then the second and the third married her, and so in the same way all seven died childless. Finally the woman also died. In the resurrection, therefore, whose wife will the woman be? For the seven had married her."
>
> Jesus said to them, "Those who belong to this age marry and are given in marriage; but those who are considered worthy of a place in that age and in the resurrection from the dead neither marry nor are given in marriage. Indeed they cannot die any more, because they are like angels and are children of God, being children of the resurrection. And the fact that the dead are raised Moses himself showed, in the story about the bush, where he speaks of the Lord as the God of Abraham, the God of Isaac, and the God of Jacob. Now he is God not of the dead, but of the living; for to him all of them are alive." Then some of the scribes answered, "Teacher, you have spoken well." For they no longer dared to ask him another question. Then he said to them, "How can they say that the Messiah is David's son? For David himself says in the book of Psalms, 'The Lord said to my Lord, "Sit at my right hand, until I make your enemies your footstool."' David thus calls him Lord; so how can he be his son?"

As mentioned above, interpretation has usually focused on Jesus' response to the question posed by the Sadducees, without really considering the mindset behind the question itself. This is not surprising, given that Bible publishers usually introduce the story with the heading "The Question about Resurrection." This risks focusing attention on Jesus' words concerning resurrection as an "after-life" event only and completely overlooking what Jesus might have been saying about what life should be like in the kingdom of God in the here and now.

Some interpreters also saw in this story a release from more "profane" pursuits. For example, Jerome and Calvin believed Jesus was challenging the Sadducees' view that any life after death would merely be a continuation of present life and would, therefore, require marriage as a way to ensure human propagation.[2] Calvin also stated that children of the resurrection would be like angels only inasmuch as they would no longer be subject to "infirmity and corruption."[3] Cyril of Alexandria believed that those driven by "fleshly lust" marry and are given in marriage, whereas those worthy of the resurrection will eschew all bodily pleasure and thereby be like the angels.[4] Matthew Henry also believed that marriage was a "preservative from sin" and a "remedy against fornication." For him, being like angels meant that people would no longer be plagued by the "delights" of their senses.[5]

More modern scholars agree that Jesus was attempting to correct the Sadducees' mistaken view on bodily resurrection,[6] a concept which would render marriage redundant.[7] They also believe Jesus was attempting to teach that resurrection life will be radically different than life as the Sadducees knew or wished it to be.[8] Levine, in her commentary on Matthew's Gospel, suggests the Sadducees were endeavoring to trick Jesus into condoning a woman having multiple husbands.[9]

Barclay suggests that another important lesson to be learned from this story is Jesus' ability to meet people where they are, using arguments and language they can understand. He argues that Jesus used Moses's experience

2. Karris, "Luke," 713; Calvin, *Harmony of the Gospels*, 3:30.
3. Calvin, *Harmony of the Gospels*, 3:31.
4. Cyril of Alexandria, "Sermon CXXXVI," 639.
5. Henry, *Matthew to John*, 1386–87.
6. Geldenhuys, *Luke*, 512.
7. Fallon, *Saint Luke*, 301.
8. Morris, *Luke*, 291.
9. Levine, "Matthew," 475.

at the burning bush because the books of Moses were the only books recognized by the Sadducees as being "canonical."[10]

Culpepper suggests that for modern audiences, Jesus' words on marriage could be either comforting or disturbing. For those who have experienced domestic violence, the words would be comforting; however, for those who have enjoyed happy marriages, not being married in the resurrection may be distressing.[11]

Beavis finds the parable disturbing, as there is no inherent criticism of levirate marriage in any version of the parable. On the other hand, she criticizes the "naïve anti-Judaism" of some feminist scholars whom she believes overstate the plight of Jewish widows and the extent to which levirate marriage was enforced.[12]

A Feminist Perspective

Over recent years, with the advent of feminist theology, there has been considerable debate concerning the portrayal of women not just in individual stories in Luke's gospel but in Luke-Acts in general. Opinions are diametrically opposed, with some commentators believing Luke-Acts to be a champion of women's rights while others decry the books as an example of how women were subjugated in the early church.

What follows is a brief summary of some of the arguments. For ease of reference, I have tried to group them under four subheadings (although, at times, there is some overlap): women portrayed as being equal to men; women given prominence over men; the ambivalence of the text regarding women; and the silencing and subordination of women.

Women Portrayed as Being Equal to Men

McWhirter states that according to Luke, Jesus and those who bore witness to him were prophets in the Old Testament tradition.[13] Forbes and Harrower agree, pointing out that as the Pentecost event was the fulfillment of the prophet Joel's prophecy that "I shall pour out my spirit on all

---

10. Barclay, *Luke*, 262.
11. Culpepper, "Luke," 390.
12. Beavis, "Feminist (and Other) Reflections," 617.
13. McWhirter, *Rejected Prophets*, 11.

flesh; your sons and your daughters shall prophesy" (Joel 2:28a), it stands to reason that women would both preach and prophesy.[14] In fact, Forbes and Harrower believe that whenever female witnesses of the gospel are mentioned in Luke-Acts, they are to be viewed as "full-orbed disciples without qualification."[15]

Indeed, women's participation in the life and fabric of the early church is evidenced by the fact that "the whole community" came together to elect the seven who would ensure the well-being of their society's widows (Acts 6:1–6) and that Paul chose Priscilla and Aquila (a married couple) as his ministry team at Ephesus. Both Priscilla and Aquila are noted as having the authority to correct Apollos when they discerned his lack of understanding of the Way (Acts 18:24–26).

Women Given Prominence over Men

For some, Luke's Gospel is the "women's Gospel." This view has largely been based on the two "bookends" of the Jesus story—Mary's version of the annunciation and the witness of the women at the tomb. It can be argued that Luke has a special emphasis on the poor and marginalized and that, as examples of these groups, women do play a prominent role. Indeed, Jesus' interactions with women would have been a scandalous breach of social convention and a challenge to first-century gender boundaries.[16]

Luke emphasizes women's equal standing in God's eyes by often pairing them with or contrasting them to male characters. For example, Mary believed and rejoiced at her annunciation (1:26–38), whereas Zechariah doubted (1:8–20); both Anna (2:36–38) and Simeon (2:25–32) recognized Jesus as the one foretold by the prophets; an unnamed woman provided Simon the Pharisee with a lesson in humility and hospitality (7:36–50); a widow had to leave herself penniless (21:1–4) while the scribes devoured her home (20:45–47); and the women who went to the tomb believed in Jesus' resurrection (24:1–10), whereas the apostles thought it to be "nonsense" and an "idle tale" (24:11).

Witherington, happy to nail his colors to the mast, states that Luke-Acts is "liberatory and positive" in its portrayal of women, giving them

---

14. Forbes and Harrower, *Raised from Obscurity*, 205.
15. Forbes and Harrower, *Raised From Obscurity*, 203.
16. Brueggemann, *Prophetic Imagination*, 86.

prominence over the male characters.[17] Other commentators are less effusive. Parvey, for example, while acknowledging that stories featuring women are more numerous than those featuring men, maintains that the reason for this was didactic—the stories were a way of instructing female converts, and the story of Martha and Mary (10:38–42) in particular showcased the roles now available to women.[18] D'Angelo agrees, stating that the Martha/Mary story was used as a way of encouraging women in the church to consider what they may be called to do in response to the gospel.[19]

The Ambivalence of the Text Regarding Women

Many commentators consider Luke-Acts as being ambivalent toward women, a fact which Gabaitse feels contributes to the polarized opinions regarding the portrayal of women in these books.[20]

D'Angelo sees this ambivalence (for example, the proliferation of stories including women, on the one hand, versus the seemingly restricted roles they were able to fulfill, on the other) as Luke's way of reassuring the Roman authorities that this new Christian sect did not pose a threat to the political status quo or encourage "un-Roman" practices.[21] Gabaitse agrees, adding that Luke's ambivalent treatment of the role of women in the fledgling church was to be expected, given the constraints inherent in a patriarchal society.[22]

While D'Angelo and Gabaitse seemingly classify this as an apparent ambivalence, other commentators such as Turid Seim and Gail O'Day see it as a real ambivalence. Seim, for example, states that Luke endeavors to silence his female characters; however, they nonetheless continue to speak through the stories Luke crafted.[23]

In summary, it is likely Luke-Acts was fashioned in such a way as to avoid antagonizing the Roman authorities, on the one hand, and the cultural mores of a patriarchal society, on the other. In so doing, Luke did not deny women's ministry but treated it with "acute discretion," a situation

17. Witherington, *Acts*, 137–38.
18. Parvey, "Leadership of Women," 141.
19. D'Angelo, "Women in Luke-Acts," 448.
20. Gabaitse, "Contextual Reading," 144.
21. D'Angelo, "Women in Luke-Acts," 443.
22. Gabaitse, "Contextual Reading," 144.
23. Seim, "Gospel of Luke," 761.

which makes these books a good source for women's history, although, some believe, "one that is to be used with the most vigilant suspicion."[24]

The Silencing and Subordination of Women

Our final group sees Luke-Acts as dangerous texts because, while they tell stories about women, these commentators believe the women themselves are silenced, subordinated, or misrepresented. Maloney and Smith, for example, refer to three lectionary texts set down for the Year of Luke[25]—the sinful woman (7:36–50), who, they say, is shown in a less favorable light than her counterpart in Mark and Matthew; Martha (10:38–42), whom Jesus rebukes when she complains about her sister, Mary; and the widow seeking justice (18:1–8), whom they say is often portrayed as strident and overly assertive—and conclude this alleged negative and inconsistent portrayal of women to be "insidious."[26]

Schüssler Fiorenza also refers to the story of Martha and Mary, suggesting that in portraying Martha as having been rebuked by Jesus, Luke was, in fact, seeking to diminish the leadership role women exercised in the early Christian church to that of the seemingly more subservient Mary.[27] She also states that Luke would have known of women who were prophets, teachers, leaders, and missionaries in the early church but chose not to depict them.[28] Schaberg echoes this sentiment, stating that in Luke, women are portrayed as the models of "subordinate service" who are excluded from power and denied significant responsibilities.[29]

As mentioned earlier, Luke-Acts has elicited varied and very strong opinions regarding the portrayal of women and their level of involvement in the early church. Personally, I am unable to agree with the two "extreme" views—that Luke-Acts is akin to a feminist manifesto or that it was a means of subjugating women and limiting their ministry in the early church.

It is entirely plausible that Luke had to fashion his documents so as not to antagonize a conservative patriarchal society or the Roman authorities.

---

24. D'Angelo, "Women in Luke-Acts," 461, 442.

25. In the Roman Catholic tradition, a liturgical year is dedicated to each of the Synoptic Gospels—Year A, Matthew; Year B, Mark; and Year C, Luke.

26. Maloney and Smith, "Year of Luke," 416–18.

27. Schüssler Fiorenza, "Martha and Mary," 21–35.

28. Schüssler Fiorenza, *In Memory of Her*, 50.

29. Schaberg, "Luke," 275.

Despite this, Luke still found a way to craft stories that succeeded in highlighting (albeit in subtle ways) the courage, humility, intelligence, tenacity, and curiosity of women.

It is also interesting to consider the work of Barbara E. Reid, who, some twenty-five years ago, wrote a book on Luke's Gospel. At that time, she concluded, amongst other things, the following: while women were portrayed as being healed and forgiven by Jesus, nothing was said about their discipleship, with the exception of Luke 8:1–3; while both men and women were present at Pentecost, it was only the men who were said to have been filled with the Spirit or directed by the Spirit; Luke's use of the term "to explain" rather than "to teach" to describe Priscilla and Aquila's interaction with Apollos (Acts 18:24–26) may have been a deliberate choice to restrict the teaching ministry to male disciples.[30]

However, Reid now believes there were some limitations in her approach, including the following: only examining texts dealing with female characters; separating chapters 1 and 2 from the rest of the Gospel; and concentrating on the ways Luke restricted women and overlooking more positive portrayals.[31]

After studying Luke as a whole rather than focusing on individual stories, Reid now argues that both men and women are largely silent in Luke's Gospel; both male and female disciples are corrected by Jesus, and they are both just as likely to make significant christological and/or theological statements; and in Luke, men and women seem to have equal speaking parts, although this changes in Acts, where Paul and Peter do take center stage.[32]

Reid also identifies the following as being noteworthy when considering Luke's treatment of women and their ministry: at the tomb, women are portrayed as faithful, persistent hearers and proclaimers of the word; the male disciples' poor reaction to their witness was a typical response to the words of a prophet, thereby affirming their role as witnesses; this, together with the stories about Elizabeth and Mary, emphasize the importance of women's ministry; and the fact that the women remembered Jesus' teachings (Luke 24:8) indicates their participation in Jesus' mission of liberating mercy.[33]

30. Reid, *Choosing the Better Part?*
31. Reid, "Luke," 6.
32. Reid, "Luke," 1, 6, 18.
33. Reid, "Luke," 1, 20, 6, 21.

Finally, there is the question of whether Luke was writing as a historian, a theologian, or both.[34] Was it Luke's aim to simply set out a historical account of Jesus' ministry and the birth and evolution of the early church, or did he describe current situations, more often than not featuring women, to make a theological point? If, as I believe, the latter is true, then rather than branding the widow as strident and bossy, perhaps Luke was commenting on the societal context that made it necessary for her to act in such a way. Perhaps the "sinful" woman was never meant to be an object lesson of repentance and humility. Maybe Luke's aim was to shine a light on the self-righteous, exclusive mindset of Simon the Pharisee and, by extension, the religious authorities of the day. Rather than silencing or sidelining women, Luke used them and their plight to highlight the historical inequities of the time and make a theological point.

The Story as Enacted Parable

Let's begin, as usual, by considering the context within which the story has been placed.

Context

As mentioned above, all three evangelists place this story within the same general context—namely, immediately following a question regarding whether it was legal to pay taxes to the emperor (Matt 22:15–22, Mark 12:13–17, Luke 20:20–27).

The political and religious landscape of the time was complicated. Politically, Palestine was under the control of the Romans. Luke sets the political scene early on by informing his readers that John the Baptist was conceived "in the days of King Herod of Judea" (1:5), that Emperor Augustus had decreed a census in which all people had to return to their own towns to be registered (2:1, 3), and that Quirinius was governor of Syria (2:2).

John the Baptist began his ministry "in the fifteenth year of the reign of Emperor Tiberius, when Pontius Pilate was governor of Judea, and Herod was ruler of Galilee, and his brother Philip ruler of the region of Ituraea and Trachonitis, and Lysanias ruler of Abilene" (3:1).

---

34. For an extensive discussion on this topic, see Marshall, *Luke*.

Whose Wife Will She Be?

While the accuracy of Luke's chronology has been a matter of some debate,[35] the fact remains that Palestine was a Roman vassal state, with a mixture of Roman and Judean law applying at the time.

Religiously, the Sadducees and Pharisees are the two main figures of authority we meet in the Gospels. Although usually mentioned together, they were politically and religiously quite different. In his commentary on Luke's Gospel, Barclay provides a very helpful summary of the main differences between these two influential groups. For our purposes, the following are most noteworthy: The Pharisees were not a political group and were content to accommodate any government which allowed them to carry out their ceremonies. The Sadducees, on the other hand, were mostly priests and aristocrats; they were the governing class and largely collaborated with Rome. As such, the Sadducees would not have wanted to risk antagonizing the Romans, as that would have endangered their comfortable existence.[36]

The Pharisees accepted the Scriptures and the myriad of regulations as stipulated in the oral and ceremonial law, whereas the Sadducees accepted only the written law of the Old Testament, stressing only the books of Moses. The Pharisees believed in the coming of the Messiah, resurrection, angels, and spirits; the Sadducees did not.[37]

In Galilee, Rome had appointed a puppet government presided over by Herod Antipas.[38] The Sadducees were supporters of this government and had no sympathy for anyone who challenged the status quo, as any disruptions would likely result in their own freedom, power, and influence being curtailed.[39]

We are told the aim of the question regarding taxes was to trap Jesus, hoping he would say something for which he could be handed over to the Roman authorities. The question was intended to create a "no-win" situation. If Jesus said it was lawful to pay taxes to the Romans, that would have been unpopular with the people, who rightly saw the Romans as invaders. On the other hand, stating it was not lawful to pay taxes to Rome would incur the wrath of the authorities, resulting in Jesus being arrested. Interestingly, Matthew and Mark identify Jesus' questioners as being both Pharisees and Herodians—very strange bedfellows indeed!

35. Geldenhuys, *Luke*, 39.
36. Barclay, *Luke*, 260–61.
37. Geldenhuys, *Luke*, 511.
38. Himes, *Christianity*, 44.
39. Fallon, *Saint Luke*, 300.

Jesus' clever answer ("Then give to the emperor the things that are the emperor's, and to God the things that are God's" [Luke 20:25]) not only confounds his questioners' intentions but also provides the teaching which will be enacted by our focus story.

A Legal Conundrum

So, the question is posed: A man who has six brothers dies, leaving no children. In accordance with the levirate law, his brother marries the widow, but he also dies leaving no children. So, too, the remaining five brothers. In the end, the widow herself dies. If there is a resurrection, whose wife will she be, as she has been married to all seven brothers? To us, this may seem a ludicrous scenario. However, given that in Matthew's version, the Sadducees preface the question by stating, "Now there were seven brothers among us" (Matt 22:25a), it may well be that levirate marriage was still practiced.

It may be helpful, at this point, to consider the position of women at the time in which this story was written. It is, of course, impossible to make a blanket statement regarding the place of women in the first century CE. Then, as now, a variety of factors needs to be taken into account, including geography, social status of the family, the overall view regarding women in any given society, and the prevailing religious traditions and beliefs.

For example, at the time that Luke-Acts was written, the education of women was deemed to be important in Rome, Egypt, and Asia Minor, whereas in Greece and Judea, it was not considered important to educate daughters.[40] Women in Asia Minor and Macedonia were able to wield religious influence, while women in Egypt were influential in both politics and religion. This was not the case in Greece and Rome.[41] Even though women were given some education and had some right to inheritance in the Greco-Roman empire, daughters were less favored than sons and were more likely to be exposed as infants.[42]

There was one group of women, however, that was considered to "enjoy" more freedom and privileges than normal, and that was the vestal virgins of the Roman Empire. Vestal virgins were emancipated from their fathers' rule, were permitted to own and administer their own property,

---

40. Forbes and Harrower, *Raised from Obscurity*, 28.
41. Forbes and Harrower, *Raised from Obscurity*, 28.
42. Forbes and Harrower, *Raised from Obscurity*, 29.

and could make a will.[43] However, given that they were chosen for their role between the ages of six and ten years of age, were expected to remain virgins (under threat of execution) and serve in the temple for thirty years, and then went back into a patriarchal society, their actual level of freedom was obviously limited.

Notwithstanding the above, it is generally accepted that in first-century Palestine, men from the ruling elite were involved in politics and the management of their estates, whereas their wives were responsible for domestic affairs and child-rearing.[44] Supposedly, a good wife was highly prized (Prov 31:10–31) and was instrumental in preserving the family honor.[45] In reality, however, things were often different. During his morning prayer, for example, a Jewish man would thank God that he was not "a gentile, a slave or a woman."[46]

Of course, things were different for the lower classes, and especially for those living on the margins: the sick, the poor, the orphan, and the widow. Life for a widow with no family was very precarious. There was no social security. If they had a skill, they may have been able to fend for themselves. However, if the widow was a young woman, this could be hazardous, as she risked being taken advantage of (Ruth 2:8–9). For those who could not provide for themselves, they were dependent on the generosity of others (Acts 6:1).

Added to this, a childless widow was still expected to fulfill her duty to her deceased husband should he not have offspring from any other woman. This resulted in her being married to a brother-in-law in order to produce an heir. As there was no requirement that the brother-in-law should be single, the possibility of friction in the family was considerable.

We are not told why the Sadducees asked the question. Perhaps they wanted to cast doubt on the whole notion of resurrection, thus making it and, by extension, the Pharisees look absurd.[47] However, as the Pharisees and Sadducees often asked Jesus what they considered to be unanswerable

---

43. *Britannica*, s.v. "Vestal Virgins," https://www.britannica.com/topic/Vestal-Virgins.
44. Stanford, *Luke's People*, 189.
45. Forbes and Harrower, *Raised from Obscurity*, 29.
46. Barclay, *Luke*, xvi.
47. Card, *Luke*, 226.

questions, this may have been a ruse to trap Jesus into saying something controversial[48] or to suggest that he was crazy, irrelevant, or dangerous.[49]

Like many of Jesus' interactions with the Pharisees and Sadducees, his response is cryptic. Indeed, it seems as though he is not answering their question at all. However, it had the effect of putting the Sadducees in their place (Luke 20:39–40). What was it in Jesus' response that chastened the religious authorities so effectively? Why were they afraid to ask him any more questions? Was it because, by praising Jesus' answer, the scribes had embarrassed the Sadducees and called their understanding of the Scriptures into question? Was it because the Sadducees realized the danger posed to their power and lifestyle if Jesus' "vision" were to become reality? Or was it because Jesus' response held a mirror up to their hypocrisy, and they didn't like what they saw? Let's take a closer look at exactly what Jesus said to them.

Jesus' Response

Interestingly, Jesus' response in Luke is considerably more polite compared to that recorded in Matthew's and Mark's accounts. In Matthew, Jesus says, "You are wrong, because you know neither the scriptures nor the power of God" (Matt 22:20), while in Mark, he challenges them by asking, "Is this not the reason you are wrong, that you know neither the scriptures nor the power of God?" (Mark 12:24). This flash of frustration may well have been a reflection of how Matthew and Mark, Jews writing for a mostly Jewish audience, felt. How could the very people who had been gifted with the "oracles of God" (Rom 3:2) be so blind to what the Scriptures taught and foretold? Luke, on the other hand, was a gentile writing to a mostly gentile audience, so he may not have felt this situation so keenly.

As mentioned above, Jesus does not seem to address the Sadducees' question at all. Instead, he talks about "this age" and "that age," about angels, burning bushes, and the patriarchs. The Sadducees' heads must have been spinning.

In his response, Jesus was challenging the very basis from which the Sadducees saw life, God's grace, God's power, the kingdom of God, and the nature of God's relationship with his people. And he begins by looking at the concept of marrying and being given in marriage.

48. Manor, "Levirate Marriage," 140.
49. Brueggemann, *Threat of Life*, 145.

Whose Wife Will She Be?
Marrying and Being Given in Marriage

As noted earlier, levirate marriage was mandated in the book of Deuteronomy. What is of importance when endeavoring to understand Jesus' response to the Sadducees' question is the language and grammatical tenses used in the Deuteronomic passage and by Jesus in his response (as related by Luke).

In the Deuteronomic passage, it is quite clear that the brother "takes" the widow in marriage (Deut 25:5). In Luke, the terminology used is "to marry" and "to be given in marriage"—the man "marries" (from the Greek *gameō* [to lead in marriage, to take a wife, to give a daughter in marriage]), whereas the woman is "given in marriage" (*ekgamiskō* [to give in marriage, to give away in marriage, as in a daughter]). Importantly, the word "marry" is in the present indicative active tense, while "given in marriage" is in the present indicative passive tense.[50] In other words, the man actively marries, but the woman is passively given in marriage.

It should be noted that a more literal rendering of verses 28–31 would read:

> Then came to him certain of the Sadducees, which deny that there is any resurrection; and they asked him, Saying, Master, Moses wrote unto us, If any man's brother die, having a wife, and he die without children, that his brother should *take* his wife, and raise up seed unto his brother. There were therefore seven brethren: and the first *took* a wife, and died without children. And the second *took* her to wife, and he died childless. And the third *took* her; and in like manner the seven also: and they left no children, and died. (KJV, my emphasis)

This is clearly more reflective of the mood in the Deuteronomic passage. Indeed, Kilgallen states that the Lucan version of the story emphasizes that the successive marriages were forced and the woman had no choice in the matter. He believes this uncovers the Sadducees' view that were there to be a resurrection, the woman would still be obliged to be a "passive breeder" even in the afterlife.[51] In his commentary on the Markan version of the story, Carter is scathing in his comments that levirate marriage "ensures the

---

50. Zodhiates, *Complete New Testament*, 536.
51. Kilgallen, "Sadducees," 479.

woman's body and reproductive capacity serve male values, and provides no space for the woman's agency, choice, will or even well-being."[52]

Seim disagrees, suggesting that Luke uses a rare middle form of the verb "to marry" which has the effect of making the woman the subject of the sentence; that is, she lets or does not let herself be married.[53] However, given the prevailing culture of the time and Luke's overarching theme of Jesus bringing good news and freedom to the poor and oppressed, this nuance of the middle voice is unlikely.

Seidler also highlights an interesting wordplay in the Deuteronomy passage. In verse 7, the *levir*, up until now referred to as "the dead man's brother," becomes "the man." In contrast, however, the woman is always referred to as "the dead man's wife."[54] This recognizes the man as a person with his own personality and desires, whereas the woman remains someone's property.

It is here that the point of Jesus' response and Luke's placement of the story (immediately following the question about paying taxes) takes on its full meaning. Luke tells us that the religious authorities are trying to prove that Jesus is a danger to both the religious (20:1–8) and the political (20:20–26) systems of the day.[55] So, they asked him whether it was lawful to pay taxes to the emperor. If he said "yes," Jesus would prove himself to be a traitor to the Jewish cause. By saying "no," he would incur the wrath of Roman authorities. Again, instead of answering their question directly, Jesus requests to see a coin and then asks his own question—whose image is on it. When the reply is that the image is of the Roman emperor, Jesus states that what belongs to the emperor should be given to the emperor, but what belongs to God should be given to God.

Immediately following this interaction, in all three Synoptic Gospels comes the question of the resurrection. The implication is clear: just as the coin is imprinted with the emperor's image and so belongs to the emperor, men and women both reflect the Maker's mark. They are made in God's image and likeness (Gen 1:26–27) and belong to God alone. The reason that they shall neither marry nor be given in marriage in the resurrection is that in the resurrection, women, made in God's image, will cease to be property.

---

52. Carter, "Mark," 339.
53. Seim, "Gospel of Luke," 759.
54. Seidler, "Forced Marriage," 445.
55. Brueggemann, *Threat of Life*, 145.

Jesus then further challenged the Sadducees by likening the children of the resurrection to angels (Luke 20:36), creatures in which the Sadducees did not believe.

Angels

As noted earlier, some commentators have suggested that Jesus' comments simply mean that because in the resurrection people will no longer die, there will no longer be a need to marry and procreate.[56] This is overly simplistic and often implies a negative view of human sexuality.

Bendoraitis believes the resurrected, like angels, are somehow associated with God in the heavenly realm.[57] Augustine agreed, stating that part of that angelic life would include seeing God face to face.[58]

Augustine also believed that God was revealed through the created order, principally through the good angels.[59] Therefore, one aspect of being like angels would seem to be that both men and women would reveal something about God and what life would be like in God's kingdom.

It is important to note the link between Jesus' comments concerning angels and his previous statement affirming they would neither marry nor be given in marriage. Jesus did not say that "they," the men, would be like angels but that both those who married and those who *were given in marriage* would be like angels. As Aquino points out, the patriarchal socioreligious laws of the time stated that because they were not circumcised, women were in a perpetual state of impurity and therefore could not belong to the holy people of God.[60] Jesus turns this notion completely on its head, stating unequivocally that both men and women would be like angels.

Note also Jesus' words that "those who *are* considered worthy for a place in *that* age" will be like angels (Luke 20:35, my emphasis). The benefits of the kingdom are not something to be yearned for at some future time, after death. The benefits of the kingdom are available now. Indeed, Jesus himself proclaimed that the "kingdom of God has come near" (Mark 1:15) and that he had come "that they may have life, and have it abundantly

---

56. Culpepper, "Luke," 389; Geldenhuys, *Luke*, 511; Fallon, *Saint Luke*, 301.
57. Bendoraitis, *Angels in Matthew*, 161.
58. Klein, *Augustine's Theology of Angels*, 89, 86.
59. Klein, *Augustine's Theology of Angels*, 112.
60. Aquino, *Our Cry for Life*, 145.

(John 10:10). When Jesus identified himself as the suffering servant, the one sent "to bring good news to the poor," "to proclaim release to the captives and recovery of sight to the blind," and "to let the oppressed go free" (Luke 4:18–19a), he also proclaimed that "today this Scripture has been fulfilled in your hearing" (Luke 4:21b). It is clear that for Luke, the kingdom of God is all about human transformation, individual and societal.[61]

Jesus' resurrection had far greater implications than his being raised from the dead. It implied that the cause he embodied had also triumphed over death. As Hunter has pointed out, the resurrection was an eschatological act of God every bit as new and amazing as creation.[62]

So, what exactly does it mean to be like angels? It means having a personal, intimate relationship with God. It means living in a society where it is acknowledged that everyone is made in God's image and treated with the respect that demands. It means no one is excluded and no one goes without. It means being a partner with God and working toward bringing to fruition God's vision of the future. As Westermann says, angels represent God's possibilities and are the means by which God's word or act touches the earth.[63]

This was a blow to the beliefs of the Sadducees, who assumed (as did the Pharisees) that any resurrection or coming of the Messiah would simply affirm the status quo and set existing societal norms in concrete.[64]

And finally, it meant that relationship with God and the benefits of the kingdom not only transcended death but were fully realized "in that age." To make this point, Jesus refers to God's ongoing relationship with the patriarchs.

The Patriarchs

Jesus now cements his arguments on the resurrection by appealing to the testimony of Moses—an authority he knew the Sadducees could not discount or refute.[65] Moses testified that at the burning bush, God had identified himself as being "the God of your father, the God of Abraham, the God

---

61. Byrne, *Hospitality of God*, 5.
62. Hunter, *New Testament Theology*, 60.
63. Westermann, *God's Angels*, 12, 58.
64. Manor, *Levirate Marriage*, 140.
65. Card, *Luke*, 226.

of Isaac, and the God of Jacob" (Exod 3:6). For them to still be children of God, they must still be alive and able to be in relationship with God.

God chose Moses to lead the Israelites out of the bonds of slavery into the freedom of a full, intimate relationship with God, a relationship that would see the creation of a society based on justice, equity, and equality. Jesus, the new Moses, came to do the same thing.

That God also chose to disclose his name to Moses (Exod 3:13–15) is an indication of the type of relationship God wished to establish with his people—a relationship based on intimacy and a willingness to make himself available and vulnerable.[66]

And as we have already seen in the chapter dealing with Sarah, when it came to grace, blessings, respect, and equality, God did not discriminate on the basis of gender. Women were just as able to enter into an intimate, loving relationship with God and to stand alongside their male counterparts as equal participants in the covenant and the creation of God's kingdom.

Thus, just as the angels live in the heavenly realm, so, too, do the patriarchs and matriarchs—they are alive in God. God's relationship with people does not end when they die; the relationship is everlasting and personal.[67] And, as Jesus' words imply, that relationship is not limited by a person's gender. Both men and women are made in God's image, so all have equal standing before God.

The Question Regarding David

Jesus now poses his own question: How can the Messiah be David's son if David himself refers to the Messiah as "my lord" (Luke 20:41–44)? Jesus is challenging his audience to imagine a world outside their narrow perceptions of traditional categories.[68] Yes, genealogically speaking, Jesus was David's son, but he was much more than that—he was the Messiah. However, he was not the type of messiah the Jewish authorities were expecting or hoping for. They were hoping for a warrior who would usher in a golden age for Israel, an age of prosperity and political power.[69]

The Scriptures of which the Sadducees and Pharisees purported to be experts made clear this was not the type of kingdom the Messiah was going

66. Sanders, *God Who Risks*, 55.
67. Geldenhuys, *Luke*, 511.
68. Culpepper, "Luke," 391.
69. Barclay, *Luke*, 263.

to inaugurate. The messianic kingdom would be a place of love, compassion, and equity—a place where all people would be treated with kindness and dignity. In short, a place where the great commandment to love God and love your neighbor as yourself would inform all decisions and aspects of society.

Jesus' question challenged the religious authorities' view of the coming Messiah and, by extension, how they viewed society's most vulnerable. In the messianic kingdom, traditional categories that resulted in women being the property of male relatives would no longer be tolerated. Yes, women bore the children and, by and large, were the homemakers. However, women were much more than that—in God's eyes, they were equal to men, participated in the covenant in their own right, and enjoyed a personal, intimate relationship with God that would transcend death.

Conclusion

Regardless of the Sadducees' motive in bringing this question to Jesus, they certainly got more than they bargained for! While Jesus did not *answer* their question *per se*, his *response* was a lesson in the power and love of God, the economy and breadth of God's kingdom, and the availability of the benefits of resurrection life in the here and now.

The Sadducees' question highlighted some aspects of their worldview: the acceptability of women being considered property and being expected to passively acquiesce to the wishes of male family members; the belief (indeed, hope) that the kingdom of God would be business as usual, except for a few improvements—enemies would be overthrown and delights multiplied;[70] the belief that death curtailed God's ability to continue relationships; and the belief that God would allow that to happen.

As the subject in this enacted parable, this hypothetical woman succeeded in highlighting the ramifications of Moses's interaction with God at the burning bush: God is a God of relationship, a relationship not even death can destroy; both men and women are made in God's image and are equal participants in the covenant; the kingdom of God has come near, and the benefits of the kingdom—justice, equity, and equality—are available now, not just after death; and in the resurrection, both men and women will, like the angels, see God face-to-face.

---

70. Morris, *Luke*, 291.

Although nameless and voiceless, this woman succeeds in demonstrating the disconnect between the worldview of the Sadducees and the economy of God's kingdom, and for that reason, she must surely be recognized as a prophet.

8

The Woman Caught in Adultery

> We must remember that the only true wealth we have is the freedom of another human, not their entrapment.
>
> —LUJAN MATUS

Introduction

As was the case with the woman with seven husbands, the story of the woman caught in adultery has traditionally been interpreted by focusing on the interaction between Jesus and the scribes and Pharisees. The woman herself has been relegated to a bit player who has very little, if anything, to do with the import of the story.

But even a cursory look at the situation in which the woman finds herself raises considerable questions. If, as the text would suggest, she was caught "in the very act," where was the man? How did he manage to escape? Was he "helped" to escape? How was it that the scribes and Pharisees just happened to be in the right place at the right time?

If, as will be argued, this story is an enacted parable, these questions will be addressed and the woman revealed as the "oracle" through whose life a light is shone on the unethical and ruthless practices to which the religious authorities were willing to go to rid themselves of their "Jesus problem."

The Woman Caught in Adultery

John 7:53—8:11—Does It Belong?

Over the years, there has been—and, indeed, continues to be—considerable discussion as to whether this passage is canonical, to which Gospel it belongs, and where in the Gospel it should appear. There is even discussion as to whether it is acceptable for a minister to base his or her sermon on this story. Before considering the passage, it would be helpful to spend some time reviewing some of these, at times, radically divergent views.

Not Johannine

The majority of commentators believe this passage is not Johannine. Carson bases his decision on the fact that the passage does not appear in the earliest versions of Syriac and Coptic gospels; any Old Latin, Old Georgian, or Armenian manuscripts; or most Greek manuscripts prior to the medieval age. He also notes that none of the church fathers cite the passage before the tenth century CE.[1] Miller agrees, stating that for the first one thousand years of the church's existence, none of the Greek fathers, with the exception of Didymus the Blind (313–98 CE), even mention the passage.[2]

Some commentators have noted that the language is more in keeping with that found in the Synoptic Gospels. Nowhere else in John, for example, is there mention of scribes (8:3) or is Jesus referred to as a teacher (8:4).[3]

Carson cites the inconsistent placement of the passage as proof of its inauthenticity—in some manuscripts, it is found either after John 7:36, 7:44, or 21:25, or after Luke 21:38.[4] Indeed, many commentators believe the passage actually belongs in Luke given that the theme of the story aligns more with those found in that Gospel.[5]

There are, of course, a variety of suggestions regarding why the story was placed at the end of chapter 7 of John's Gospel. O'Day believes it was inserted as an example of the increasing conflict between Jesus and his opponents as described in chapters 7 and 8, whereas Temple stated it was used as an illustration of John 8:15 ("You judge by human standards; I judge no

---

1. Carson, *John*, 333.
2. Miller, "Text-Criticism," 372.
3. E.g., O'Day, "Gospel of John," 628; Morris, *John*, 883.
4. Carson, *John*, 333.
5. E.g., Sanders and Mastin, *John*, 461; Temple, *St John's Gospel*, 128; Morris, *Luke*, 147.

one").[6] Other commentators, while not considering the story to be true, nonetheless believe it to be true to the character of Jesus[7] and consistent with other Jesus traditions previously judged to be authentic,[8] and therefore worthy of inclusion in the canon.

There is a view, however, that while the story is not Johannine, it does relate a situation that actually happened,[9] because, as Kaczorowski states, it is unlikely the early church would have made up a story that potentially showed Jesus as being soft on adultery, given the moralistic mood of the church at that time.[10] Kaczorowski also believes the passage to be canonically sound because it meets the tests of apostolicity, antiquity, historical authenticity, orthodoxy, usage, and spiritual power.[11]

On the other hand, Miller and Wallace believe that as it is possible to argue against the passage's authenticity and apostolicity, it would be preferable that it not appear in Bibles at all, with Wallace citing "a continued tradition of timidity" pervading the printing of modern versions of the Bible as the reason that it still does.[12] Miller, therefore, suggests that pastors faced with this reading begin by explaining the canonical difficulties of the text before proceeding to preach on the truths contained in the narrative but citing other canonical texts in support of their comments. In this way, he says, pastors can confidently say they are preaching God's word.[13] Harris agrees, stating that if any teaching were to depend solely on this passage for its support, then that teaching could not claim to have spiritual authority.[14]

Johannine

Although vastly outnumbered, there are commentators who believe the passage to be Johannine, because rather than interrupting the flow (as Thompson argues[15]), it either contributes to the Gospel's unfolding story or

---

6. O'Day, "Gospel of John," 614; Temple, *St John's Gospel*, 145.
7. Morris, *John*, 883.
8. Kaczorowski, "Pericope," 327.
9. Temple, *St John's Gospel*, 145; Tasker, *John*, 110; Kaczorowski, "Pericope," 327.
10. Kaczorowski, "Pericope," 330.
11. Kaczorowski, "Pericope," 333.
12. Miller; "Text-Criticism," 381; Wallace, "Bart," 336.
13. Miller; "Text-Criticism," 384.
14. Harris, *John*, 166.
15. Thompson, *John*, 178–79.

represents the pinnacle of several themes John introduced and explored in preceding chapters.

Hodges, for example, believes the passage follows on naturally from verse 52, because as it was the end of the Feast of Tabernacles, observant Jews would have been returning home after spending the last seven days in "booths." He also states that any arguments against its authenticity based on its omission from some manuscripts are inconclusive, as it is possible it was deliberately omitted because of its controversial nature.[16]

Disagreeing with commentators who cite linguistic considerations as proof the passage is not Johannine, Heil believes there to be "striking" linguistic links that prove the story to be both Johannine and in the right place, because it contributes to the narrative progression of chapters 7 and 8. Firstly, Heil cites the theme of picking up stones in order to kill (John 8:7, 59), noting that when the Pharisees do take up stones, it is to kill Jesus, ironically revealing that to be their true intent all along. Heil also maintains that Jesus' command to go and sin no more (5:14, 8:11) was an invitation to recognize his true identity, thereby receiving eternal life, which was John's main purpose in writing his Gospel (20:31).[17]

Baylis believes the story is an inseparable part of chapters 7 and 8, as it provides proof that Jesus is the prophet promised by Moses (Deut 18:15). Baylis maintains that the first seven chapters of John's Gospel serve to contrast Jesus and Moses. The comparison begins in the prologue: the prophet revealed God's word, while Jesus is God's Word incarnate; Moses gave the law through which humanity was condemned, while Jesus did not come to condemn but to provide grace and forgiveness; the symbolic lamb of the Passover protected the Israelites from God's wrath, while Jesus was the Lamb of God through whose sacrifice humanity was reconciled to God.[18]

Baylis further expands his theme by highlighting the following comparisons: while Moses turned water into the blood of judgment (Exod 7:19), Jesus turned water into celebratory wine at Cana; Moses parted the waters of the Red Sea, whereas Jesus was able to walk on water; the manna provided to Moses did not stop the ancestors from dying, but Jesus was the living bread guaranteed to give eternal life. The Pharisees' aim was to trap Jesus into contradicting the law of Moses, thereby proving to the people

---

16. Hodges, "Woman Taken in Adultery," 42, 41.
17. Heil, "Jesus and the Adulteress," 182–91.
18. Baylis, "Woman Caught in Adultery," 171–84.

that he was not a prophet, but by turning the tables on them, Jesus, according to Baylis, proved that he was.[19]

Ramifications

While this ongoing discussion may be quite interesting, could it have wider ramifications? What questions does it raise in people's minds about the text's orthodoxy when, in their Bibles, it appears inside parentheses, with a footnote regarding either its omission in some ancient manuscripts and/or its placement in others?[20]

Similarly, what effect does it have when commentators seem to treat the passage as though it were "extracanonical"? For example, in their various commentaries, Bultman ignores the story altogether; Morris and Sanders and Mastin treat it as an appendix at the end of their commentaries; Carson treats it as an excursus; and Beasley-Murray and Temple discuss it after their comments on chapter 8.

And, perhaps most importantly, when a commentator approaches a text with a preconceived opinion as to its authenticity and canonicity, how does that affect their engagement with the text, their willingness to learn lessons from it, and the conclusions to which they ultimately come?

These disagreements, while they may seem to be purely academic in nature, have not only raised questions regarding the text's authenticity, but they have also caused some commentators and preachers to believe the text should only be proclaimed with heavy "caveats". Indeed, as we have seen, there is even a view that the story should not appear in the Bible at all.

Clearly, this does not have a negative effect on Jesus, the scribes, or the Pharisees—they appear in lots of other stories. But what does it do to the perceived "bit player"? These discussions could well have the effect of silencing the woman completely and rendering her totally invisible—nameless, manipulated, and all but voiceless in the story. However, given the power of her message, some may have welcomed that as a pleasing consequence.

---

19. Baylis, "Woman Caught in Adultery," 171–84.

20. The RSV omitted this passage from its publication in the 1950s until 1971, when the New Testament was revised.

The Woman Caught in Adultery

The Story

Before going on to discuss whether the passage is an enacted parable, let us firstly reacquaint ourselves with the story and some of the more traditional interpretations:

> Then each of them went home, while Jesus went to the Mount of Olives. Early in the morning he came again to the temple. All the people came to him and he sat down and began to teach them. The scribes and the Pharisees brought a woman who had been caught in adultery; and making her stand before all of them, they said to him, "Teacher, this woman was caught in the very act of committing adultery. Now in the law Moses commanded us to stone such women. Now what do you say?" They said this to test him, so that they might have some charge to bring against him. Jesus bent down and wrote with his finger on the ground. When they kept on questioning him, he straightened up and said to them, "Let anyone among you who is without sin be the first to throw a stone at her." And once again he bent down and wrote on the ground. When they heard it, they went away, one by one, beginning with the elders; and Jesus was left alone with the woman standing before him. Jesus straightened up and said to her, "Woman, where are they? Has no one condemned you?" She said, "No one, sir." And Jesus said, "Neither do I condemn you. Go your way, and from now on do not sin again." (John 7:53—8:11)

Given what we have seen in previous chapters of this book, it should come as no surprise that most commentators focus on the interaction between Jesus and the Pharisees, almost totally disregarding the woman and what her situation might convey. Broadly speaking, the most common interpretation is that the Pharisees' actions, despite their protestations to the contrary, were not concerned with the law or justice but rather were politically motivated.[21] Temple and Hodges argue that by posing what they thought to be an unanswerable question, the Pharisees sought to trap Jesus, while Barclay argues that their aim was to discredit him.[22] If Jesus upheld the letter of the law, he would effectively be pitting himself against the Roman authorities, as they were the only ones able to execute the death

---

21. O'Day argues that the Pharisees were not concerned with the law or justice, and Tasker states that their motives were politically motivated. See O'Day, "Study in Misreading," 632; Tasker, *John*, 111.

22. Temple, *St John's Gospel*, 146; Hodges, "Woman Taken in Adultery," 44; Barclay, *John*, 1.

penalty. This would probably result in him being arrested for revolutionary activities and would also ensure he lost favor with the people.[23] On the other hand, if Jesus said the woman should not be stoned, he would be seen to be contradicting the law of Moses, thus proving, as far as the Pharisees were concerned, that he was not a prophet.

Other commentators, however, placed more emphasis on the crime of which the woman was accused and Jesus' handling of the situation, rather than the Pharisees' motives and probable orchestration of the entire episode. Augustine, for example, described the scene after the Pharisees had departed as "there remained alone they two, a wretch and Mercy."[24] This simplistic interpretation does the story a grave disservice, ignoring the complexity of what is going on. Not only does it suggest the woman is somehow irredeemable, it also effectively makes the story all about her sin, rather than Jesus' challenge to the status quo and his deteriorating relationship with the Jewish authorities. The question arises, therefore, of whether the complexity of the story was deliberately sacrificed because, as Augustine wrote, men were afraid "lest their wives should gain impunity in sin."[25]

This possibility was also uppermost in Calvin's mind. He, too, emphasized the societal upheaval that would result should Jesus be seen to be condoning adultery, going to great pains to point out that although Jesus did forgive the woman, he did not seek to abolish the sentences or punishments in force at the time. This was considered to be of utmost importance, because if adultery was seen not to be a serious crime, then the door would be "thrown open to every kind of treachery" and would potentially result in property being passed on to an illegitimate child, all of which would bring disgrace to the husband, the greatest evil of all.[26]

A Feminist Perspective

Broadly speaking, recent scholarship still tends to focus on the motives behind the Pharisees' actions in bringing the woman before Jesus and the significance of Jesus' physical and verbal responses. Unfortunately, this continues to cast the woman as peripheral to the real action. For example, in her article "Nameless Women in the Canonical Gospels," Pellegrini, who

23. Sanders and Mastin, *John*, 464.
24. Augustine, *Homilies*, 477.
25. Augustine, qtd. in Sanders and Mastin, *John*, 462.
26. Calvin, *St John*, 209.

argues that the evangelists chose not to name some women in order to make their message more powerful, does not mention this woman in the body of her article at all, only including her in an appendix and simply identifying her as "the adulteress."[27] As suggested above, perhaps the discussion regarding the authenticity and canonicity of this passage has succeeded in silencing this woman even more than would be expected.

O'Day, however, does place the woman center stage, believing that Jesus does not simply speak to the woman and his opponents in this interaction but primarily to the situation in which each finds themselves, thus treating everyone as "theological equals." As such, she argues that Jesus is challenging the accepted authority of the Pharisees and offering them and the woman the opportunity of a new beginning.[28] This is the same dynamic that was at work in the story of the forgiven woman. Jesus offers those who perceive themselves to be superior and beyond reproach the opportunity to realize the error of their ways and contribute to the establishment of a society based on kingdom values.

O'Day also points out that traditional "misreadings" of the passage are based on an unhealthy interest in the woman's sin, thereby objectifying and dehumanizing her. She concludes that the various misreadings all stem from "androcentric fears" of what could happen if women's sexuality passed out of the control of their husbands, a fear that resulted in them going to extraordinary lengths to sanitize the passage in order to retain control of their women and "save Jesus from himself."[29]

The Story as Enacted Parable

Let us now turn our attention to whether this story can be interpreted as an enacted parable, with the woman fulfilling the role of prophet.

Context

As we have seen in previous chapters, it was not unusual for the evangelists to use an enacted parable as a physical demonstration of the disconnect

---

27. Pellegrini, "Nameless Women," 387–430.
28. O'Day, "John," 630.
29. O'Day, "Study in Misreading," 634–35.

between the situation as it was and what God expected it to be, a demonstration provided by this passage.

Immediately prior to this story (John 7:45–52), we learn that the Pharisees had sent the temple police to arrest Jesus. They had not done so, having been impressed by the way Jesus spoke. The Pharisees then accused the police of having been deceived by Jesus, much like the crowds, who—they stated—were accursed and ignorant of the law. Nicodemus, himself a Pharisee, pointed out that under the law of Moses, it was illegal to judge someone without first giving them a hearing, an argument summarily discounted by the Pharisees.

It is immediately following this interaction that John presents us with the story of the woman caught in adultery. A woman not given the opportunity to speak a word, let alone defend herself; a woman whose fate had been sealed well before she was allegedly caught *in flagrante delicto*.

The next scene (8:12–20) is a conversation between Jesus and the Pharisees which again focuses on what constitutes valid and invalid testimony, this time pertaining to Jesus' claims about himself and from where he came. The interaction sees Jesus reiterating the stipulation that two or more witnesses are required before a charge can be brought to trial.

Characters

Traditionally, it has been the scribes, the Pharisees, and Jesus who have been considered to be the main players in this scene. There is no doubt as to the motives of Jesus' opponents, John having dedicated much of the preceding seven chapters to establishing the growing antagonism between the parties.

Not surprisingly, the woman has been viewed as being merely a prop to help along the flow of the action. As we will soon discover, however, she and Jesus join forces to deliver a profound prophetic message.

Another "collective" character is the crowd that had gathered in the temple to listen to Jesus' teachings. Having witnessed the shocking events unfold, it is a reasonable assumption that even though the scribes and Pharisees left the scene, the crowd would have stayed to see what ended up happening.

Then, we have the woman herself—again, nameless and, if not totally silent, effectively silenced. We know nothing of her. Like the forgiven woman, she is considered a nonperson, defined by what she is said to have done, not by who she is.

The Woman Caught in Adultery

Placement

The action of this enacted parable takes place in the temple, the place where Jewish people came to be taught the law of Moses. The Pharisees make a spectacular entrance, dragging in a woman, placing her where she was the center of attention, and thereby interrupting Jesus' teaching. Given that the Pharisees' aim was not simply to prove Jesus was not a prophet but to ensure he was arrested and killed, their calling him "teacher" was disingenuous, to say the least.

It is also important to note the placement of the scribes and Pharisees in connection to the woman. The scribes and Pharisees deposited the woman "in their midst" (8:3 KJV): they surround her; she is trapped, hemmed in by them and their accusations.

Surrounding these characters is the crowd, certainly getting more than they bargained for. Reactions would, logically, have been varied—shock at this intrusion into a holy place, disgust at the heinous crime being uncovered, curiosity regarding what would happen next, anticipation of the sentence being carried out, excitement at being able to take part in the execution, and perhaps even compassion for the woman.

The "Crime" and the "Time"

The charge was adultery, a crime punishable by death (Deut 22:22, Lev 20:10). However, even if we assume there was no doubt as to her "guilt," questions still remain. If she was caught in the act, where was the man? How did he get away? Was he allowed to escape? If, as Morris suggests, it was the Pharisees who were the witnesses, how did they happen to discover the crime?[30] Had they entrapped the woman in order to entrap Jesus?

The Pharisees charge the woman with the crime for which she has been arrested and then go on to proclaim that "the law of Moses commanded us to *stone such women*" (John 8:5, my emphasis). There are two interesting issues here. Firstly, the law clearly stated that in cases of adultery, *both* the man and the woman were to be *executed* (Deut 22:22).

Secondly, the only instance where stoning is prescribed as the means of execution for both parties is when a betrothed virgin is raped in the town. She is executed because had she cried out, someone would have heard her and come to her assistance (Deut 22:23–24). On the other hand, if a betrothed virgin is raped in the open country, only the man is to be executed,

---

30. Morris, *John*, 885.

because even if she had cried out, there may not have been anyone there to hear her and come to her aid (Deut 22:25–27).

Are we to infer, therefore, that the woman the Pharisees chose to use as a pawn in their quest to have Jesus killed was a betrothed virgin who, given the traditions of that society, would have probably been just into her teens? Or, even more disturbingly, given the section of the law cited by the Pharisees themselves, are we to deduce the woman (girl) was actually a victim of rape? Does this scenario make sense of the Pharisees' comment that *such women* were to be stoned?

After accusing the woman, passing judgment on her without a trial or giving her the opportunity to speak on her own behalf, and proclaiming what the sentence should be, the Pharisees then demanded a ruling from Jesus.

Jesus' Physical Response

As usual, Jesus chose not to play the Pharisees' game, instead bending down and writing on the ground, a move that must have both perplexed and infuriated his interlocutors. Unsurprisingly, there has been a lot of speculation as to what it was that Jesus wrote, if anything.

Temple, for example, believes Jesus didn't write anything but was so horrified by what was going on in the temple that he stooped down in order to hide his agitation.[31] Barclay suggests it is possible that Jesus listed the Pharisees' sins. As evidence of this view, he cites an Armenian manuscript which reads, "He himself, bowing his head, was writing with his finger on the earth to declare their sins and they were seeing their several sins on the stones."[32]

Derrett suggests Jesus wrote two passages from Scripture, the first being "You shall not join hands with the wicked to act as a malicious witness (Exod 23:1b) and the second, "Keep far from a false charge, and do not kill the innocent and those in the right, for I will not acquit the guilty" (Exod 23:7).[33] Carson believes Jesus wrote part of Jer 17:13: "Those who turn away from you shall be recorded in the underworld, for they have forsaken the fountain of living water, the Lord."[34] Finally, Card points out a connection

---

31. Temple, *St John's Gospel*, 146.
32. Barclay, *John*, 3.
33. Derrett, *Law*, 187.
34. Carson, *John*, 335.

to Prov 20:9 ("Who can say, 'I have made my heart clean; I am pure from my sin'?"), a connection he states also points to the passage being Johannine, given John's use of the wisdom writings elsewhere in his Gospel.[35]

Sanders and Mastin believe Jesus was mirroring the custom of Roman magistrates, who wrote down their sentences before pronouncing them.[36] Both Hodges and Baylis draw a parallel between Jesus writing on the ground and the finger of God inscribing the law onto the tablets (Exod 31:18), with Baylis citing this as further proof that John used this passage to prove Jesus was the prophet predicted by Moses.[37]

While interesting, all speculation is ultimately academic, as—apart from showing frustration—the scribes and Pharisees did not react to what Jesus did but rather to what he said. As O'Day points out, Jesus' refusal to respond verbally was an indication he was well aware of the trap they were setting for him. In their hubris, his opponents could not imagine how he could avoid springing the trap on himself, so they persisted in their questioning. She also states that focusing on just that small segment of the story shows a dissatisfaction and distrust in the story as written, effectively shifting the focus away from the fact that Jesus treated the woman as a social equal to the Pharisees.[38]

Jesus' First Verbal Response—Setting the Scene

Given that John didn't shy away from portraying the extent of the animosity between the Pharisees and Jesus (5:39–47, 8:23–29), this interaction is almost anticlimactic. Jesus simply straightens up, invites anyone who is without sin to throw the first stone, and then stoops down again and writes on the ground, indicating he has said all he intends to say on the matter.

Not surprisingly, there have been a variety of suggestions regarding what Jesus meant when he said "without sin." Sanders and Mastin believe it meant being without sin at all, the aim being to teach the Pharisees how presumptuous they were in believing themselves worthy to sit in judgment in place of God, whereas Barclay believes Jesus was referring to sinful

---

35. Card, *John*, 105.
36. Sanders and Mastin, *John*, 465.
37. Hodges, "Woman Taken in Adultery," 46; Baylis, "Woman Caught in Adultery," 180.
38. O'Day, "Study in Misreading," 632, 636.

desires.[39] Carson and Hodges believe the sin in question to be more specific, suggesting Jesus was actually referring to adultery, thus cutting through the double standards that existed in that society.[40]

All the above interpretations assume the Pharisees took the opportunity to examine their lives and motives, realized their own sinfulness, repented, and left the scene with their tails between their legs, a situation not borne out in the remainder of the Gospel. Yes, they did leave the scene with their tails between their legs, but only to regroup and continue their quest to trap Jesus and have him killed. More likely, they were thinking of that inconvenient part of the law that states the following:

> A single witness shall not suffice to convict a person of any crime or wrongdoing in connection with any offense that may be committed. Only on the evidence of two or three witnesses shall a charge be sustained. If a malicious witness comes forward to accuse someone of wrongdoing, then both parties to the dispute shall appear before the Lord, before the priests and the judges who are in office in those days, and the judges shall make a thorough inquiry. If the witness is a false witness, having testified falsely against another, then you shall do to the false witness just as the false witness had meant to do to the other. So you shall purge the evil from your midst. The rest shall hear and be afraid, and a crime such as this shall never again be committed among you. Show no pity: life for life, eye for eye, tooth for tooth, hand for hand, foot for foot. (Deut 19:15–21)

The Outcome

This is where the reversal in our enacted parable begins to take place, heralded by a dramatic change in the scene. The scribes and Pharisees, who refused to allow the woman to speak on her own behalf, are themselves silenced. They who believed it was their right to decide who was or was not worthy to be in the temple are the ones who are forced to leave one by one, slowly dismantling the circle they had formed around the woman. In the end, only Jesus and the woman remain "center stage." Although Jesus stoops and stands twice in the course of the story, he and the woman are effectively the only two characters able to stand their ground. This is an

---

39. Sanders and Mastin, *John*, 465; Barclay, *John*, 4.
40. Carson, *John*, 336; Hodges, "Woman Taken in Adultery," 48.

incredibly powerful image, something that would not have been lost on members of the crowd.

As we saw in the story of the forgiven woman, there has been a dramatic reversal of roles. Those who saw themselves as the arbiters of the law were displaced by someone whom they considered to be dispensable: a chattel, a pawn, a sinner, a mere woman.

Jesus and the Woman—The Scene Continues

The remaining characters in this enacted parable are Jesus, the woman, and the members of the crowd who stay to see what will happen next. It is important to remember that it is only the reader who is aware of the Pharisees' plot to trap Jesus. As far as the crowd is concerned, the woman is guilty as charged—it is, after all, Pharisees who have accused her. What is going through their minds? If the woman has been caught in the act, why have the Pharisees not carried out the sentence, as is their duty? What does it mean that they have instead left the temple in silence? What will happen to the woman now? It is for their benefit that the scene continues to be played out.

Although Jesus must be aware of what is going on around him, he nonetheless asks the woman where her accusers are and whether any have condemned her. Jesus thus passes the baton to the woman, leaving it to her to deliver the prophetic message.

The Woman's Response

Historically, not much—if anything—has been written about the woman's response. It is important to note, however, that the woman uses the same word (in Greek, *oedeís*) in her response to Jesus as he uses in his question to her. The conversation between Jesus and the woman can more literally be rendered: "Woman, where are they? Has *not even one* condemned you?" "*Not even one*, sir." The more modern translation of "no one" waters down the emphatic tone of the interaction and obscures the fact that this is another example of engrossed acting.

The woman now finds herself joining forces with Jesus as a fellow actor in this enacted parable. Once the epicenter of condemnation, the woman is now the one through whom God's compassion and freedom are being demonstrated and offered.

Before You Were Born, I Anointed You

An Offer of Freedom

Many commentators believe that because Jesus told the woman to "go your way, and from now on do not sin again," it confirms her guilt (John 8:11).[41] Indeed, the NIV translates Jesus' comment as "Leave your life of sin," suggesting her to be a serial adulteress. This is not borne out in the Greek, which simply encourages the woman to go and sin no longer. Again, we are confronted with this "bipolar" portrayal of women—they are either virgins or whores.

To our ears, it sounds unconscionable that a woman who had been, at best, entrapped or, at worst, raped would have to be forgiven. However, do we need to understand Jesus' words in this way? There are several instances where Jesus "forgives" people in situations where no "sin" has been identified. The paralytic, whose friends bring him to Jesus, is told that his sins are forgiven and that he should take up his bed and walk (Matt 9:2–8, Mark 2:1–12, Luke 5:17–26). Interestingly, in Matthew's version, Jesus is recorded as encouraging the man to "take heart" (9:2), from the Greek root *tharsos*, which means "daring," "boldness," or "courage."[42]

Also of note is the man Jesus healed at the pool at Bethzatha, who had been paralyzed for thirty-eight years (John 5:1–18). Jesus prefaced his encouragement for the man to sin no more with the words "See, you have been made well!" (John 5:14b). The Greek root is *hygiēs*, which, while it can mean "whole in body," can also mean "true in doctrine."[43] Because of his encounter with Jesus, this man was made right with God and, like the paralytic in Matthew, could now go out boldly to begin a new life.

The woman finds herself in a similar situation. Even if she had been guilty of adultery, she was also the victim of a cynical attempt at entrapment. Unlike the Pharisees, Jesus was always more interested in fulfilling the spirit of the law rather than the letter of the law. The man at the pool was, after all, one of Jesus' "Sabbath healings."

As the focal character in this enacted parable, the woman demonstrated to the people in the crowd the extent of God's mercy and love. Her situation also confronted them with how they had automatically "seen" her and compared that with how Jesus saw her. The woman symbolized, in her

---

41. Carson, *John*, 337; Sanders and Mastin, *John*, 466; Temple, *St John's Gospel*, 146; Morris, *John*, 886.

42. Zodhiates, *Complete New Testament*, 718.

43. Zodhiates, *Complete New Testament*, 1403.

being, the freedom and healing offered to her and, by extension, to all people. Tragically, Jesus' words of forgiveness, healing, and liberty, while meant for everyone who had been present, were not heard by those who needed to hear them most—the Pharisees had already left to continue their plotting.

Conclusion

With their seemingly unanswerable question, the Jewish authorities were intent on either discrediting Jesus in the eyes of his followers or having him arrested (and perhaps executed) by the Roman authorities. To achieve this, they were prepared to sacrifice a nameless, voiceless woman.

The circumstances which surrounded her arrest raise a variety of very unsettling questions. How could the Pharisees have been witnesses to an act of adultery, and what role had they played in ensuring she committed the crime? And perhaps most disturbing of all, was the woman (or, indeed, young girl) the victim of rape? Regardless of what the answers to these questions might be, the fact remains that the woman was simply a "means to an end"—a pawn in the Pharisees' political game. That, to them, she was worthless and dispensable is evidenced by the fact that she was not afforded the opportunity to defend herself against the accusations, something that was clearly against the Mosaic law.

As we have already seen, the evangelists often used an enacted parable as a dramatic representation of a situation that had just been described. In this case, our story of a voiceless, nameless woman who had been framed highlights the lengths to which the Pharisees were willing to go in order to protect their power and privilege.

John never speaks of Jesus performing miracles; in his Gospel, they are signs (2:11, 23; 4:54; 6:14; 12:37; 20:30)—signs that point to the fact that "Jesus is the Messiah, the Son of God, and that through believing you may have life in his name" (20:31).

As the focal character in the enacted parable, the woman's placement within a circle of hostile men all but baying for her blood highlights the psychological and economic captivity experienced by the most vulnerable in a society governed by those who were only interested in preserving the freedom their own status afforded them. This is held up in sharp contrast to the freedom and new life God offers to each person, regardless of gender, social standing, wealth, or perceived worthiness.

Jesus and the woman joined forces in this tableau. She was the sign proclaiming that in God's eyes, *no one* is expendable, *no one* is irredeemable, *no one* is to be used as a pawn—*not even one*. She was the one through whom God's invitation to choose light over darkness, life over death, was extended. And for this, she, too, must be numbered among the prophets.

9

The Canaanite Woman

> Well behaved women seldom make history
> —LAUREL THATCHER ULRICH

Introduction

Over the last few chapters, we have met a number of nameless, silent women who, because of the situations in which they found themselves, shone a light on the inequities and injustices of their time. Becoming the subjects of enacted parables, they are revealed as being prophets in the Old Testament understanding of the role.

A widow shows up the unfairness of the temple tax and the hypocrisy of some of the Jewish authorities; a gate-crasher exposes the attitudes of superiority and entitlement which render anyone perceived as being "other" as unworthy of forgiveness and inclusion; the subject of a hypothetical theological conundrum highlights the endemic sexism that has no issue with women being treated as breeding stock; and a woman entrapped sheds light on the length some Pharisees were prepared to go to rid themselves of their "Jesus problem."

Our next prophet, while being nameless, is anything but silent. Known only as "a Canaanite woman," she engages in a frank and fearless conversation with Jesus which results in amazing transformations.

The Story

The story of the Canaanite woman appears in two Gospels, Matthew and Mark. While the basic elements of the stories are the same, there are some notable differences. To make comparison easier, the passages are set out below, side by side:

Matt 15:21–29	Mark 7:24–31
21 Jesus left that place and went away to the district of Tyre and Sidon.	24 From there he set out and went away to the region of Tyre. He entered a house and did not want anyone to know he was there. Yet he could not escape notice,
22 Just then a Canaanite woman from that region came out and began to cry out, saying, "Have mercy on me, Lord, Son of David; my daughter is tormented by a demon." 23 But he did not answer her at all. And his disciples came and urged him, saying, "Send her away, for she keeps shouting after us."	25 but a woman whose little daughter had an unclean spirit immediately heard about him, and she came and bowed down at his feet. 26 Now the woman was a Gentile, of Syrophoenician origin. She begged him to cast the demon out of her daughter.
24 He answered, "I was sent only to the lost sheep of the house of Israel." 25 But she came and knelt before him, saying, "Lord, help me!" 26 He answered, "It is not fair to take the children's food and throw it to the dogs." 27 She said, "Yes, Lord, yet even the dogs eat the crumbs which fall from their masters' table."	27 He said to her, "Let the children be fed first, for it is not fair to take the children's food and throw it to the dogs." 28 But she answered him, "Sir, even the dogs under the table eat the children's crumbs."
28 Then Jesus answered her, "Woman, great is your faith! Let it be done for you as you wish." And her daughter was healed instantly.	29 Then he said to her, "For saying that, you may go—the demon has left your daughter." 30 So she went home, found the child lying on the bed, and the demon gone.
29 After Jesus had left that place, he passed along the Sea of Galilee, and he went up the mountain, where he sat down.	31 Then he returned from the region of Tyre, and went by way of Sidon towards the Sea of Galilee, in the region of the Decapolis.

As mentioned above, while largely similar, there are some differences in how Matthew and Mark chose to relate the story. Firstly, in Mark's version, Jesus is in someone's home, and the Canaanite woman approaches him there. As a consequence, there are no witnesses to the exchange, whereas in

The Canaanite Woman

Matthew's version, Jesus is not said to be in a house, and the disciples are present.

Secondly, in Matthew's version, Jesus seems to imply that he has no mission to the gentiles at all, whereas in Mark's version, the implication is that while he did have a mission to the gentiles, their time had not yet come. Finally, Mark provides an interesting piece of extra information when he states that the woman discovered her healed daughter lying on a bed. We will address these differences in more detail later in the chapter.

This story has the potential to be very disturbing. What are we to make of Jesus' treatment of the woman—a mother who was pleading for her daughter to be cured? Unlike the situation in the parable of the forgiven woman, where Simon was excluding someone he considered to be beneath his contempt, in this story, it is Jesus who seems to be the villain. How can we reconcile this behavior with the overall image of Jesus as being compassionate and welcoming and an advocate for the poor and marginalized? I believe that if we interpret this story as an enacted parable, with the woman taking on the role of prophet, all these difficulties are resolved.

Firstly, however, let us consider how some commentators have interpreted this story.

Allegory

Some of the church fathers interpreted this story as an allegory. Origen, for example, stated that the food represents Jesus' teaching, disinterest and neglect of those teachings makes people "dogs," and the Canaanite woman represents the evolving human soul. With this interpretation, the woman, representing the human soul, is emerging from a place of humiliation and degradation to seek healing from Jesus.[1]

Jerome, on the other hand, saw the story as being an allegory of the faith, patience, and humility of the Christian church, which, he stated, is not a wild dog (like the pagans) but a domesticated pet waiting under the table for Jesus' crumbs. The daughter represents the pagan souls that were to remain tormented until such time as the church interceded on their behalf.[2]

The validity of allegorical interpretations has long been a matter of debate, even amongst the church fathers. The Antiochian school, for example, insisted on the priority of linguistic considerations, whereas the

---

1. Klancher, *Canaanite Woman*, 55–57.
2. Klancher, *Canaanite Woman*, 74–75.

Alexandrian school sought to discover what the spirit of the story might be. Later, reacting to what they saw as being unnecessary layers of pious tradition, Luther insisted that the primary and grammatical meaning of the Bible is clear, and Calvin stated that there is only one meaning to a passage, not many.[3]

A Call to Perseverance in Prayer

The story of the Canaanite woman has often been used as a didactic tool to highlight the benefits available if one perseveres in prayer. This interpretation rests on grammatical considerations focusing on the tenses used in the story. The use of the aorist tense suggests that Jesus refused the woman's request only once, whereas the woman kept asking Jesus to heal her daughter (the verbs being in a tense suggesting a recurring action).[4] Her perseverance seemingly won the day, and her daughter was healed.

This view is held by Ryle, who states that the purpose of the story is to highlight the importance of praying for others, and that having to wait for prayer to be answered is a good thing because suffering leads a person to God.[5] Henry agrees, stating that the moral of the story is the efficacy of earnestness in prayer.[6]

Healy (commenting on Matthew's version) also cites perseverance in prayer as the moral of the story, stating that the Canaanite woman's perseverance caused Jesus to change his mind and give the children's food to the gentiles ahead of schedule.[7]

A Matter of Timing

Like Healy, other commentators have concluded that Jesus refused the Canaanite woman's plea because of the divinely ordained precedence of the Jews.[8] Calvin believed the mission to the gentiles would only begin after the resurrection, whereas Hill states that Jesus delayed granting the woman's

---

3. For a more detailed discussion, see Thiselton, "Hermeneutics," 293–97.
4. Zodhiates, *Complete New Testament*, 863, 867.
5. Ryle, *Expository Thoughts*, 146, 180.
6. Henry, *Matthew to John*, 391.
7. Healy, *Mark*, 145.
8. E.g., Burkill, "Historical Development," 167; Morris, *Matthew*, 404.

wish until she recognized the divinely ordained division between God's people and the gentiles.[9] Robinson agrees, stating that Jesus refused her request in such an offensive way to teach her that his mission was to the Jews first and that her "pushy" Canaanite ways would not work with him.[10]

Derrett, in an attempt to explain what he sees as the inconsistent way Jesus dealt with the woman, suggests the story is an example of midrash.[11] He argues that because of the Jews' precedence, Jesus could only grant the woman's request if some form of reciprocity was demanded. According to Derrett, this reciprocity was indeed due to the woman because the widow of Zarephath had saved Elijah's life by giving him the last of her food (1 Kgs 17:8–16). Derrett also argues that the woman's response to Jesus is itself a midrash—if her daughter was to "eat," the demon must first be expelled, for a table cannot be laid for demons (1 Cor 10:21).[12]

An Example of Faith

Another view is that the Canaanite woman was a foil to the dullness/intransigence of Jesus' disciples in particular[13] and the Jews in general.[14] The Jews had failed in the mission God had set them—to be a light to the nations. Insofar as the disciples were concerned, they wanted Jesus to grant her request not because they cared about her or her daughter but because she was being a nuisance (Matt 15:23). The woman's great faith (Matt 15:28) is contrasted with the disciples' little faith (Matt 6:30, 8:26, 14:31, 16:8, 17:20).

A Socioeconomic Approach

Perkins and Chinen suggest that Jesus' harsh retort stemmed from the fact that farmers from Upper Galilee exported food to more prosperous non-Jewish areas. In times of food shortage, this resulted in the gentiles (dogs) being fed from the food which, in their view, belonged by right to

---

9. Calvin, *Harmony of the Gospels*, 2:170; Hill, *Matthew*, 254.

10. Robinson, *Mind and Heart*, 283.

11. Midrash is an early Jewish interpretation of or commentary on a biblical text, clarifying or expounding a point of law or developing or illustrating a moral principle.

12. Derrett, "Syro-Phoenician Woman," 167.

13. Barclay, *Matthew*, 134.

14. Calvin, *Harmony of the Gospels*, 2:166.

the children (the Jews).[15] Kinukawa agrees, stating that the Tyrians exercised oppressive political and economic power over the Galileans, which accounts for Jesus' bitter words to the woman.[16] As can be imagined, this may well have caused considerable resentment toward the gentiles, a resentment which could have spilled over into the racially mixed communities to which Matthew and Mark were writing.

A Test

Witherington suggests Jesus' aim was to either test the woman's faith or his disciples' characters. With regard to the latter suggestion, he cites the fact that Jesus' comment that he was sent only to the lost sheep of Israel (Mark 15:24) was directed primarily to the disciples, who had requested he grant the woman's request solely as a way of getting rid of her. Jesus was, according to Witherington, giving the disciples the opportunity to react to the situation in a more appropriate way. If this is the case, then clearly, the woman passed the test but the disciples did not.[17]

An Example of Humility and Wisdom

Commentators ranging from some of the church fathers to more modern scholars consider the woman as a "type" used by the evangelists as an example of humility, in contrast to the Jews, who were puffed up with pride because they were descendants of Abraham.[18] However, other commentators have taken their arguments an important step further, concluding that the story is *as much* about the woman as it is about Jesus.[19] This means the focus is now on both parties in the exchange rather than just on one of the protagonists over and above the other.

Harrington and Keenan make the important—and, given the details of the story, somewhat surprising—comment that both the woman and Jesus exhibit the humility necessary to enable people to enter into meaningful discourse with each other rather than attempting to control the

---

15. Perkins, "Mark," 610; Chinen, "Crumbs," 12.
16. Kinukawa, "Mark's Syrophoenician Woman," 81.
17. Witherington, *Genesis of Christianity*, 75.
18. E.g,. Augustine, "Sermon 27," para. 11; Anderson, *Mark*, 191–92.
19. Alt, "Humility and Wisdom," 1.

interaction.[20] But how can this be the case when Jesus seemingly rebuffs the woman's heartfelt plea for her daughter on the grounds that she and her kind are not entitled to God's grace simply because of their ethnicity? As will be discussed later, this apparently illogical conclusion is indeed possible if the story is viewed as an enacted parable.

A Feminist Perspective

Again, the advent of liberation and, in particular, feminist theology has seen the focus shift away from Jesus to the words and actions of the Canaanite woman. Some suggested interpretations follow.

The Woman as Teacher

Aquino believes the Canaanite woman demonstrated that her being not just a woman but a non-Jewish woman did not justify her exclusion from the community Jesus was endeavoring to initiate. Indeed, Aquino sees her determination and response to Jesus' comments as a turning point in Jesus' understanding of his own ministry, emphasizing that God's kingdom was open to all, and not just those belonging to the house of Israel.[21] O'Day agrees, stating that it was the Canaanite woman's faith in Jesus that freed him to be fully who he was meant to be.[22]

Witherington also states that Jesus' interaction with the woman and his healing of her daughter served a didactic purpose, counteracting the many Jewish warnings against dealing not just with women in general but with foreign women in particular. This, Witherington believes, made possible more open relationships between men and women and facilitated non-Jewish women joining Christian communities in the early church.[23]

Authority for Gentile Mission

Getty-Sullivan believes that the aim of the story is to contrast the woman's willingness to believe and accept Jesus with the disbelief and rejection he

---

20. Harrington and Keenan, *Paul and Virtue Ethics*, 146.
21. Aquino, *Our Cry for Life*, 146.
22. O'Day, "Surprised by Faith," 125.
23. Witherington, *Genesis of Christianity*, 86.

encountered from his own people.[24] The woman, a Canaanite, would be expected to be hostile to Jesus and all he stood for. Instead, she bowed down before him (Matt 15:25) in much the same way as the magi (Matt 2:11), the leper whom Jesus healed (Matt 8:2), and the women at the tomb (Matt 28:9). The Canaanite woman, as a representative of marginalized people believed to be excluded from God's kingdom, highlights the legitimacy of Jesus' mission to the gentiles.[25]

Rocchietti agrees, stating that the woman's perseverance in demanding what she deserved not only resulted in her daughter's healing but was also instrumental in opening the door for the inclusion of gentiles in the early church.[26]

Burkill has suggested that the story served to emphasize to the evangelists' audience that the church continued to have a mission to the gentiles. Pointing out the liturgical/sacramental language of the passage, Burkill suggests that the role of the Canaanite woman was parabolic—she highlighted that gentiles could also be inspired to recognize Christ as the one who gave himself as the bread of life for the salvation of the world.[27]

This is an important point, because the issue was not simply whether or not it was necessary to adopt certain customs before being able to join a Christian community; it was actually about ethnic identity. Smith argues that by declaring all foods clean (Matt 15:10–11, Mark 7:18–19) and by crossing over into gentile territory, Jesus was not declaring that ethnic boundaries should no longer exist. What Jesus was showing was that those boundaries no longer had the power to limit the coming of God's kingdom into areas and among ethnic groups where it was presumed to be absent.[28] Note, importantly, Smith's assertion that God's kingdom was "presumed" to have been absent. The implication is that God's mission was always to the world, but it was through the *agency* of the Jews that this was to take place.

Indeed, Boring suggests, the evangelists may have crafted their stories in such a way as to challenge their readers to place themselves in the role of the other, rethink their perceptions, and confront their sexism and racism.[29]

---

24. Getty-Sullivan, *Women*, 85.
25. Getty-Sullivan, *Women*, 88.
26. Rocchietti, "Women," 107.
27. Burkill, "Syrophoenician Woman," 28.
28. Smith, "Construction of Identity," 477.
29. Boring, "Matthew," 338.

The Canaanite Woman

Intersectionality

Glancy sees this story as an example of intersectionality,[30] comparing the ways Jesus responded to the Canaanite woman with the way he responded to Jairus (Mark 5:22–24a). Jairus, a leader of the synagogue, fell at Jesus' feet, begging him repeatedly to cure his "little daughter," who was gravely ill. This view suggests Jesus responded by immediately following Jairus to his home in order to cure the child. Glancy suggests Jesus responded with disdain to the woman's plea because of her gender and ethnicity, whereas he responded positively to Jairus, whom he considered to be culturally superior to the woman.[31]

While this would appear to be the case, it is important to keep in mind that Jesus did interrupt his trip to Jairus's house in order to speak to and acknowledge the faith of the woman who had been hemorrhaging for twelve years (Mark 5:25–34). This woman was rendered perpetually unclean by her affliction. She was also destitute and, because she approached Jesus on her own and was not identified as "belonging" to a male relative, was probably isolated, shunned, and alone. In effect, she was just as much an object of disdain as the Canaanite woman, yet Jesus chose to delay his trip to Jairus's home in order to speak with her.

Winners and Losers

While it must be admitted that liberation and feminist theology have gone a long way in making known the plight of marginalized and vulnerable people and giving them a voice, it is also the case that, at times, the language used can be counterproductive. Take, for example, some of the descriptions used to describe the outcome of the interaction between the Canaanite woman and Jesus: the woman defeated Jesus,[32] the woman confronted Jesus and bested him,[33] and the woman won the contest.[34]

---

30. Intersectionality is an analytical framework for understanding how aspects of a person's social and political identities combine to create different modes of discrimination and privilege. Examples of these aspects include gender, caste, race, class, sexuality, religion, disability, and physical appearance.
31. Glancy, "First Century Bodies," 342–63.
32. Nelavala, "Smart Syrophoenician Woman," 68.
33. Alt, "Humility and Wisdom," 6.
34. Schüssler Fiorenza, *In Memory of Her*, 137.

In many cases, Jesus is seen as a representative of the kyriarchal system of his day (the rule of the lord, master, father, and husband),[35] with Kinukawa believing the passage highlights the response of a woman who had been subjugated from birth, because if a modern Western woman had been treated so badly, she would rather have borne her daughter's suffering than speak to the person insulting her.[36]

Nelavala believes that although Jesus attributed "secondary-ness" to the woman, she nevertheless defeated him, and her victory rectified his mistaken attitude of Jews first, gentiles second.[37] Other interpretations include the following: Jesus' initial response (in Matthew) indicated he had no intention of helping the woman and he simply used the precedence of the Jews as a way of avoiding having to help her at all;[38] the woman helped Jesus understand that his mission was universal;[39] and the woman changed Jesus' mind by her wit and cleverness.[40]

Siker, who believes Jesus considered the woman to be a gentile dog and not even fully human, states that it was Jesus who was the sinner and the woman caused him to repent of his initial dismissal of her and her daughter.[41]

Clearly, this type of language is adversarial and suggests that for there to be "winners," there must be "losers." The danger is that in seeking to liberate one group of people, another group is demonized and marginalized in the process. For there to be real progress, liberation must be sought for both parties, as the oppressors need to be liberated just as much as the oppressed. Commenting on liberation theology's "basic polarity" between liberation and oppression, Volf states that the goal must be to find a way that binds conflicting parties together rather than pulling them apart. This binding, or "embrace," as Volf calls it, should lead to both parties seeing the world through the eyes of the other person.[42]

---

35. Tuohy, "Rhetoric and Transformation," 1.
36. Kinukawa, *Women and Jesus*, 58.
37. Nelavala, "Smart Syrophoenician Woman," 67.
38. Van Den Eynde, "Teacher Becomes a Student," 276.
39. E.g., Wainwright, "Voice from the Margin," 152; Schüssler Fiorenza, *In Memory of Her*, 137.
40. Ringe, "Gentile Woman's Story," 71.
41. Siker, *Jesus, Sin, and Perfection*, 169–70.
42. Volf, "Conversations," 72.

Alison refers to this as the "intelligence of the victim"—an intelligence, or knowledge, that can only be gained when we see situations through the eyes of the victim and which will be the foundation of a new unity of humanity—a unity in which no one seeks to gain "over-against" anyone else.[43]

Reciprocal Service

Of course, shifting the main focus to the Canaanite woman is definitely a positive move. What is needed, however, is a way of interpreting the story that both respects what Scripture tells us about Jesus' character and his mission to proclaim the gospel to all people, and also does justice to the dignity and intelligence of the woman and sees her as integral to the meaning of the story rather than merely a "bit player." Thurston has begun this process, stating that in this story, we see an example of something quite characteristic in Jesus' ministry—reciprocal service.[44] Thurston considers it ironic that most scholars comment on the woman's humility, when it is, she says, Jesus who demonstrates humility by recognizing and acknowledging the woman's insight. At the end of the encounter, no character is left unchanged.[45]

The Story as Enacted Parable

Again, in order to discern whether this story is an enacted parable, we need to take into account the somewhat complex context within which it is situated.

Context

The context within which the story of the Canaanite woman is placed is largely the same in both Gospels. To appreciate fully the meaning and importance of the story, we need to go back to the story of the feeding of the five thousand (Matt 14:13–21, Mark 6:30–44). Here, Jesus was in Jewish territory. After a day of Jesus preaching and curing people, the disciples encouraged him to dismiss the crowds to enable them to go into the villages

---

43. Alison, *Knowing Jesus*, 90.
44. Thurston, *Knowing Her Place*, 28.
45. Thurston, *Knowing Her Place*, 31.

and obtain food. Jesus, after challenging the disciples to provide food for the crowd themselves, miraculously provided enough food not only for five thousand men and an undisclosed number of women and children but also enough to fill twelve baskets after everyone had eaten their fill.

This feeding miracle is itself an enacted parable, indicating the extent of God's grace and generosity. The fact that there were twelve baskets of food left over marks this as a "Jewish miracle," the number of baskets corresponding to the number of the tribes of Israel.

Both Gospels then relate Jesus walking on water (Matt 14:22–33, Mark 6:45–52) and curing numerous people at Gennesaret (Matt 14:34–36, Mark 6:53–56). The next story describes Jesus' confrontation with the Pharisees and scribes regarding the burden they were placing on people by insisting the letter of the law be strictly followed rather than the spirit of the law (Matt 15:1–20, Mark 7:1–23). The religious authorities had ceased to be shepherds to the people, instead becoming hard taskmasters, enforcing rules that often resulted in people suffering hardship. The poor widow we met in an earlier chapter is a good example of this. Indeed, Jesus also suggested the letter of the law was being used by some to shirk their responsibilities (Matt 15:1–6, Mark 7:10–13).

To highlight his argument, Jesus takes on the Jewish laws of dietary purity, stating that people were not rendered unclean by anything they ate. Rather, they were rendered unclean if their actions were unlawful, cruel, thoughtless, or unethical. It is important to remember that not all Pharisees or scribes were bad people. Most were just trying to uphold the law as they saw it. Unfortunately, this had resulted in them putting their faith in adherence to a set of rules and regulations rather than in the mercy and loving-kindness of the God of their ancestors—a God of love, relationship, and inclusion.

Immediately after Jesus had proclaimed all food to be clean, we have the story of the Canaanite woman (Matt 15:21–28, Mark 7:24–30). This nameless woman approaches Jesus, asking that he cure her daughter. Following a rather remarkable and very controversial conversation with Jesus, her daughter is, indeed, cured. We will consider the details of this story shortly.

Jesus then proceeds to cure many more people (Matt 15:29–31, Mark 7:31–37[46]). Importantly, it is evident from Matthew's rendition of the story

---

46. Although in Mark, we are only told of Jesus curing a deaf man.

The Canaanite Woman

that those cured by Jesus were, in fact, gentiles, as they are said to praise "the God of Israel" following the miracles.

Then follows another feeding miracle (Matt 15:32–39, Mark 8:1–10). This miracle took place in gentile territory, involved four thousand men (the women and children again not being counted) and resulted in seven baskets of food being left over after all had eaten their fill.

The number of baskets left over from both feeding miracles is important. As already mentioned, the twelve baskets from the first miracle are believed to represent the twelve tribes of Israel. However, it is the relevance of the seven baskets left over from the second miracle that is notable for our purposes. In the book of Deuteronomy (7:1–4), there is a list of seven nations that the Israelites must destroy. They are also banned from making treaties with these nations or intermarrying with them. These nations are the Hittites, the Girgashites, the Amorites, the Perizzites, the Hivites, the Jebusites, and the Canaanites.

LeMarquand believes the story of the Canaanite woman is to be seen as a reversal of this Canaanite conquest narrative.[47] Interestingly, scripturally speaking, the number seven signifies perfection and completion. The second feeding miracle, therefore, emphasizes that the type of kingdom Jesus has come to inaugurate will include not only God's chosen people, the Israelites, but also citizens of the nations who had historically been the sworn enemies of the Israelites. The Canaanite woman is not only the parabolic bridge linking the feeding stories, but she also embodies the message.

The final story we need to consider to appreciate fully the importance of the Canaanite woman is the description of Jesus warning the disciples against the "yeast of the Pharisees and Sadducees" and the disciples' mistaken belief that he was simply referring to the fact that they had forgotten to bring any bread to eat (Matt 16:1–12, Mark 8:11–21). Not only had the Pharisees imposed impossible burdens on their own people, but they were also failing to be a light to the gentiles. Their actions were not enticing people to trust in the God of Israel, a compassionate, gentle shepherd to his people. Instead, gentiles were often viewed with contempt and disdain. Jesus' two feeding miracles were enacted parables meant to embody the generosity and inclusiveness of God's kingdom—a message Jesus' disciples clearly did not understand.

It is now time to take a closer look at the story of the Canaanite woman and consider whether she fulfills the role of prophet.

---

47. LeMarquand, "Canaanite Conquest," 243.

Characters

The "cast" of this enacted parable is small—either two or three, depending on which Gospel you are reading. In Mark, the only characters are the woman and Jesus. In Matthew, we can add another "collective" cast member: the disciples.

The "Placement" of Jesus and the Woman

In the chapter dealing with the forgiven woman, we noted the interplay between the woman and Simon, with them being either "in place" or "out of place." The woman began by being out of place in a male-only environment, but ended up "displacing" Simon and taking over his role as host.

Here, it can be argued that both Jesus and the woman are out of place. Both Gospels place Jesus in gentile territory, a place where his Jewish heritage makes him an outsider and where his religious identity as a rabbi means nothing.[48] For her part, the woman, while being in her own territory, is portrayed as being alone. She is not linked to a male and dares to approach a man, a stranger, a Jew—behavior which would have been regarded as scandalous.

The Approach

Commentators are divided as to whether the woman approached Jesus because she believed him to be the Messiah[49] or simply because, on the basis of what she had heard of him, she had faith he would grant her request.[50] Clearly, she had heard of Jesus and his reputation. Perhaps the more pragmatic reason was that she was a desperate mother who was willing to try anything in the hope of saving her daughter.

In Matthew's Gospel, the woman approached Jesus in the presence of an undisclosed number of his disciples, who encouraged Jesus to grant her wish not because they felt any compassion for her or her daughter but because she was annoying them.

---

48. Monro, *Erotic Transgression*, 146.

49. E.g., Healy, *Mark*, 145. Calvin, *Harmony of the Gospels*, 2:170.

50. E.g., Rhoads, "Syrophoenician Woman," 346; Hill, *Matthew*, 254; Boring, "Matthew," 336.

The Canaanite Woman

As already noted, Witherington sees what follows as Jesus' way of challenging the typical Jewish male's attitude toward women (as evidenced by his disciples), stating that Jesus declined to respond to the woman in order to give his disciples time to react to the situation.[51]

Mark has the woman approaching Jesus in a house. As was ascertained earlier, for an enacted parable to be efficacious, there is no need for there to be an audience. Here we are faced with several unanswered questions. Whose house was it? Why was Jesus, a Jew, able to enter a house in gentile territory? Did the woman have permission to enter the house or, like the forgiven woman, did she "gate-crash"? Regardless of what the answers to these questions might be, we are left with the conclusion that the Canaanite woman was acting "outrageously" by demanding to be heard and daring to step outside the position constructed for her by the patriarchal society.[52]

What is important, however, is the imagery evoked by this enacted parable. While both Jesus and the woman may have been out of place, by joining forces, they demonstrated that God's "house" was big enough to accommodate all people and that nobody should be expected to go without or be satisfied with the crumbs.

The Conversation

The conversation between Jesus and the Canaanite woman has elicited considerable consternation over the years, raising, as it does, questions regarding Jesus' apparently brutal treatment of the woman, his knowledge regarding the extent of his mission, and his willingness to fulfill that mission given the disdain in which women and gentiles were held in first-century Israel.[53] Over the centuries, in an attempt to answer these questions satisfactorily, exegesis of these passages has resulted in a wide range of opinions as to how Jesus' seemingly offensive behavior could be reconciled with the image of Jesus as Isaiah's suffering servant who was to "bring forth justice to the nations" (Isa 42:1b).[54]

---

51. Witherington, *Ministry of Jesus*, 64.
52. Saunders, *Outrageous Women*, 2.
53. For the disdain in which first-century women were held in Israel, see Jeremias, *Jerusalem*, 359. For the disdain in which gentiles were held, see Hurlburt, *Romance with Romans*, 29.
54. E.g., North, "Isaiah," 741; Buelt, *New Friendship*, 140.

In my view, the argument that Jesus regarded his mission as being only to the Jews is difficult to maintain given the scriptural evidence against it. Firstly, both Matthew and Mark portray Jesus as having healed gentiles before this particular story (Matt 8:28–34, Mark 5:1–13). Of note, also, is Jesus' healing of the centurion's servant (Matt 8:5–13). Not only does this seem to have taken place prior to the curing of the Canaanite woman's daughter, but Jesus expressly states that "many will come from east and west and will eat with Abraham and Isaac and Jacob in the kingdom of heaven" (Matt 8:11)—an indication that Jesus saw his mission as universal.[55]

In John, Jesus refers to the sheep he must bring in that are not of his fold (John 10:16), and Luke ties Jesus' ministry to that of the suffering servant of Isaiah, whose mission it was to be a light to the nations in order that God's salvation could reach to the ends of the earth (Luke 4:18–19, Isa 49:6).

Indeed, in Genesis we see God as the God of all nations well before the call of Abraham. This call was not so God could have a particular people for himself, excluding all other nations. Abraham's mission—and that of the Israelites—was to be a light to the world so that through the Israelites' example "all the families of the earth shall be blessed" (Gen 12:3b). The Israelites had taken their status as God's chosen people and made it into an exclusive club from which all others were excluded—however, as Scott points out, "favoritism need not imply exclusivism."[56]

It was this "calling" to be a light to the world that informed Jesus' thinking and the mission of the early Christian community. In the Letter to the Romans, Paul links the salvation of the Jews to his mission to the gentiles, stating that the Jews who had rejected Jesus would ultimately believe and be saved as a result of seeing the faith the gentiles had in Jesus and the joy that faith brought them (Rom 11:1–16).

So, if it cannot be argued that Jesus was either unaware of the universality of his mission or unwilling to fulfill it, how can we adequately explain his treatment of the Canaanite woman? I believe the answer must be that the story is an enacted parable.

It cannot be denied that the conversation between the Canaanite woman and Jesus is jarring. A mother asks Jesus to cure her sick daughter. His response seemingly equates helping her with taking food from more deserving children and throwing it to the dogs. While the Israelites used

---

55. Humphries-Brooks, "Canaanite Woman," 143.
56. Scott, "Gentiles," 165.

dogs to guard houses (Isa 56:10) and flocks (Job 30:1), the fact remains that by and large, they were despised as scavengers and were seldom house pets.[57] The term "dog" was also used pejoratively to denote anything of little or no worth (2 Kgs 8:13) or euphemistically when referring to a male prostitute.[58] Indeed, the only positive portrayal of a dog in Scripture can be found in the book of Tobit, where an enigmatic and unnamed dog accompanies and protects the hero of the story as he strives to vanquish demons and murderous fish in order to win the hand of a fair maiden.[59]

It is important, however, to consider the particular word for "dog" both evangelists chose to use. The Greek word is *kynarion*, which denotes a small dog, a puppy, or a household pet. Both Jesus and the woman use this form of the word, and nowhere else in Scripture is it used when referring to dogs. It is clear from her response that the woman was not cowed by Jesus' remark. Rather, she points out that it was usual for the dogs to be nourished by what the children let fall from the table, a comment that succeeded in changing the image of the dogs from dirty outsiders to members of the family who already have a place in the master's home.

Thurston has rightly pointed out that the woman "is given the lines" we would normally expect to come from the mouth of Jesus.[60] This whole interaction feels like a scene in a play, with both the woman and Jesus playing a particular part. It is always difficult to gauge the tenor of a conversation solely by the written word. So much is lost—body language, facial expressions, tone of voice. What was the expression on Jesus' face when he spoke to the woman? Was it, as we so often assume, hard and disapproving, or was there an unspoken invitation for her to become, as did the forgiven woman, a coconspirator in the scene about to be enacted? If this was an enacted parable, then the latter must be the case.

Going back to our discussion of the various types of organismic involvement, this is an example of engrossed acting, as was the conversation between David and the prophet Nathan. However, I believe that instead of Jesus being the one who was forced to see the error of his ways (as was the case with David), the enacted parable was performed to emphasize the equal status of women and non-Jewish people in God's kingdom. It was

---

57. Smith, *Animals and Birds*, 15.
58. Strong, "Hebrew and Chaldee Dictionary," 55.
59. Beresford, "Feathers, Fins and Fur," 100–101.
60. Thurston, *Knowing Her Place*, 32.

through the words and actions of the Canaanite woman that the reality of God's reign was revealed.

This story is also an example of alterity. Monro describes alterity as the voluntary "de-privileging" of a person of greater status (whom she calls "A") and the "privileging" of a person of lesser status (whom she calls "non-A") to enable an interaction between two people who are now of equal status.[61] This is not a role reversal. In the story of the Canaanite woman, Jesus does not become marginalized in order for the woman to be privileged; they are now interacting as equals, with the usual give and take that involves.

Moyer calls this a "role-reversing interlude" and states that it is used widely in biblical literature as a highly expressive means of focusing on and highlighting the central character in a given story, with a view to exploring their rich human complexity.[62] I suggest there needs to be more notice taken of these "interludes," as they give a voice to often-nameless characters who are seen merely as peripheral to the action or whose only function is as a foil to the words and actions of Jesus or other male protagonists, rather than being, as they are in many cases, the central character in a prophetic drama.

Earlier, we noted that it was not unusual for objects or people to be the "example" in an enacted parable. This is one such case. By participating in (or, indeed, instigating) a frank and feisty discussion with Jesus, the woman becomes, like many Old Testament prophets before her, the personification of the message of the enacted parable. In this case, the Canaanite woman became the sign of what the status of women would look like in God's kingdom. No longer marginalized or silenced, women would be equal to men in all aspects of their lives.

Some commentators have already stated that the Canaanite woman's response is the hinge on which the whole story turns and that it is she who delivers the "*mot juste*" and not Jesus.[63] Alt, using Mark's version, identifies the story as a chiasm, with the woman's response as the hinge:

Jesus' arrival near Tyre and effort to escape notice
The woman approaches
The woman's petition
Jesus' response
The woman's retort

---

61. Monro, *Erotic Transgression*, 153.
62. Moyer, "Who Is the Prophet," 183, 169.
63. Witherington, *New Testament Rhetoric*, 29; McKenzie, "Matthew," 90.

The Canaanite Woman

Jesus' second response
The woman's petition is granted
The woman returns home and finds her daughter healed
Jesus' return from the region of Tyre[64]

Other commentators have drawn parallels between the Canaanite woman and other Old Testament characters. Smith likens the Canaanite woman to Hannah (1 Sam 1:9–18). Both women are distressed, both request a miracle, and both are rebuked. Instead of slinking away, humiliated, both Hannah and the Canaanite woman correct the one who had rebuked them and, subsequently, are rewarded by having their prayers answered.[65]

Both women also change the trajectory of history.[66] Hannah's son, Samuel, became the prophet who anointed kings, whereas the Canaanite woman (and her daughter) were the fulcra after which it should have been impossible to argue that the gifts of God's kingdom were available to only those of a certain gender, age, or ethnicity. Sanders sees similarities with one of the patriarchs, Jacob (Gen 32:24–30). Both he and the Canaanite woman wrestled with God, refusing to let him go until they had received the blessing each had requested.[67]

The Outcome

Immediately following the woman's retort, Jesus proclaims her daughter to have been healed, a fact confirmed by the woman on her return to her home, where she finds her daughter lying on "the bed," the demon having left her (Mark 7:30). Cadwallader rightly points out that it cannot be interpreted that the child was lying in bed due to "post-exorcism distress." Were this to be the case, it would not tie in with other healing miracles described in Mark's gospel to be complete and decisive (1:21–28, 9:14–29, 8:22–26). It would only confirm that the woman had to make do with "a fragment of a miracle, a crumby remainder."[68]

Importantly, the Greek word translated as "bed" (*klínē*) can also be used to describe a couch, sofa, or divan used for sitting or reclining.

---

64. Alt, "Humility and Wisdom," 3. This chiasm is taken verbatim from Alt.
65. Smith, "Double Portion," 126.
66. Smith, "Double Portion," 138.
67. Sanders, *God Who Risks*, 99.
68. Cadwallader, *Beyond the Word*, 263.

Zodhiates points out that in this passage, *klínē* may be taken in the sense of triclinium, "the couch or sofa on which the ancients reclined at meals."[69] When Zodhiates states that the "ancients" reclined at meals, what he means is that the men reclined at meals, never women or children.[70] The Canaanite woman's daughter, no longer tormented, is instead taking her place at the banquet table, and not long after, so did four thousand gentile men and an undisclosed number of women and children.

The Canaanite woman and her daughter personify the generosity and inclusiveness of God's kingdom. As Brueggemann points out, Jesus' healing miracles did not happen "to those who held on to the old order, but to those who yearned because the old order had failed them or squeezed them out."[71] The enacted parable has been efficacious—the Canaanite woman, her daughter, and the multitudes from other nations are no longer expected to make do with someone's leftover crumbs. As Chinen points out, any outcome where some are at the table while others are not, or where some have food while others only get the crumbs, is unacceptable.[72]

Conclusion

Again, this story presents us with several unanswered questions and confronting situations. Who is this woman? Why was Jesus in gentile territory and in whose house was he? Why did Jesus treat this woman so harshly? Was he unaware of his mission or unwilling to fulfill it?

The only way to answer these questions adequately is to treat the story as an enacted parable. When considered within its extensive and instructive context, we see that the Canaanite woman provides the bridge which links the two feeding miracles—the first miracle indicating that God's mercy and abundance is sufficient for all Jewish people, the second providing visual proof of the overturning of the strictures against the gentile nations.

Even though there is dialogue involved, the story still meets the criteria of an enacted parable. Like the interaction between David and the prophet Nathan, the story of the Canaanite woman is an example of engrossed acting because it is structured like a set piece—a tableau. It is also, as we have seen, an example of alterity—Jesus deliberately "de-privileges" himself

---

69. Zodhiates, *Complete New Testament*, 871.
70. Cadwallader, *Beyond the Word*, 272–73.
71. Brueggemann, *Prophetic Imagination*, 111.
72. Chinen, "Crumbs," 4.

so that the woman can become the focus of the story. This results in the woman playing the role not of a victim or an adversary but of a prophet—the one through whom the word of God is proclaimed and through whose actions healing and reconciliation are achieved. Interpreting the story as an enacted parable highlights the tendency to view those who are different from us as "other" or, as Schüssler Fiorenza puts it, as "non-persons."[73]

As discussed in previous chapters, parables are meant to shock, and enacted parables are designed to confront people who have become so hard-hearted they are immune to the morals and teachings of the spoken parables. In the case of the Canaanite woman, the offense caused to her *in* the story, therefore, is meant to elicit shock in readers *of* the story[74]—that is where the power of the enacted parable lies. This shock elicits many uncomfortable questions about Jesus and his motivation. It is only when the story is viewed as an enacted parable that adequate responses to those questions can be found.

In summary, recognizing this story as an enacted parable allows us to see the Canaanite woman for who she really is. No longer a "bit player" who can be effectively silenced and whose message can be made "safe"; no longer a victim or an adversary. She emerges as the prophet through whose words and actions healing, freedom, and belonging is won not only for herself and her daughter but for all who are considered to be unworthy of God's love and a seat at his table.

---

73. Schüssler Fiorenza, *But She Said*, 21.
74. McCracken, *Scandal*, 22.

10

Conclusion—Why Is This Important?

> The poor are always prophetic.... That is why we should take time to listen to them. And that means staying near them, because they speak quietly and infrequently; they are afraid to speak out, they lack confidence in themselves because they have been broken and oppressed. But if we listen to them, they will bring us back to the essential.
>
> —JEAN VANIER

A Quick Recap

Over the last several chapters, we've attempted to challenge a number of traditionally held beliefs concerning the prophetic ministry, who exercised it, how they exercised it, and whether John the Baptist was the last of the Old Testament-style prophets. This has been done to form the foundation on which to build an argument that demonstrates that women fulfilled a prophetic ministry more often, and with greater effectiveness, than has previously been recognized.

In our first chapter, we considered the role of the prophet and reviewed how this has been understood and interpreted over the years. Based on the work of Walter Brueggemann, we suggested that the role of the prophet can best be described as challenging the "royal consciousness," an attitude that abhors vulnerability and renders society not only unwilling to see the plight

Conclusion—Why Is This Important?

of the marginalized but unable to do so.[1] It was possibly this type of "blindness" that Luke was describing in his story of Lazarus and Dives (Luke 16:19–31)—Lazarus lay at the gate of Dives's property, but Dives seemed unable to see him. In this chapter, we also discussed the difference between being a prophet and acting in a prophetic manner, as well as the different ways men and women tend to behave in given situations.

In chapter 2, we discussed the attributes of a parable and its function of placing two "ways of being" side by side, often promoting behaviors that were counterintuitive. While, on the one hand, this invited people to join with God to reimagine and recreate a world where people lived in accordance with God's will, it also threatened the status quo, something that often made life very difficult for the prophet.

Given their importance in demonstrating the ways in which women fulfilled a prophetic ministry, particular emphasis was placed on enacted parables, the various forms of organismic involvement employed in these stories, and the use of objects or people as the "props," or "signs," in these parables.

In chapter 3, we took a closer look at some of the grammatical, linguistic, editorial, and sociological issues which may have contributed to an inaccurate view of who a prophet could be. We then considered the stories of the women either named as prophets in Scripture or acknowledged as such in Jewish tradition. We noted that of these ten women, Anna was the only prophetess named in the New Testament, and only Deborah, Huldah, and possibly Noadiah can be considered to have exercised a recognized leadership role. The others either used trickery, psychology, and manipulation or exercised the authority they had within their own households to achieve their aims.

In the next chapter, we encountered two more groups of women who, for the purposes of this book, we called the "tricksters" and the "dismissed." The tricksters, as the term suggests, were forced to use trickery, subterfuge, and, in many cases, their sexuality in order to simply survive. In so doing, they highlighted how far society had strayed from its covenantal responsibilities. They also succeeded in helping some of God's plans come to fruition.

The "dismissed" prophetesses were examples of women whom society believed it could use and then, when they had served their purpose (like

---

1. Brueggemann, *Prophetic Imagination*, 35.

Hagar) discard. This category also included women who were largely unseen and whose contribution to society was not properly appreciated.

What all these women had in common is that while they were vulnerable, marginalized, or largely ignored, they were not victims. They were skilled, resourceful, and feisty. They recognized their own worth and did what they needed to do in order to survive.

Succeeding chapters introduced us to some New Testament prophetesses—women who were the "signs" in enacted parables: a widow whose last penny had been devoured by the religious system; a gate-crasher who succeeded in teaching a pious Pharisee a lesson in generosity and hospitality; a woman who was the subject of a theological hypothesis but who shone a light on a system that considered women to be property and of no greater value than a breeding cow; a woman who was used in a sting operation devised to entrap Jesus; and a feisty foreigner whose clever repartee demonstrated that God's love and compassion is available to all people, regardless of gender or ethnicity.

We've been on quite a journey so far. Some of the stories have been far-fetched, rollicking good yarns; others have been confronting and depressing. While certainly not perfect, these women were strong and inspirational—fighting a patriarchal system to claim the rights and privileges of which God deemed them deserving. I believe little doubt remains that they were indeed prophets in the Old Testament understanding of the role.

But these stories describe contexts and events dating back at least two thousand years. Why is it important to revisit these stories now? I believe the answer is twofold—it is important to try to understand exactly what the evangelists were trying to impart (exegesis) so that we can apply those lessons to our own lives and contexts (hermeneutics).

Exegetical Importance

Each Gospel was written to a particular audience for a particular purpose. While they describe events in the life of Jesus, they are not like modern biographies, which often provide a blow-by-blow description of the subject's life, often commencing with stories regarding their parents and sometimes even previous generations. By contrast, in Mark's Gospel, Jesus appears as a grown man ready to commence his earthly mission, while in John's Gospel, Jesus is identified as the preexisting Logos through whom everything was created. John also tells us his purpose in writing his Gospel is to provide

Conclusion—Why Is This Important?

"signs" pointing to who Jesus is so that readers might believe "that Jesus is the Messiah, the Son of God, and that through believing you may have life in his name" (John 20:31).

Jesus himself said he came so that people might have abundant life (John 10:10)—the end result of living in a way that is congruent with the will of God and a main theme in all four Gospels.

The purpose of the written "good news" was to testify to Jesus' divinity, his mission to inaugurate the kingdom of God, and the societal changes that would entail. As such, no story, no character, is simply padding. There are no "bit players." Each character has his or her story to tell and lesson to impart. In a society where so many were rendered voiceless and nameless by overzealous purity laws or patriarchal societal constructs, it makes sense for the evangelists to have used voiceless and nameless characters to highlight the entrenched discrimination in society and set alongside it the alternative "kingdom economy" Jesus had come to initiate and promote.

The situations in which our female prophets found themselves are so alien to the lives of those of us who live in more affluent, Western countries that it is easy to discount them as being exaggerated or hyperbolic. It is almost impossible for us to believe a woman could be forced to have a child and then, when the situation changes, that both she and her child are driven from the only home they have; or that a woman could be handed down from brother to brother, afforded no more dignity than a farm animal.

While we have uncovered a number of feisty prophetesses who take center stage in their respective enacted parables, like their male counterparts, it is not, in the end, all about them. They are the signs that at one and the same time shine a light on the inequities of society and offer an alternative where everyone is of value. As Brueggemann points out, it is only the denied ones who can do this, as those caught up in the royal consciousness are unable to do so.[2]

While the stories contained in the various books of the Bible describe situations that occurred within a particular time and context, the Bible itself, as a whole, is a timeless document. If modern readers cease to find its message relevant, meaningful, and helpful in their own context, that is because there is a failure to understand the stories within the contexts in which they were written. When our prophetesses are relegated to the role of bit players, the messages they are embodying are often overlooked. Unfortunately, prior to the rise of liberation theologies, it was often the case that

---

2. Brueggemann, *Prophetic Imagination*, 65.

middle-class, middle-aged, white male theologians focused mainly on the words and actions of Jesus and other male protagonists, often obscuring the messages the evangelists were trying to convey.

Far from being mere bit players, our women were indeed authentic prophets. The situations in which they found themselves, and the decisions they were forced to make, function like an icon: we are able to look through them, into the reality they reveal—a reality that is often very uncomfortable and confronting. This is why careful exegesis is so important.

Hermeneutical Importance

As mentioned above, the Bible is a timeless document, meant to be as relevant today as it was to the various people for whom and to whom it was written, in the myriad situations in which they found themselves. While the authors had no concept of "modern" issues such as weapons of mass destruction, IVF, or gender diversity, the basic premise remains the same—the creation of a society that is based on the commandments to love God and love neighbor and that, as a result, is compassionate, equitable, and just.

If our "hidden" prophetesses have taught us anything, it is that the societies in which they lived were often anything but compassionate, equitable, and just. It was precisely in these circumstances that prophets were called by God to effect change. By allowing these women to shine a light on the inequities of their time, we are able to ask ourselves two very important questions: Who (or what) are the hidden prophets in our time? And what should be done to give them a voice and address the issues they bring into the light?

Who (or What) Are Our Prophets?

If we take our definition of prophet as being someone who, by their very being and circumstances, shines a light on the inequities and hard-heartedness of the society in which they live, then we are left with several uncomfortable questions. From the perspective of living in an affluent, first-world country like Australia, my set of questions would include the following: Why is an average of one woman per week losing her life at the hands of a current or former partner? Why, in such an affluent country, are so many people sleeping rough? Why are women over the age of fifty the fastest growing demographic in terms of homelessness? Why is the life expectancy of Australia's indigenous population so much lower than that of other people? Why are our indigenous people so disproportionately represented in areas such as incarceration, mental health, and suicide? And that is just in Australia. Each country, of course, has its own set of uncomfortable questions.

Globally, we may ask: Why are thousands of children dying of hunger in some countries, while in other countries, tons of food are wasted each week? What should be done to resolve conflicts that, at times, have gone on for generations and have caused so much death, displacement, and suffering? How can we resolve the refugee problem? How can we guarantee equity and justice when it comes to access to food, clean water, and vaccines?

Of course, we must not ignore what is, arguably, the most all-pervasive "prophet" of our time—the environment. How many animals need to become endangered or extinct, how much ice needs to melt, or how many disasters caused by extreme weather events need to occur before we "see" the link between these issues and humankind's pillaging of the earth?

How to Respond to These Prophets

Unfortunately, when confronted by the issues faced by the vulnerable and marginalized in our world, the response is often the same as was experienced by the prophets of old—Band-Aid solutions at best, denial and hostility at worst. Of course, as Brueggemann would point out, that is only to be expected of a society that has become a slave to the royal consciousness.

When Jesus saw an injustice, he not only acted to alleviate the suffering of the person involved, but he also challenged the societal structures that caused the suffering in the first place and allowed it to continue. That's what made him so unpopular with the authorities and contributed to his execution.

It is not enough to simply "throw money" at a problem like violence against women. Of course, it is vital to provide adequate crisis accommodation and counseling, and that does cost money. But that is only a short-term solution. What has to be addressed is the attitude that violence is an appropriate response, that it's okay to bully and intimidate women and children.

It is vital to supply enough money to address the physical and mental health issues of Australia's indigenous population. However, it is more important to address the feelings of despair and hopelessness caused by a history of dispossession, attempted genocide, and theft of their children.

It is hard to go into these dark places, but real progress cannot be made until we, as a society, do so. Some denounce this approach as a "black armband" view of history, but the denied ones tell us time and again that unless their pain is recognized and validated, healing cannot commence. Not just their own healing, but that of the whole of society.

Just as Simon the Pharisee was given the opportunity to learn and grow by his encounter with the forgiven woman, so, too, are we being given the same opportunity each time we "see" the hidden prophets in our midst.

The whole basis of liberation theology is see (or observe), judge, act.[3] This type of seeing involves discernment and analysis. We are to judge based on prior discernment—no assumptions or knee-jerk reactions. And finally, we act. This is a twofold activity. Firstly, we act to alleviate immediate danger, pain, or hardship. Then we must take on the task of advocacy in an attempt to dismantle the structures that perpetuate the injustices, replacing them with structures that promote a society where all people are safe, included, and valued.

Conclusion

Over the course of this book, we have encountered several inspirational women—women who, as we have seen, were prophets in their own right. If we allow them to, these women can speak to us across the centuries and despite differences in customs and traditions. Through their lived experiences, they invite us to open our eyes and *see* our own prophets, *judge* what it is we need to do, and then, in conjunction with our "denied ones," *act* to create a society based on justice, compassion, and equity; a society that values each individual and takes seriously our stewardship of the earth and its resources.

This is the invitation extended to Simon the Pharisee by the forgiven woman, and to each person present in the temple by the woman caught in adultery. The authors of these stories did not tell us whether those people accepted the invitation . . .

Will we?

---

3. Farmer, "Health, Healing," 201–6.

Bibliography

Ackerman, Susan. "Why Is Miriam Also among the Prophets? (And Is Zipporah among the Priests?)." *Journal of Biblical Literature* 121.1 (Spring 2002) 47–80. https://scholarlypublishingcollective.org/sblpress/jbl/article/121/1/47/181772.

Alison, James. *Knowing Jesus*. London: SPCK, 1993.

Alt, Christopher E. "The Dynamic of Humility and Wisdom: The Syrophoenician Woman and Jesus in Mark 7:24–31a." *Lumen et Vita* 2 (2012) 1–13. https://ejournals.bc.edu/index.php/lumenetvita/article/view/1901/1908.

Anderson, B. W. "Signs and Wonders." In *The Interpreter's Dictionary of the Bible: R–Z*, edited by George Arthur Buttrick et al., 348–51. Nashville: Abingdon, 1962.

Anderson, Hugh. *The Gospel of Mark*. The New Century Bible Commentary. Grand Rapids: Eerdmans, 1976.

Aquino, Maria Pilar. *Our Cry for Life: Feminist Theology from Latin America*. Maryknoll, NY: Orbis, 1993.

Augustine. *Homilies on the Gospel according to John and His First Epistle*. Vol. 1. A Library of the Fathers of the Holy Catholic Church: Anterior to the Division of the East and West. Oxford: J. H. Parker, 1848. https://www.google.com.au/books/edition/Homilies_on_the_Gospel_According_to_St_J/-UsMAAAAIAAJ?hl=en.

———. "Sermon 27 on the New Testament." New Advent. https://www.newadvent.org/fathers/160327.htm.

Bach, Alice. "The Pleasure of Her Text." *Union Seminary Quarterly Review* 43 (1989) 41–58. https://doi.org/10.7916/d8-3fj7-gp22.

Bailey, Kenneth E. *Poet & Peasant and through Peasant Eyes: A Literary-Cultural Approach to the Parables in Luke*. Combined ed. Grand Rapids: Eerdmans, 1983.

Baldwin, Joyce G. *1 and 2 Samuel: An Introduction and Commentary*. Tyndale Old Testament Commentaries 8. Downers Grove, IL: InterVarsity, 1988.

Barclay, William. *The Gospel of John*. Vol 2. Rev. ed. The Daily Study Bible Series. Edinburgh: Saint Andrew, 1975.

———. *The Gospel of Luke*. The Daily Study Bible Series. Edinburgh: Saint Andrew, 1955.

———. *The Gospel of Matthew*. Vol 2. The Daily Study Bible Series. Edinburgh: Saint Andrew, 1957.

Barton, John. "Ethics in Isaiah of Jerusalem." In *This Place Is Too Small for Us: The Israelite Prophets in Recent Scholarship*, edited by Robert P. Gordon, 80–97. Winona Lake, IN: Eisenbrauns, 1995.

Batten, Loring Woart. *Ezra and Nehemiah*. Edinburgh: T. & T. Clark, 1913.

Bibliography

Baylis, Charles P. "The Woman Caught in Adultery: A Test of Jesus as the Greater Prophet." *Bibliotheca Sacra* 146 (1989) 171–84. https://ixtheo.de/Record/1637270941.

Beavis, Mary Ann. "Feminist (and Other) Reflections on the Woman with Seven Husbands (Mark 12:20–23): A Neglected Synoptic Parable." *Hermeneutik der Gleichnisse Jesu: Methodische Neuansätze zum Verstehen Urchristlicher Parabeltexte (Wissenschaftliche Untersuchungen zum Neuen Testament* 231) (2008) 603–17. https://ixtheo.de/Record/1445158124.

Bendoraitis, Kristian A. *"Behold, the Angels Came and Served Him": A Compositional Analysis of Angels in Matthew*. London: T. & T. Clark, 2015.

Beresford, Anna. "Feathers, Fins and Fur: The Significance of the Animals in the Book of Tobit." *St Mark's Review* 248 (January 2019) 91–104. EBSCOhost.

———. "Whose Wife Will She Be? A Feminist Interpretation of Luke 20:27–38." *Priscilla Papers* 35.4 (Autumn 2021) 6–13. https://www.cbeinternational.org/sites/default/files/2021-10/PP35.4Web.pdf.

Berkhof, Louis. *Systematic Theology*. Grand Rapids: Eerdmans, 1938.

Bingemer, Maria Clara. "Reflections on the Trinity." In *Through Her Eyes: Women's Theology from Latin America*, edited by Elsa Tamez, 56–80. Maryknoll, NY: Orbis, 1989.

Birch, Bruce C. "The First and Second Books of Samuel." In *The New Interpreter's Bible: A Commentary in Twelve Volumes*, edited by Leander E. Keck et al., 949–1383. Vol. 2. Nashville: Abingdon, 1998.

Blank, S. H. "Fable." In *The Interpreter's Dictionary of the Bible: E–J*, edited by George Arthur Butterick, 221. Nashville: Abingdon, 1962.

Blomberg, Craig L. "The Miracles as Parables." In *The Miracles of Jesus*, edited by David Wenham and Craig Blomberg, 327–59. Vol. 6 of *Gospel Perspectives*. Sheffield, UK: Journal for the Study of the Old Testament, 1986.

———. "New Testament Miracles and Higher Criticism: Climbing up the Slippery Slope." *Journal of the Evangelical Theological Society* 27.4 (December 1984) 425–38. https://www.etsjets.org/files/JETS-PDFs/27/27-4/27-4-pp425-438_JETS.pdf.

Blue, Debbie. "The Book of Esther Laughs at Empire: Biblical Farce." *Christian Century*, January 12, 2016, 32–33. https://www.christiancentury.org/article/2015-12/biblical-farce.

Boring, M. Eugene. "The Gospel of Matthew." In *The New Interpreter's Bible: A Commentary in Twelve Volumes*, edited by Leander E. Keck et al., 89–505. Vol. 8. Nashville: Abingdon, 1995.

Bovan, François. *Luke 1: A Commentary on the Gospel of Luke 1:1—9:50*. Hermeneia: A Critical and Historical Commentary on the Bible. Translated by Christine M. Thomas. Minneapolis: Fortress, 2002.

Brenneman, Laura L. "Your Daughters Shall Prophesy: How Can We Keep Silent?" *Conrad Grebel Review* 28.2 (Spring 2010) 52–61. https://uwaterloo.ca/grebel/publications/conrad-grebel-review/issues/spring-2010/your-daughters-shall-prophesy-how-can-we-keep.

Bridge, Edward J. "Desperation to a Desperado: Abigail's Request to David in 1 Samuel 25." *Australian Biblical Review* 63 (2015) 14–28. EBSCOhost.

Brueggemann, Walter. "The Book of Jeremiah: Portrait of the Prophet." *Interpretation* 37 (1983) 130–45. https://doi.org/10.1177/002096438303700203.

———. *The Prophetic Imagination*. Minneapolis: Fortress, 2001.

BIBLIOGRAPHY

———. *The Threat of Life: Sermons on Pain, Power, and Weakness*. Edited by Charles L. Campbell. Minneapolis: Fortress, 1996.

———. "Truth-Telling and Peacemaking: A Reflection on Ezekiel." *Christian Century*, November 30, 1998, 1096–98. https://www.religion-online.org/article/truth-telling-and-peacemaking-a-reflection-on-ezekiel/.

Buckland, Collin Blake. *Jesus and the Thoughts of Many Hearts*. London: T. & T. Clark, 2015.

Buelt, Edward. *A New Friendship: The Spirituality and Ministry of the Deacon*. Collegeville, MN: Liturgical, 2011.

Burkill, T. A. "The Historical Development of the Story of the Syrophoenician Woman (Mark vii:24–31)." *Novum Testamentum* 9.3 (1967) 161–77. https://brill.com/view/journals/nt/9/3/article-p161_1.xml.

———. "The Syrophoenician Woman: The Congruence of Mark 7:24–31." *Zeitschrift für die Neutestamentliche Wissenschaft* 57 (1966) 23–37. https://doi.org/10.1515/zntw.1966.57.1-2.23.

Burrows, Millar. "Levirate Marriage in Israel." *Journal of Biblical Literature* 59.1 (March 1940) 23–33. https://doi.org/10.2307/3262301.

Byrne, Brendan. *The Hospitality of God: A Reading of Luke's Gospel*. Strathfield, Australia: St Paul's, 2000.

Cadwallader, Alan H. *Beyond the Word of a Woman: Recovering the Bodies of the Syrophoenician Woman*. Adelaide, Australia: ATF, 2008.

Callaghan, Josiah M. "Covenant Partners: An Egalitarian Reading of Genesis 17:15–16." *Priscilla Papers* 33.4 (Fall 2019) 18–21. https://www.galaxie.com/article/pp33-4-06.

Calvin, John. *The Gospel according to St John: Part One, 1–10*. Calvin's New Testament Commentaries 4. Translated by T. H. L. Parker. Edited by David W. Torrance and Thomas F. Torrance. Grand Rapids: Eerdmans, 1961.

———. *A Harmony of the Gospels Matthew, Mark & Luke and James and Jude*. Vol. 3 of Calvin's New Testament Commentaries. Translated by A. W. Morrison. Edited by David W. Torrance and Thomas F. Torrance. Grand Rapids: Eerdmans, 1978.

———. *A Harmony of the Gospels Matthew, Mark & Luke*. Vol. 2 of Calvin's New Testament Commentaries. Translated by T. H. L. Parker. Edited by David W. Torrance and Thomas Forsyth Torrance. Edinburgh: Saint Andrew, 1972.

Card, Michael. *John: The Gospel of Wisdom*. Downers Grove, IL: InterVarsity, 2014.

———. *Luke: The Gospel of Amazement*. Downers Grove, IL: InterVarsity, 2011.

Carman, Amy Smith. "Abigail: The Wise Woman of Carmel." *Stone-Campbell Journal* 18.1 (Spring 2015) 47–60. http://www.stone-campbelljournal.com/the_journal/research/volume-18-issue-1/180104/.

Carson, Donald Arthur. *The Gospel according to John*. The Pillar New Testament Commentary.Grand Rapids: Eerdmans, 1991.

Carter, Warren. *Mark*. Edited by Sarah J. Tanzer. The Wisdom Commentary 42, edited by Barbara E. Reid. Collegeville, MN: Liturgical, 2019.

Cassidy, Richard J. *Jesus, Politics, and Society: A Study of Luke's Gospel*. Maryknoll, NY: Orbis, 1978.

Cavalcanti, Tereza. "The Prophetic Ministry of Women in the Hebrew Bible." In *Through Her Eyes: Women's Theology from Latin America*, edited by Elsa Tamez, 118–39. Maryknoll, NY: Orbis, 1989.

Bibliography

Chinen, Mark A. "Crumbs from the Table: The Syrophoenician Woman and International Law." *Journal of Law and Religion* 27.1 (2011–12) 1–57. https://www.jstor.org/stable/41428276.

Chisholm, Robert B., Jr. *Handbook of the Prophets*. Grand Rapids: Baker Academic, 2002.

Claassens, L. Juliana M. "Calling the Keeners: The Image of the Wailing Woman as a Symbol of Survival in a Traumatized World." *Journal of Feminist Studies in Religion* 26.1 (2010) 63–77. https://www.researchgate.net/publication/236718430_Calling_the_Keeners_The_Image_of_the_Wailing_Woman_As_Symbol_of_Survival_in_a_Traumatized_World.

———. *Mourner, Mother, Midwife: Reimagining God's Delivering Presence in the Old Testament*. Louisville: Westminster John Knox, 2012.

Coats, George W. "Parable, Fable, and Anecdote: Storytelling in the Succession Narrative." *Interpretation: A Journal of Bible and Theology* 35.4 (October 1981) 368–82. https://doi.org/10.1177/002096438103500404.

Cosgrove, Charles H. "A Woman's Unbound Hair in the Greco-Roman World, with Special Reference to the Story of the 'Sinful Woman' in Luke 7:36–50." *Journal of Biblical Literature* 124.4 (Winter 2005) 675–92. https://doi.org/10.2307/30041064.

Crabbe, Kylie. "A Sinner and a Pharisee: Challenges at Simon's Table in Luke 7:36–50." *Pacifica: Australasian Theological Studies* 24 (October 2011) 247–66. https://doi.org/10.1177/1030570X1102400303.

Crossan, John Dominic. *In Parables: The Challenge of the Historical Jesus*. New York: Harper & Row, 1973.

Culpepper, R. Alan. "The Gospel of Luke." In *The New Interpreter's Bible: A Commentary in Twelve Volumes*, edited by Leander E. Keck et al., 3–490. Vol. 9. Nashville: Abingdon, 1995.

Cyril of Alexandria, "Sermon CXXXVI." In *Commentary on Luke*, 636–40. http://tertullian.org/fathers/cyril_on_luke_13_sermons_135_145.htm.

D'Angelo, Mary Rose. "Women in Luke-Acts: A Redactional View." *Journal of Biblical Literature* 109.3 (1990) 441–61. https://doi.org/10.2307/3267051.

Darr, Katheryn Pfisterer. *Far More Precious than Jewels: Perspectives on Biblical Women*. Louisville: Westminster John Knox, 1991.

del Prado, Consuelo. "I Sense God in Another Way." In *Through Her Eyes: Women's Theology from Latin America*, edited by Elsa Tamez, 140–49. Maryknoll, NY: Orbis, 1989.

Dennis, Trevor. *Sarah Laughed: Women's Voices in the Old Testament*. London: SPCK, 1994.

Derrett, J. Duncan M. *Law in the New Testament*. London: Darton, Longman & Todd, 1970.

———. "Law in the New Testament: The Syro-Phoenician Woman and the Centurion of Capernaum." *Novum Testamentum* 15 (July 1973) 161–86. https://doi.org/10.2307/1560339.

DiCicco, Mario. "What Can One Give in Exchange for One's Life? A Narrative-Critical Study of the Widow and her Offering, Mark 12:41–44." *Currents in Theology and Mission* 25.6 (December 1998) 441–49. EBSCOhost.

Dinkler, Michal Beth. *Silent Statements: Narrative Representations of Speech and Silence in the Gospel of Luke*. Berlin: De Gruyter, 2013.

Bibliography

Doat, David. "Disability, Theology, and Human Evolution: An Original Hypothesis Based on the Spiritual Experience of L'Arche Communities." *Journal of Religion, Disability & Health* 17.2 (2013) 125–68. https://doi.org/10.1080/15228967.2012.731879.

Driver, Samuel Rolles. *A Critical and Exegetical Commentary on Deuteronomy.* The International Critical Commentary. New York: Charles Scribner & Sons, 1895. https://www.google.com.au/books/edition/A_Critical_and_Exegetical_Commentary_on/vmJgGpJZBw0C?hl=en.

Dunn, J. D. G. "Myth." In *Dictionary of Jesus and the Gospels*, edited by Joel B. Green et al., 566–69. Downers Grove, IL: InterVarsity, 1992.

Dyck, Bruno. *Management and the Gospel: Luke's Radical Message for the First and Twenty-First Centuries.* Basingstoke, UK: Palgrave Macmillan, 2013.

Erzberger, Johanna. "Prophetic Sign Acts as Performance." In *Jeremiah Invented: Constructions and Deconstructions of Jeremiah*, edited by Else K. Holt and Carolyn J. Sharp, 104–16. London: Bloomsbury, 2015.

Esposito, Thomas. *Jesus' Meals with Pharisees and Their Liturgical Roots.* Rome: Gregorian & Biblical, 2015.

Eza, Tonya. "How to Tell a True Prophetess from a False One." *Lutheran Forum* (Fall 2007) 9–11. EBSCOhost.

Fadiman, Clifton, ed. *The Little, Brown Book of Anecdotes.* Toronto: Little, Brown & Company, 1985.

Faley, Roland J. "Leviticus." In *The New Jerome Biblical Commentary*, edited by Raymond E. Brown et al., 61–79. London: Geoffrey Chapman, 1990.

Fallon, Michael. *The Gospel according to Saint Luke.* Kensington, Australia: Chevalier, 2007.

Farmer, Paul. "Health, Healing and Social Justice: Insights from Liberation Theology." In *The Preferential Option for the Poor beyond Theology*, edited by Daniel G. Groody and Gustavo Gutiérrez, 199–228. Notre Dame, IN: University of Notre Dame Press, 2014.

Fischer, Irmtraud. *Des femmes messagères de Dieu: Prophètes et prophétesses dans la Bible hébraïque.* Paris: Médiaspaul, 2002.

———. *Women Who Wrestled with God: Biblical Stories of Israel's Beginnings.* Collegeville, MN: Liturgical, 2005.

Forbes, Greg W., and Scott D. Harrower. *Raised from Obscurity: A Narrative and Theological Study of the Characterisation of Women in Luke-Acts.* Eugene, OR: Pickwick, 2015.

Fretheim, Terence E. "The Book of Genesis." In *The New Interpreter's Bible: A Commentary in Twelve Volumes*, edited by Leander E Keck et al., 321–674. Vol. 1. Nashville: Abingdon, 1994.

———. "What Biblical Scholars Wish Pastors Would Start and Stop Doing about Ethical Issues in the Old Testament." *Word & World* 31.3 (Summer 2011) 297–306. https://wordandworld.luthersem.edu/issues.aspx?article_id=1569.

Friebel, K. G. "Sign Acts." In *Dictionary of Old Testament Prophets*, edited by Mark J. Boda and J. Gordon McConville, 707–13. Nottingham, UK: InterVarsity, 2012.

Gabaitse, Rosinah Mmannana. "Contextual Reading of Luke-Acts with Pentecostal Women in Botswana." In *Luke-Acts*, edited by James P. Grimshaw, 137–54. London: T. & T. Clark, 2019.

Bibliography

Gafney, Wilda. "A Prophet-Terrorist(a) and an Imperial Sympathizer: An Empire-Critical, Postcolonial Reading of the No'adyah/Nechemyah Conflict." *Black Theology: An International Journal* 9.2 (2011) 161–76. https://doi.org/10.1558/blth.v9i2.161.

Gaster, T. H. "Myth, Mythology." In *The Interpreter's Dictionary of the Bible: K–Q*, edited by George Arthur Butterick, 481–87. Nashville: Abingdon, 1962.

Geldenhuys, Norval. *Commentary on the Gospel of Luke*. The New International Commentary on the New Testament. Grand Rapids: Eerdmans, 1975.

Getty-Sullivan, Mary Ann. *Women in the New Testament*. Collegeville, MN: Liturgical, 2001.

Glancy, Jennifer A. "Jesus, the Syrophoenician Woman, and Other First Century Bodies." *Biblical Interpretation: A Journal of Contemporary Approaches* 18 (2010) 342–63. https://doi.org/10.1163/156851510X517582.

Goldsmith, Galen L. "The Cutting Edge of Prophetic Imagery." *Journal of Biblical and Pneumatological Research* 3 (2011) 3–18. https://www.academia.edu/11950184/The_Cutting_Edge_of_Prophetic_Imagery.

Grassi, Joseph A. *God Makes Me Laugh: A New Approach to Luke*. Wilmington, DE: Michael Glazier, 1986.

———. *Peace on Earth: Roots and Practices from Luke's Gospel*. Collegeville, MN: Liturgical, 2004.

Hamilton, Victor P. *The Book of Genesis: Chapters 1–17*. The New International Commentary on the Old Testament. Grand Rapids: Eerdmans, 1990.

Hamori, Esther J. "The Prophet and the Necromancer: Women's Divination for Kings." *Journal of Biblical Literature* 132.4 (2013) 827–43. https://doi.org/10.2307/42912469.

Harrington, Daniel J. "An Enacted Parable." *America: The Jesuit Review*, July 21, 2008, 47. https://www.americamagazine.org/content/the-word/enacted-parable.

Harrington, Daniel J., and James F. Keenan. *Paul and Virtue Ethics*. Chicago: Sheed & Ward, 2002.

Harris, Murray J. *John*. Exegetical Guide to the Greek New Testament. Edited by Andreas J. Köstenberger and Robert W. Yarborough. Nashville: B. & H. Academic, 2015.

Harris, Sarah. "Letting (H)Anna Speak: An Intertextual Reading of the New Testament Prophetess (Luke 2:36–38)." *Feminist Theology* 27.1 (2018) 60–74. https://doi.org/10.1177/0966735018794483.

Healy, Mary. *The Gospel of Mark*. Grand Rapids: Baker Academic, 2008.

Heil, John Paul. "The Story of Jesus and the Adulteress (John 7,53—8,11) Reconsidered." *Biblica* 72.2 (1991) 182–91. https://www.jstor.org/stable/42611174.

Henry, Matthew. *Matthew to John*. Vol. 5 of *Commentary on the Whole Bible*. Grand Rapids: Christian Classics Ethereal Library, n.d. https://www.ccel.org/ccel/h/henry/mhc5/cache/mhc5.pdf.

Higgs, Liz Curtis. "The Forgiven Woman: An Outpouring of Grace: Luke 7:36–50." *Today's Christian Woman* 28.5 (September/October 2006) 30. https://www.todayschristianwoman.com/articles/2006/september/8.30.html.

Hill, David. *The Gospel of Matthew*. The New Century Bible Commentary. Edited by Matthew Black. Grand Rapids: Eerdmans, 1972.

Himes, Kenneth R. *Christianity and the Political Order: Conflict, Cooptation, and Cooperation*. Maryknoll, NY: Orbis, 2013.

Hitchens, Christopher. *Love, Poverty, and War: Journeys and Essays*. New York: Nation, 2004.

BIBLIOGRAPHY

Hodges, Zane C. "The Woman Taken in Adultery (John 7:53—8:11)." *Bibliotheca Sacra* 137.545 (January 1980) 41–53. https://www.galaxie.com/article/bsac137-545-04.

Holladay, John S. "Assyrian Statecraft and the Prophets of Israel." In *Prophecy in Israel*, edited by David L. Petersen, 122–43. London: SPCK, 1987.

Hooker, Morna D. *The Signs of a Prophet: The Prophetic Actions of Jesus*. London: SCM, 1997.

Hornsby, Teresa J. "The Woman Is a Sinner/The Sinner Is a Woman." In *A Feminist Companion to Luke*, edited by Amy-Jill Levine and Marianne Blickenstaff, 121–32. London: Sheffield Academic Press, 2002.

Houston, Walter. "What Did the Prophets Think They Were Doing? Speech Acts and Prophetic Discourse in the Old Testament." *Biblical Interpretation: A Journal of Contemporary Approaches* 1.2 (1993) 167–88. https://doi.org/10.1163/156851593X00043.

Hubbard, Mallonee. "The Woman Who Never Stopped Menstruating." *Daughters of Sarah* 11.6 (November–December 1985) 8–10. EBSCOhost.

Humphries-Brooks, Stephenson. "The Canaanite Woman in Matthew." In *A Feminist Companion to Matthew*, edited by Amy-Jill Levine, 138–56. Sheffield, UK: Sheffield Academic, 2011.

Hunter, A. M. *Interpreting the Parables*. London: SCM, 1960.

———. *Introducing New Testament Theology*. London: SCM, 1957.

———. *The Parables Then and Now*. Philadelphia: Westminster, 1971.

Hurlburt, Ted E. *Romance with Romans*. Enumclaw, WA: Pleasant Word, 2010.

Irwin, Brian P. "Yahweh's Suspension of Free Will in the Old Testament: Divine Immorality or Sign-Act?" *Tyndale Bulletin* 54.2 (2003) 55–62. https://hdl.handle.net/1807/73634.

Jackson, Melissa A. *Comedy and the Feminist Interpretation of the Hebrew Bible*. Oxford: Oxford University Press, 2012.

Janssen, Rosalind. "A New Reading of Shiphrah and Puah—Recovering their Voices." *Feminist Theology* Vol 27.1 (2018) 9–25. https://doi.org/10.1177/0966735018789129.

Jeremias, Joachim. *Jerusalem in the Time of Jesus*. Translated by F. H. and C. H. Cave. London: SCM, 1969.

Johnson, Luke Timothy. *The Gospel of Luke*. Sacra Pagina 3, edited by Daniel J. Harrington. Collegeville, MN: Liturgical, 1991.

Jost, Renate. "The Daughters of Your People Prophesy." In *Prophets and Daniel: A Feminist Companion to the Bible*, edited by Athalya Brenner, 70–76. London: Sheffield Academic, 2001.

Kaczorowski, Scott J. "The Pericope of the Woman Caught in Adultery: An Inspired Text Inserted into an Inspired Text?" *Journal of the Evangelical Theological Society* 61.2 (2018) 321–37. https://www.etsjets.org/files/JETS-PDFs/61/61-2/JETS_61.2_321-337_Kaczorowski.pdf.

Kalmanofsky, Amy. *Dangerous Sisters of the Hebrew Bible*. Minneapolis: Fortress, 2014.

Karris, Robert J. *Eating Your Way through Luke's Gospel*. Collegeville, MN: Liturgical, 2006.

———. "The Gospel according to Luke." In *The New Jerome Biblical Commentary*, edited by Raymond E. Brown et al., 675–721. London: Cassell, 1990.

Keil, C. F., and F. Delitzsch. "Deuteronomy." In *The Pentateuch*, 269–517. Vol. 1 of *Commentary on the Old Testament in Ten Volumes*. Translated by James Martin. Grand Rapids: Eerdmans, 1980.

Bibliography

Kessler, Rainer. "Miriam and the Prophecy of the Persian Period." In *Prophets and Daniel: A Feminist Companion to the Bible*, edited by Athalya Brenner, 77–86. London: Sheffield Academic, 2001.

Kidner, Derek. *Ezra and Nehemiah*. Dowers Grove: InterVarsity, 1979.

Kilgallen, J. J. "The Sadducees and Resurrection from the Dead: Luke 20:27–40." *Biblica* 67 (1986) 478–95. https://www.jstor.org/stable/42611054.

Kinukawa, Hisako. "The Journey of a Girl Who Talks Back: Mark's Syrophoenician Woman." In *Faith and Feminism: Ecumenical Essays*, edited by D. Diane Lipsett and Phyllis Trible, 69–97. Louisville: Westminster John Knox, 2014.

———. *Women and Jesus in Mark*. Maryknoll, NY: Orbis, 1994.

Kirkpatrick, A. F. *The First Book of Samuel*. Cambridge: Cambridge University Press, 1918.

Klancher, Nancy. *The Taming of the Canaanite Woman: Constructions of Christian Identity in the Afterlife of Matthew 15:21–28*. Studies of the Bible and Its Reception 1. Berlin: De Gruyter, 2013.

Klein, Elizabeth. *Augustine's Theology of Angels*. Cambridge: Cambridge University Press, 2018.

Klein, Ralph W. "The Books of Ezra & Nehemiah." In *The New Interpreter's Bible: A Commentary in Twelve Volumes*, edited by Leander E. Keck et al., 663–851. Vol. 3. Nashville: Abingdon, 1999.

Kreider, Glenn R. "Jesus the Messiah as Prophet, Priest, and King." *Bibliotheca Sacra* 176.702 (2019) 174–87. EBSCOhost.

LaCocque, André. *The Feminine Unconventional: Four Subversive Figures in Israel's Tradition*. Minneapolis: Fortress, 1990.

Lane, William L. *Commentary on the Gospel of Mark*. Grand Rapids: Eerdmans, 1975.

Laney, J. Carl. "The Role of the Prophets in God's Case against Israel." *Bibliotheca Sacra* 138.552 (1981) 313–25. EBSCOhost.

Lange, Armin. "Greek Seers and Israelite-Jewish Prophets." *Vetus Testamentum* 57 (2007) 461–82. https://www.jstor.org/stable/20504277.

Lapsley, Jacqueline E. "Look! The Children and I Are Signs and Portents in Israel: Children in Isaiah." In *The Child in the Bible*, edited by Marcia J. Bunge, 82–102. Grand Rapids: Eerdmans, 2008.

Lederman-Daniely, Dvora. "Revealing Miriam's Prophecy." *Feminist Theology* 25.1 (2016) 8–28. https://doi.org/10.1177/0966735016657704.

———. "And Sarah Heard It in the Tent Door (Genesis 18, 10): Uncovering Sarah's Covenant." *Feminist Theology* 27.1 (2018) 26–42. https://doi.org/10.1177/0966735018789134.

LeMarquand, Grant. "The Canaanite Conquest of Jesus (Mt 15:21–28)." *Journal of the Faculty of Religious Studies*, McGill, Vol 33 (2005) 237–247. EBSCOhost.

Lessing, Reed. "Preaching Like the Prophets: Using Rhetorical Criticism in the Appropriation of Old Testament Prophetic Literature." *Concordia Journal* (October 2002) 391–408. https://www.csl.edu/wp-content/uploads/2010/12/October-2002.pdf.

Levine, Amy-Jill. "Matthew." In *The Women's Bible Commentary: Twentieth Anniversary Edition*, edited by Carol A. Newsom et al., 465–77. Louisville: Westminster John Knox, 2012.

Lewis, Jack P. *The Minor Prophets*. Grand Rapids: Baker Book House, 1966.

"Life." http://www.twainquotes.com/Life.html.

Malchow, Bruce V. *Social Justice in the Hebrew Bible*. Collegeville, MN: Liturgical, 1996.

Bibliography

Maloney, Linda M., and Elizabeth J. Smith. "The Year of Luke: A Feminist Perspective." *Currents in Theology and Mission* 21.6 (November 1994) 415–23. EBSCOhost.

Manor, Dale W. "A Brief History of Levirate Marriage as It Relates to the Bible." *Restoration Quarterly* 27.3 (1984) 129–42. EBSCOhost.

Marchetti, Christine. "Women Prophets in the Old Testament." *Priscilla Papers* 32.2 (Spring 2018) 9–13. https://issuu.com/mutualitymag/docs/pp322-web.

Marshall, I. Howard. *Luke: Historian & Theologian*. Exeter, UK: Paternoster, 1970.

Matthews, V. H. "Prophecy and Society." In *Dictionary of the Old Testament Prophets*, edited by Mark J. Boda and J. Gordon McConville, 623–34. Nottingham, UK: InterVarsity, 2012.

Mays, James L. "Justice: Perspectives from the Prophetic Tradition." In *Prophecy in Israel*, edited by David L. Petersen, 144–58. London: SPCK, 1987.

McCracken, David. *The Scandal of the Gospels: Jesus, Story, and Offense*. New York: Oxford University Press, 1994.

McFague, Sallie. "Parable." In *A Dictionary of Christian Theology*, edited by Alan Richardson and John Bowden, 425–26. London: SCM, 1983.

McKenzie, John L. "The Gospel According to Matthew." In *The Jerome Biblical Commentary*, edited by Raymond E. Brown et al., 62–114. London: Cassell, 1968.

McWhirter, Jocelyn. *Rejected Prophets: Jesus and His Witnesses in Luke-Acts*. Minneapolis: Fortress, 2013.

Mendenhall, George E. "Covenant." In *The Interpreter's Dictionary of the Bible: A–D*, edited by George Arthur Buttrick, 714–23. Nashville: Abingdon, 1962.

Miller, Patrick D. "The Book of Jeremiah." In *The New Interpreter's Bible: A Commentary in Twelve Volumes*, edited by Leander E. Keck et al., 555–926. Vol. 6. Nashville: Abingdon, 2001.

Miller, Timothy E. "Text-Criticism and the Pulpit: Should One Preach about the Woman Caught in Adultery?" *Themelios* 45.2 (2020) 368–84. https://www.thegospelcoalition.org/themelios/article/text-criticism-and-the-pulpit-should-one-preach-about-the-woman-caught-in-adultery/.

Milton, John. *Paradise Regained*. The Project Gutenberg. https://www.gutenberg.org/files/58/58-h/58-h.htm.

Monro, Anita. *Resurrecting Erotic Transgression: Subjecting Ambiguity in Theology*. London: Equinox, 2006.

Morgan, G. Campbell. *Voices of Twelve Hebrew Prophets*. Grand Rapids: Baker Book House, 1975.

Morgenstern, Julian. *The Book of the Covenant*. Eugene, OR: Wipf & Stock, 2007.

Morris, Leon. *The Gospel according to John*. Grand Rapids: Eerdmans, 1971.

———. *The Gospel according to Matthew*. Grand Rapids: Eerdmans, 1992.

———. *Luke: An Introduction and Commentary*. Leicester, UK: InterVarsity, 1974.

Mowry, M. Lucetta. "Allegory." In *The Interpreter's Dictionary of the Bible: A–D*, edited by George Arthur Buttrick, 82–84. Nashville: Abingdon, 1962.

———. "Parable." In *The Interpreter's Dictionary of the Bible: K–Q*, edited by George Arthur Buttrick, 649–54. Nashville: Abingdon, 1962.

Moyer, Clifton J. "Who Is the Prophet, and Who the Ass? Role-Reversing Interludes and the Unity of the Balaam Narrative (Numbers 22–24)." *Journal for the Study of the Old Testament* 37.2 (2012) 167–83. https://doi.org/10.1177/0309089212455568.

Mullen, J. Patrick. *Dining with Pharisees*. Collegeville, MN: Liturgical, 2004.

Mullins, Michael. *The Gospel of Luke: A Commentary*. Dublin: Columba, 2010.

Bibliography

Myers, Carol L. *Discovering Eve: Ancient Israelite Women in Context.* New York: Oxford University Press, 1988.

Napier, B. D. "Prophet, Prophetism." In *The Interpreter's Dictionary of the Bible: K–Q,* edited by George Arthur Buttrick, 896–919. Nashville: Abingdon, 1962.

Neale, David A. *None but the Sinners: Religious Categories in the Gospel of Luke.* Sheffield: JSOT, 1991.

Nelavala, Surekha. "Smart Syrophoenician Woman: A Dalit Feminist Reading of Mark 7:24–31." *Expository Times* 118.2 (2006) 64–69. https://doi.org/10.1177/0014524606070856.

Niditch, Susan. "Folklore, Feminism, and the Ambiguity of Power." In *Faith and Feminism: Ecumenical Essays,* edited by B. Diane Lipsett and Phyllis Trible, 55–67. Louisville: Westminster John Knox, 2014.

Nogalski, James D. *Interpreting Prophetic Literature: Historical and Exegetical Tools for Reading the Prophets.* Louisville: Westminster John Knox, 2015.

North, C. R. "Isaiah." In *The Interpreter's Dictionary of the Bible: E–J,* edited by George Arthur Buttrick, 731–44. Nashville: Abingdon, 1962.

O'Day, Gail R. "The Gospel of John." In *The New Interpreter's Bible: A Commentary in Twelve Volumes,* edited by Leander E. Keck et al., 491–865. Vol. 9. Nashville: Abingdon, 1995.

———. "John 7:53—8:11: A Study in Misreading." *Journal of Biblical Literature* 111.4 (Winter 1992) 631–40. https://doi.org/10.2307/3267436.

———. "Surprised by Faith: Jesus and the Canaanite Woman." In *A Feminist Companion to Matthew,* edited by Amy-Jill Levine, 114–25. Sheffield, UK: Sheffield Academic Press, 2001.

Oladejo, Olusayo Bosun. "Prophetic Guilds in the Old Testament as a Paradigm for Socio-Political Transformation in Africa." *Ogbomoso Journal of Theology* 16.3 (2011) 115–36. EBSCOhost.

Olanisebe, Samson O. "Levirate Marriage amongst the Hebrews and Widow's Inheritance amongst the Yoruba: A Comparative Investigation." *Verbum et Ecclesia* 35.1 (2014) 1–7. https://doi.org/10.4102/ve.v35i1.826.

Oswalt, John N. "Is There Anything Unique in the Israelite Prophets?" *Bibliotheca Sacra* 172.685 (January–March 2015) 67–84. https://www.galaxie.com/article/bsac172-685-05.

Otwell, John H. *And Sarah Laughed: The Status of Women in the Old Testament.* Philadelphia: Westminster, 1977.

Parvey, Constance F. "The Theology and Leadership of Women in the New Testament." In *Religion and Sexism,* edited by Rosemary Radford Reuther, 139–46. New York: Simon & Schuster, 1974.

Patterson, Richard D. "The Old Testament Use of an Archetype: The Trickster." *Journal of the Evangelical Theological Society* 42.3 (September 1999) 385–94. https://www.galaxie.com/article/jets42-3-01.

Pellegrini, Silvia. "Nameless Women in the Canonical Gospels." *Gospels: Narrative and History,* edited by Mercedes Navarro Puerto and Marinella Perroni, 387–430. Atlanta: SBL, 2015.

Perkins, Pheme. "The Gospel of Mark." In *The New Interpreter's Bible: A Commentary in Twelve Volumes,* edited by Leander E. Keck et al., 509–733. Vol. 8. Nashville: Abingdon, 1995.

Bibliography

Petersen, David L. "Introduction to Prophetic Literature." In *The New Interpreter's Bible: A Commentary in Twelve Volume*, edited by Leander E. Keck et al., 1–23. Vol. 6. Nashville: Abingdon, 2001.

———. *The Role of Israel's Prophets*. Sheffield, UK: Journal for the Study of the Old Testament, 1981.

———. "Ways of Thinking about Israel's Prophet." In *Prophecy in Israel*, edited by David L. Petersen, 1–21. London: SPCK, 1987.

Peterson, Brian Neil. *John's Use of Ezekiel: Understanding the Unique Perspective of the Fourth Gospel*. Minneapolis: Fortress, 2015.

Polzin, Robert. *Samuel and the Deuteronomist: 1 Samuel*. Pt. 2 of *A Literary Study of the Deuteronomic History*. San Francisco: Harper & Row, 1989.

Porter, Jeanne. *Leading Ladies: Transformative Biblical Images for Women's Leadership*. Philadelphia: Innisfree, 2000.

Powell, Mark Allan. *What Are They Saying about Luke?* New York: Paulist, 1989.

Prahlow, Jacob J. "Women in the Apostolic Fathers: Paranetic Women in 1 Clement (Part II). *Pursuing Veritas* (blog). April 21, 2016. https://pursuingveritas.com/2016/04/21/women-in-the-apostolic-fathers-paranetic-women-in-1-clement-part-ii/.

Reid, Barbara E. *Choosing the Better Part? Women in the Gospel of Luke*. Collegeville, MN: Liturgical, 1996.

———. "Do You See This Woman? A Liberative Look at Luke 7:36–50 and Strategies for Reading Other Lukan Stories against the Grain." In *A Feminist Companion to Luke*, edited by Amy-Jill Levine and Marianne Blickenstaff, 106–20. London: Sheffield Academic Press, 2002.

———. "Do You See This Woman? Luke 7:36–50 as a Paradigm for Feminist Hermeneutics." *Biblical Research* 40 (1995) 37–49. EBSCOhost.

———. "The Gospel of Luke: Friend or Foe of Women Proclaimers of the Word?" *Catholic Biblical Quarterly* 78.1 (January 2016) 1–23. https://www.jstor.org/stable/43900808.

Rhoads, David. "Jesus and the Syrophoenician Woman in Mark: A Narrative-Critical Study." *Journal of the American Academy of Religion* 62.2 (Summer 1994) 343–75. https://www.jstor.org/stable/1465270.

Ringe, Sharon H. "A Gentile Woman's Story." In *Feminist Interpretation of the Bible*, edited by Letty M. Russell, 65–72. Louisville: Westminster John Knox, 1985.

Ritchie, Nelly. "Women and Christology." In *Through Her Eyes: Women's Theology from Latin America*, edited by Elsa Tamez, 81–95. Maryknoll, NY: Orbis, 1989.

Robinson, Geoffrey. *A Change of Mind and Heart: The Good News according to Mark*. Revesby, Australia: Parish Ministry, 1994.

Rocchietti, Aracely de. "Women and the People of God." In *Through Her Eyes: Women's Theology from Latin America*, edited by Elsa Tamez, 96–117. Maryknoll, NY: Orbis, 1989.

Romero, Oscar. *A Prophetic Bishop Speaks to His People*. Vol. 1 of *The Complete Homilies of Archbishop Oscar Arnulfo Romero*. Translated by Joseph Owens. Miami: Convivium, 2015.

Ross, James F. "The Prophet as Yahweh's Messenger." In *Prophecy in Israel*, edited by David L. Petersen, 112–21. London: SPCK, 1987.

Ryle, John Charles. *Expository Thoughts on the Gospels: Mark*. Cambridge: James Clarke & Co., 1973.

———. *Expository Thoughts on the Gospels: Matthew*. Cambridge: James Clarke & Co., 1974.

Bibliography

Sanders, J. N., and B. A. Mastin. *The Gospel according to John*. Black's New Testament Commentaries. London: A. & C. Black, 1968.

Sanders, Jack T. *The Jews in Luke-Acts*. London: SCM, 1987.

Sanders, John. *The God Who Risks: A Theology of Divine Providence*. Rev. ed. Downers Grove, IL: InterVarsity, 2007.

Saunders, Ross. *Outrageous Women, Outrageous God: Women in the First Two Generations of Christianity*. Alexandria, Australia: E. J. Dwyer, 1996.

———. *She Has Washed My Feet with Her Tears*. Berkeley, CA: Seastone, 1998.

Schaberg, Jane. "Luke." In *The Women's Bible Commentary*, edited by Carol Newsom and Sharon Ringe, 75–292. Louisville: Westminster John Knox, 1992.

Schipper, Jeremy. *Parables and Conflict in the Hebrew Bible*. Cambridge: Cambridge University Press, 2009.

Schoors, Antoon. *I Am God Your Saviour: A Form-Critical Study of the Main Genres in Is. xl–lv*. Supplements to Vetus Testamentum 24. Leiden, Netherlands: Brill, 1973.

Schüssler Fiorenza, Elisabeth. *But She Said: Feminist Practices of Biblical Interpretation*. Boston: Beacon, 1992.

———. "A Feminist Critical Interpretation for Liberation: Martha and Mary; Luke 10:38–42." *Religion and Intellectual Life* 3 (1986) 21–35. EBSCOhost.

———. *In Memory of Her: A Feminist Theological Reconstruction of Christian Origins*. New York: Crossroad, 1983.

Scott, J. Julius, Jr. "Gentiles and the Ministry of Jesus: Further Observations on Matt 10:5–6; 15:21–28." *Journal of the Evangelical Theological Society* 33.2 (June 1990) 161–69. https://www.galaxie.com/article/jets33-2-03.

Seidler, Ayelet. "The Law of Levirate and Forced Marriage—Widow vs Levir in Deuteronomy 25:5–10." *Journal for the Study of the Old Testament* 42.4 (2018) 435–56. https://doi.org/10.1177/0309089216692180.

Seim, Turid Karlsen. "The Gospel of Luke." In *Searching the Scriptures: A Feminist Commentary*, edited by Elisabeth Schüssler Fiorenza, 728–62. Vol. 2. New York: Crossroad, 1994.

Shepherd, David. "Prophetaphobia: Fear and False Prophecy in Nehemiah VI." *Vetus Testamentum* 55 (April 2005) 232–50. https://www.jstor.org/stable/1519469.

Siker, Jeffrey S. *Jesus, Sin, and Perfection in Early Christianity*. New York: Cambridge University Press, 2015.

Simon, Uriel. "The Poor Man's Ewe-Lamb: An Example of a Juridical Parable." *Biblica* 48.2 (1967) 207–42. https://www.jstor.org/stable/42618475.

Smith, Gary V. *Interpreting the Prophetic Books: An Exegetical Handbook*. Grand Rapids: Kregel Academic, 2014.

Smith, Geoffrey. "A Closer Look at the Widow's Offering: Mark 12:41–44." *Journal of the Evangelical Theological Society* 40.1 (March 1997) 27–36. https://www.etsjets.org/files/JETS-PDFs/40/40-1/40-1-pp027-036_JETS.pdf.

Smith, Julie M. "A Double Portion: An Intertextual Reading of Hannah (1 Samuel 1–2) and Mark's Greek Woman (Mark 7:24–30)." *Dialogue: A Journal of Mormon Thought* 50.2 (2017) 125–38. https://doi.org/10.5406/dialjmormthou.50.2.0125.

Smith, Julien C. H. "The Construction of Identity in Mark 7:24–30: The Syrophoenician Woman and the Problem of Ethnicity." *Biblical Interpretation: A Journal of Contemporary Approaches* 20 (2012) 458–81. EBSCOhost.

Smith, Willard S. *Animals and Birds of the Bible*. Nashville: Abingdon, 1989.

Bibliography

Snodgrass, Klyne. "Parable." In *The Dictionary of Jesus and the Gospels*, edited by Joel B. Green and Scot McKnight, 591–601. Downers Grove, IL: InterVarsity, 1992.

———. "Prophets, Parables, and Theologians." *Bulletin for Biblical Research* 18.1 (2008) 45–77. https://www.jstor.org/stable/26423728.

Song, C. S. *In the Beginning Were Stories, Not Texts*. Eugene, OR: Cascade, 2011.

Stacey, W. D. *Prophetic Drama in the Old Testament*. London: Epworth, 1990.

Stanford, Thomas J. F. *Luke's People: The Men and Women Who Met Jesus and the Apostles*. Eugene, OR: Wipf & Stock, 2014.

Stanglin, Keith D. "Spiritus Propheticus: Spirit and Prophecy in Calvin's Old Testament Exegesis." *Calvin Theological Journal* 50 (2015) 23–42. https://www.researchgate.net/publication/282289557_Spiritus_propheticus_Spirit_and_prophecy_in_Calvin's_old_testament_exegesis.

Stein, Robert H. "Parables." In *The Oxford Companion to the Bible*, edited by Bruce M. Metzger and Michael D. Coogan, 567–70. New York: Oxford University Press, 1993.

Strong, James. "Hebrew and Chaldee Dictionary." In *The Complete Word Study Old Testament*, written by Warren Patrick Baker and edited by Spiros Zodhiates, 2485–2611 (1–126). Chattanooga: AMG, 1994.

Swartley, Willard M. "Politics and Peace (Eirēnē) in Luke's Gospel." In *Political Issues in Luke-Acts*, edited by Richard J. Cassidy and Philip J. Scharper, 18–37. Maryknoll, NY: Orbis, 1983.

Sweeney, Marvin A. "Introduction to the Prophetic Books." In *New Oxford Annotated Bible*, edited by Michael D. Coogan, 961–64. New York: Oxford University Press, 2010.

Tamez, Elsa. "Women's Lives as Sacred Text." In *Women's Sacred Scriptures*, edited by Kwok Pui-Lan and Elisabeth Schüssler Fiorenza, 57–64. London: SCM, 1998.

Tannehill, Robert C. "Should We Love Simon the Pharisee? Hermeneutical Reflections on the Pharisees in Luke." *Currents in Theology and Mission* 21 (1994) 424–33. EBSCOhost.

Tannen, Deborah. "You Just Don't Understand: Women and Men in Conversation." *Sintagma Revista de Lingüística*, January 1992, 110–15. https://www.researchgate.net/publication/46314186_Tannen_D_1991_You_just_don%27t_understand_Women_and_men_in_conversation.

Tasker, R. V. G. *John: An Introduction and Commentary*. Tyndale New Testament Commentaries. Edited by R. V. G. Tasker. London: InterVarsity, 1960.

———. "Parable." In *The New Bible Dictionary*, edited by J. D. Douglas et al., 932–34. Leicester, UK: InterVarsity, 1976.

Temple, William. *Readings in St John's Gospel: First and Second Series*. London: Macmillan, 1939.

Tew, W. Mark. *Luke: Gospel to the Nameless and Faceless*. Eugene, OR: Wipf & Stock, 2012.

Thiselton, A. C. "Hermeneutics." In *The New Dictionary of Theology*, edited by Sinclair B. Ferguson et al., 293–97. Leicester, UK: InterVarsity, 1988.

Thompson, John L. *Writing the Wrongs: Women of the Old Testament among Biblical Scholars from Philo through the Reformation*. New York: Oxford University Press, 2001.

Thompson, Marianne. *John: A Commentary*. Louisville: Westminster John Knox, 2015.

Thurston, Anne. *Knowing Her Place: Gender and the Gospels*. Mahwah: Paulist, 1998.

Bibliography

Tiemeier, Tracy S. "Catholic Feminism and Asian Religious Traditions: Rethinking Christ's Offices of Priest, Prophet, and King." *Greek Orthodox Theological Review* 60 (2015) 49–74. EBSCOhost.

Tucker, Gene M. "The Book of Isaiah 1–39." In *The New Interpreter's Bible: A Commentary in Twelve Volumes*, edited by Leander E. Keck et al., 27–305. Vol. 6. Nashville: Abingdon, 2001.

———. "The Role of the Prophets and the Role of the Church." In *Prophecy in Israel*, edited by David L. Petersen, 159–76. London: SPCK, 1987.

Tuohy, Anne. "Rhetoric and Transformation: The Feminist Theology of Elisabeth Schüssler Fiorenza." *Australian eJournal of Theology* 5 (August 2005) 1–8. https://acuresearchbank.acu.edu.au/download/91eed47573fdab3140854dde5941354cd1154d57f9fb3566948acf35dacb0cd5/644575/OA_Tuohy_2005_Rhetoric_and_transformation_the_feminist.pdf.

Tupek, Michael. *Torah of Sin and Grace: How the Hebrew Prophets Understood the Torah*. Eugene, OR: Resource, 2012.

Van Den Eynde, Sabine. "When a Teacher Becomes a Student: The Challenge of the Syrophoenician Woman (Mark 7.24–31)." *Theology* 103.814 (2000) 274–79. https://doi.org/10.1177/0040571X0010300406.

Van Til, Kent A. "Three Anointings and One Offering: The Sinful Woman in Luke 7.36–50." *Journal of Pentecostal Theology* 15.1 (2006) 73–82. https://brill.com/view/journals/pent/15/1/article-p73_3.xml.

Van Wolde, Ellen J. *Ruth and Naomi*. London: SCM, 1997.

Vine, W. E. "Allegory." In *Vine's Expository Dictionary of Old & New Testament Words*, 39. Nashville: Thomas Nelson 1996.

Volf, Miroslav. "Conversations with Miroslav Volf on His Book *Exclusion and Embrace: A Theological Exploration of Identity, Otherness, and Reconciliation* (1996)." *Conrad Grebel Review* 18.3 (Fall 2000) 71–82. https://uwaterloo.ca/grebel/publications/conrad-grebel-review/issues/fall-2000/conversations-miroslav-volf-his-book-exclusion-and-embrace.

Wainwright, Elaine M. "A Voice from the Margin: Reading Matthew 15:21–28 in an Australian Feminist Key." In *Reading from This Place: Social Location and Biblical Interpretation in Global Perspective*, edited by Fernando F. Segovia and Mary Ann Tolbert, 131–53. Vol. 2. Minneapolis: Fortress, 1995.

Wallace, Daniel B. "The Gospel according to Bart: A Review Article of *Misquoting Jesus* by Bart Ehrman." *Journal of the Evangelical Theological Society* 49.2 (June 2006) 327–49. https://www.galaxie.com/article/jets49-2-07.

Warren Jr., William F. "Parables: How Should We Understand them?" *Theological Educator* 56 (Fall 1997) 38–48. EBSCOhost.

Weber, Max. "The Prophet." In *Prophecy in Israel*, edited by David L. Petersen, 99–111. London: SPCK, 1987.

Weisberg, Dvora E. "The Widow of Our Discontent: Levirate Marriage in the Bible and Ancient Israel." *Journal for the Study of the Old Testament* 28.4 (2004) 403–29. https://doi.org/10.1177/030908920402800402.

Westermann, Claus. *God's Angels Need No Wings*. Translated by David L. Scheidt. Philadelphia: Fortress, 1979.

Weyermann, Andrew M. "Christ-Centred Preaching." *Currents in Theology and Mission* 28.6 (December 2001) 594–99. EBSCOhost.

Bibliography

Willett, Elizabeth Ann R. "Unveiling Old Testament Women with Accurate Translation." *Priscilla Papers* 33.4 (Fall 2019) 13–17. https://www.galaxie.com/article/pp33-4-05.

Williams, James G. "The Prophetic 'Father': A Brief Explanation of the Term 'Sons of the Prophets.'" *Journal of Biblical Literature* 85.3 (September 1966) 344–48. https://doi.org/10.2307/3264248.

Wire, Antoinette Clark. *The Corinthian Women Prophets: A Reconstruction through Paul's Rhetoric*. Minneapolis: Fortress, 1990.

Witherington, Ben, III. *The Acts of the Apostles: A Socio-Rhetorical Commentary*. Grand Rapids: Eerdmans, 1988.

———. *New Testament Rhetoric: An Introductory Guide to the Art of Persuasion in and of the New Testament*. Eugene, OR: Cascade, 2009.

———. *Women and the Genesis of Christianity*. Cambridge: Cambridge University Press, 1990.

———. *Women in the Ministry of Jesus*. Cambridge: Cambridge University Press, 1984.

Wolff, Hans Walter. "Prophets and Institutions in the Old Testament." *Currents in Theology and Mission* 13.1 (1986) 5–12. EBSCOhost.

Wray, T. J. *Good Girls, Bad Girls: The Enduring Lessons of Twelve Women of the Old Testament*. Lanham, MD: Rowman & Littlefield, 2008.

Yates, Gary. "Prophetic Sign Acts." Lecture 17 of *Jeremiah*. 2013. http://www.essaydocs.org/jeremiah-by-dr-gary-yates.html?page=18.

York, John O. *The Last Shall Be First: The Rhetoric of Reversal in Luke*. Sheffield, UK: Journal for the Study of the Old Testament, 1991.

Zodhiates, Spiros, ed. *The Complete New Testament Word Study Dictionary*. Iowa Falls, IA: World Bible, 1994.

———, comp. *The Complete Word Study New Testament*. Chattanooga, TN: AMG, 1991.

Name/Subject Index

A
Aaron, 47
Abigail, prophet, 2n5, 48, 51–52
Abraham, 49, 67–68
Achior, 65, 66
acting, ritual. *See* ritual acting
Adam, 4
Adonijah, 5
adultery, 127–28
    See also woman caught in adultery, story of
advising, role of, 14
Agabus, 39–40, 41
Ahasuerus, king, 52–53
allegories, 20, 81, 137–38
alterity, 152
Amos, prophet, 2, 13
anecdotes, 19, 20
angels, 8, 67–68, 100, 113–14
Anna, prophet, 41–42
anti-prophets, 26
apostles, 40
Asherah, prophets of, 2
audience. *See* witnesses

B
Baal, prophets of, 2
banquets, 27
    See also food; meals
Bathsheba, xii, 5
Bible, translations of, 35–37
    See also Scripture
bizarreness, 24
Boaz, xii, 62–63

C
Canaanite woman, story of
    as allegory, 137–38
    Canaanite woman as prophet in, 154–55
    Canaanite woman as teacher in, 141
    Canaanite woman generally in, 149–54
    Canaanite woman's approach in, 148–49
    Canaanite woman's faith in, 139, 140
    as chiasm, 152–53
    context of, 145–47
    conversation in, 149–53
    as didactic, 138
    disciples and, 140
    economics and, 139–40
    as enacted parable, 145–55
    feminist interpretations of, 141–45
    healing in, 153–54
    humility in, 140–41, 145
    as intersectional, 143
    Jesus' response in, 148–54
    in Matthew and Mark, 136–37
    mission to Jews and gentiles and, 138–39, 141–42, 149–54
    prayer and, 138
    rivalry in, 143–45
    setting for, 148
    spatial relations in, 148–49
    various interpretations of, 137–41
charisma, 4

Name/Subject Index

cheek, turning the other, 22–23
classical hypnotic role taking, 13, 31, 71, 96
commandments, ten, 87
communication, 17, 38
compassion, 12
consciousness, 11–12
convention, 22–23
conversion, 6–7
covenant, Mosaic, 5–6
crime, 130

D

Daniel, prophet, 2, 11
David, king, xii, 4, 30, 51–52, 115–16
Deborah, prophet, xi, 2, 37, 45–46, 48
    "palm" of, 46
disciples, 75, 140
"dismissed," the, 67–70
divination, 9

E

Eli, 50
Elijah, prophet, 45, 68, 74
emancipation narratives, 48
embodiment, 95–96
enacted parables
    allure of, 25
    bizarreness in, 24
    efficacy of, 25, 28
    Jesus and, 26–27, 28
    miracles as, 26–27
    purposes of, 27
    sign acts and, 25n34, 29
    spoken parables and, 17, 25
    symbols in, 28
    time and, 27
    types of, 29–31
    witnesses and, 27–28
    See also Canaanite woman, story of; forgiven woman, story of; widow at treasury, story of; woman caught in adultery, story of; woman who had had seven husbands, story of
engrossed acting, 13, 30–31, 96
Esther, prophet, xi, 2n5, 14, 48, 52–53

ethics, 23
    See also morals
Exodus event, 11, 26
extravagance, 21
Ezekiel, prophet, xiii, 1, 2, 11, 24, 29–30, 37, 42, 69
    wife of, 42

F

fables, 18–19, 20
female prophets
    calling of, 37
    communication styles of, 38
    in imagination, 34, 38, 70
    in Jewish tradition, 48–53
    lives of, 37
    in New Testament, 41–42
    not named as prophets in Bible, 57–58, 61–70
    occurrence of, 35
    in Old Testament, 42–48
    in Scripture or tradition, 53–55
    visibility of, 37–38
    See also prophets
feminine wiles, 53, 57, 63
food, 146–47
    See also banquets; meals
foretelling, 11
forgiven woman, story of
    as allegory, 81
    as chiasm, 91
    context of, 86–87
    as didactic, 82
    discipleship in, 84
    economics and, 83
    embodiment and, 85–86, 95–96
    as enacted parable, 86–97
    equality in, 85
    feminist interpretations of, 83–86
    forgiven woman as prophet in, 96–97
    forgiven woman generally in, 88, 89–92
    forgiveness in, 82–83, 93–94
    gratitude in, 81, 85
    hospitality in, 92–93
    Jesus' response in, 91–95

Name/Subject Index

John the Baptist and, 97
key moment in, 91–92
in Luke, 79–81
marginalized persons and, 84, 85–86
meal in, 88–89
parable nested within, 91
reversals in, 94–95
service, humility and, 82, 85
Simon the Pharisee in, 78–83, 85, 88–96
social identity and, 84
various interpretations of, 81–83
forgiveness, 91, 93–94
See also forgiven woman, story of

G
Gad, 9
gender, 35–37
gentiles, 51, 138–39, 141–42, 149–54
gifts of the Spirit, 39
God
for all nations, 69
angels and, 67–68
"feminine" face of, 69
hand of, 31
heralds of word of, 8
imagination of, 11
judgment of, 69
kingdom of, 22, 23, 27, 113–14, 115–16
messengers of, 7–8, 28–29
names for, 49–50, 68
grammar, 35

H
Habakkuk, prophet, 2, 43
Hagar, 39, 48–49, 67–68
Haggai, prophet, 2
Haman, 52–53
Hannah, prophet, 2n5, 48, 50–51, 153
Heman, 9
Hilkiah, 43
history, 54
histrionic neurosis, 13, 31
Holofernes, 65–66
hope, 12, 28

Hosea, prophet, 2, 13, 26
hospitality, 92–93
Huldah, prophet, 2, 37, 43, 48

I
Iddo, 9
imagination, 11–12, 23
interludes, 152
Isaiah, prophet, xiii, 1, 2, 24, 37
"wife" of, 42, 48
Ishmael, 67

J
Jael, 57
Jehozabad, 36
Jeremiah, prophet, xiii, 2, 13, 24, 37, 43
loincloth of, 30
Jesus
Canaanite woman and, 148–54
Deborah and, 45–46
enacted parables and, 26–27, 28
forgiven woman and, 91–95
King David and, 115–16
miracles and, 26–27
Moses and, 121–22
as prophet, 4, 8, 40, 79, 83
solidarity of, 12
spoken parables and, 18, 22, 23
wailing women and, 70
widow at treasury and, 75
woman caught in adultery and, 128–33
woman who had been hemorrhaging and, 143
woman who had had seven husbands and, 110–16
Jezebel, 44, 68
Joash, king, 36
Joel, prophet, 2
John the Baptist, 1–2, 39, 97
Jonah, prophet, 2, 13, 26
Josiah, king, 43
Judah, 61–62
Judith, xi, 14, 65–66
justice. *See* social justice

Name/Subject Index

K
king, office of, 3
kingdom of God, 22, 23, 27, 113–14, 115–16

L
lamentation, 69–70
law, 5, 45
leadership, 39, 69
liberation theology, 162
Lot's daughters, xii, 57
Luke-Acts, 101–6

M
Malachi, prophet, 2
manipulation, 53
marginalized persons, xi, 4–5, 9–10, 11–12, 54, 84, 85–86
marriage, 100, 101, 111–13
    levirate, 58–61, 101, 108
Mary, xii
matriarchs, 115
    See also specific matriarchs
meals, 88–89
    See also banquets; food
mediation, 47, 48
Melchizedek, 4
men, communication styles of, 38
mercy, 132–33
messengers, God's, 7–8, 28–29
Messiah, 4, 115–16
metaphors, 22
Micah, prophet, 2, 47
midwives, Hebrew, 64–65
miracles, 26–27, 146–47
Miriam, prophet, 2, 46–48
mission, 138–39, 141–42, 149–54
monarchy, 53–54
morals, xiii, 19
    See also ethics
Mordecai, 52–53
Moses, 4, 12, 45, 46, 47, 114–15, 121–22
Mount Tabor, 45–46
mourning, 69–70
mundaneness, 21
mustard seed, parable of the, 22

myths, 19, 20

N
Nabal, 51–52
Nahum, prophet, 2, 43
names, 49–50, 68
Naomi, xii, 62–64
Nathan, 5, 30, 51–52
Nehemiah, governor, 44–45
Noadiah, prophet, 2, 44–45, 48

O
Obadiah, prophet, 2
observation, 91–92
offices, Old Testament, 3
Onan, 61
oracles, 8, 76
oratory, 7, 17
"organismic involvement," 29

P
Palestine, 106–7
parables, xiii
    characteristics of, 21
    definition of, 17
    as function of stories, 23–24
    as genre, 20, 23–24
    juridical, 20
    as metaphors, 22
    purposes of, 18, 23, 24
    spoken, 17, 18, 22, 23, 25
    stories and, 18–20
    teaching and, 22
    trickery in, 57
    twists in, 21
    See also enacted parables
patriarchs, 114–15
    See also specific patriarchs
Paul, apostle, 40, 41
Pharisees, 86–87, 107, 109–10, 118, 123–30
    See also Simon the Pharisee
Pharoah, 26, 64–65
Philip's daughters, 41
plays, 30–31
poetry, 9–10
politics, 7
prayer, 138

Name/Subject Index

predictions, 11
priesthood, 3–4, 47
prophecy
    acting prophetically and, 12–14, 17, 38–39
    cessation of, 39
    fulfillment of, 3
    gift of, 40
    imagination of, 11–12
    law and, 45
    poetry and, 9–10
prophetesses, 2, 42
    See also female prophets
prophets
    apostles and, 40
    attitudes toward, 3, 4–5
    authority of, 4
    books of, 2
    calling of, 4, 37
    as conservative, 6
    definition of, 3, 160
    false, 44
    in imagination, 1–2
    lives of, 37
    major or minor, 2
    marginalized persons and, 4–5
    New Testament, 1–2, 2–3, 39–40
    number of, 2, 14
    office of, 3–4
    Old Testament, 1
    roles of, xiii, 2, 3–14, 39–40
    schools of, 13
    social justice and, 6
    of today, 160–62
    word of God and, 25–26
    writing or non-writing, 2
    See also female prophets; *specific prophets*
props, 17, 26
Puah, 64–65

R
Rahab, xii, 39, 57
rapport, 38
Rebecca, 39, 58
Rebekah, 57
Rechabites, 28

repentance, 6–7, 9–10, 69, 125
reporting, 38
resurrection, 100, 112, 114, 115
rhetoric, 7, 17
righteousness, 10, 87
ritual acting, 13, 29–30
role theory, 13
Ruth, Moabite, xi, xii, 14, 62–64

S
Sadducees, 98–101, 107, 109–10, 113
Samuel, prophet, 9, 46, 50, 51
Sarah, prophet, 2n5, 48–50, 67–68
schools, prophets,' 13
scribes, 118, 126
Scripture
    authorization of, 43
    masculinization of, 36
    message of, 159–60
see, judge, act, 92, 162
seeing, 91–92
seers, 8–9
Shaphan, 43
Shelah, 61–62
Shemaiah, 44
Shimeath, 36
Shimrith, 36
Shiprah, 64–65
sign acts. *See* enacted parables
signs, 31
    See also symbols
Simeon, 41
Simon the Pharisee, 40, 78–83, 85, 88–96
social justice, 6, 10–11
Solomon, king, 5
"son of man," 36
sower, parable of the, 21
Spirit, gifts of the, 39
staged events, 29–30
stories
    emancipation, 48
    females in, xi–xii
    types of, 18–20
    See also Canaanite woman, story of; forgiven woman, story of; widow at treasury, story of;

stories (*continued*)
    See also (*continued*)
        woman caught in adultery, story of; woman who had had seven husbands, story of
symbols, 28
    See also signs
Syrophoenician woman, 51
    See also Canaanite woman, story of

T

Tamar, xii, 14, 39, 58, 61–62
taxes, 107–8
theocracy, 2
theology, xi, 162
time, 27
trickery, 48, 57–58, 61–66

U

Uriah the Hittite, 30
Uzziah, 65

V

vestal virgins, 108–9
victory songs, 36, 47, 51
visions, 31, 71–72
vulnerability, 54
vulnerable persons, xii, 12
    See also marginalized persons

W

warnings, 24
widow at treasury, story of
    context of, 74–75
    disciples in, 75
    as enacted parable, 75–76
    Jesus' response in, 75
    in Mark and Luke, 72
    preferred interpretation of, 75–76
    various interpretations of, 73–74
    widow as prophet in, 75–76
widow of Zarephath, 74
widows (nonspecific), 58–61, 109
wisdom, 22, 87
witnesses, 27–28, 130
woman, Canaanite. See Canaanite woman, story of
woman, Syrophoenician, 51
    See also Canaanite woman, story of
woman caught in adultery, story of
    caught woman as prophet in, 133–34
    caught woman generally in, 131–33
    context of, 125–26
    crime in, 127–28
    crowd in, 131
    as enacted parable, 125–34
    feminist interpretations of, 124–25
    Jesus' response in, 128–33
    in John, 123
    Pharisees in, 123–30
    provenance of, 119–22
    reversals in, 130–31
    setting for, 127
    spatial relations in, 127
    various interpretations of, 123–24
woman who had been hemorrhaging, 143
woman who had had seven husbands, story of
    context of, 106–9, 112
    as enacted parable, 106–17
    feminist interpretations of, 101–6
    Jesus' response to, 110–16
    in Luke, 99
    Sadducees in, 98–101, 107, 109–10, 113
    various interpretations of, 100–101
    woman as prophet in, 116–17
women (nonspecific)
    abuse of, 133
    ambivalence toward, 103–4
    communication styles of, 38
    as equal to men, 101–2, 116
    monarchy and, 53–54
    in Near East in 1st century CE, 108–9, 111–12
    as prominent over men, 102–3
    scriptural visibility of, 36–37
    silencing of, 104–6, 122, 125
    stereotypes about, 89–90, 96–97

Name/Subject Index

wailing, 69–70
See also specific women
word of God, 28–29

Z

Zabad, 36
Zechariah, prophet, 2, 11
Zephaniah, prophet, 2, 43

Scripture Index

OLD TESTAMENT

Genesis

1:26–27	112
2:24	30
12:3b	150
12:10–20	49
16:1–2	61n20
16:2, 5, 6	68
16:7	68
16:10	67, 68
16:11–12	68
17:5, 15	49
17:16	49
17:25	67
18:1–15	68
19:8	57
19:30–38	xii
19:33–35	63
19:34	57
20:1–18	49
21:13	68
21:15–16	68
21:19	68
22:9–10	68
22:11–14	68
27	58
30:4	61n20
30:9	61n20
30:15–16	63
32:22–32	68
32:24–30	153
38	58
38:7, 10	61
38:8–10	60
38:9a	61
38:12–26	60

Exodus

1:15–20	64
2:1–10	46–48
3:6	115
3:13–15	49, 115
7:19	121
15:20–21	36, 46–48
20:1–17	87
20:2	6
20:3–11	6
20:12–18	6
22:21–24	45
22:22–24	75
23:1b	128
23:7	128
23:9	6
23:10–12	6
31:18	129

Leviticus

18	63
18:16	59
19:9–10	75
20:21	59
23:22	75

Scripture Index

Numbers
12:1–16	46–48
20:1–13	46–48

Deuteronomy
5:33	41
7:1–4	147
14:28–29	75
18:9–14	9
18:15	121
19:15–21	130
22:22	127
22:23–24	127
22:25–27	128
23:3–6	66
24:1–4	60
24:19–21	75
25:5–10	59
25:5	111
25:6	60
25:7–10	60
27:20	63
29:29	63

Joshua
2:1–7	57

Judges | xi, 50
4	13
4:4–23	45–46
4:5a	46
4:6–7	37, 46
4:17–22	57
5:7	46
17:10	46
18:19	46
21:25	50

Ruth | xi, 50
1:1	50
2:3	75
2:8–9	109
3	63
3:1–15	60
3:7b	63
3:8	63
4:7	60

1 Samuel | 50
1:1–2:21	50–51
1:1–2	61n21
1:9–18	153
2:10b	51
5:11	31
7:15–17	46
9:1–10	13
9:9	9
9:19	9
19:18–24	13
24:3	63
25:1	51
25:3	51
25:3–42	51–52
25:14–17	51
25:17, 36	51
25:18–19	51
25:28	52
25:30	52
25:36	51

2 Samuel
7:1–17	52
12:1–15	20
12:1–6	30–31
12:4–14	5
14	20
24:11	9

1 Kings
1:5–31	5
1:34	13
14:1–18	13
17:8–24	13
17:8–16	139
17:16	73
18:19	2
19:4	68
19:6	68
20:35–43	20
22:6	2

Scripture Index

2 Kings

2:3, 5, 7	2
8:13	151
22:10	43
22:13a	43
22:14–20	43
22:15–20	37
22:15	43
25:21	63

1 Chronicles

25:1–3	13
25:5	9

2 Chronicles

9:29	9
13:22	13
24:26	36
28:9–15	13
34:22–28	43

Ezra

9–10	44–45

Nehemiah

6:10–13	44
6:14	44, 45
13:3	45

Tobit 151

Judith xi, 65–66

1	65
2–3	65
2:6	65
3:5–9	65
3:8	66
4:2	65
4:8–15	65
5	65
6	65
7	65
8–10	66
11–13	66
14–16	66
14:10	66

Esther xi, 52–53

4:11	53
4:14	53
4:16	53
8:11–13	53

Job

19:21	31
30:1	151
40	66

Psalms

59:10–12	21
68	36
68:11	36
91:16	41
111:10a	87

Proverbs

3:27–31	87
16:31	41
29:9	129
31:10–31	51, 109

Song of Songs 81

Wisdom

27–28	87

Sirach

1:11–12	87

Isaiah xii

2:2–4	22
5:1–7	20
5:1–6	24
6:8	7–8
8:1–4	42
8:3	2
20:3	1, 24
30:9–10	9

Scripture Index

Isaiah (*continued*)
40:5	63
42:1b	149
49:6	150
53:1	63
56:10	151

Jeremiah
1:1	13
1:8	8
4:3	7
5:29	8
9:1–16	69
9:17–20	69
9:17	70
13:1–11	24, 27, 30
15:17–18	31
17:13	128
24:3	31, 71
35	28
38:4–6	5
42:4	13
52:27	63
Baruch	2n2

Ezekiel
4:1–17	24
4:1–8	1
4:1–3	24
4:4–8	29–30
8:1	31
15:25	63
22:26	5
24:3–5	24
24:18	42
32:1	69
32:16	69

Daniel
7:1–8	31, 72
7:14	36

Joel
2:28a	101–2

Amos
4:1	5
7:8	31, 71
7:14	13, 37

Micah
1:1	37
4:1–2	22
6:4	47

Zechariah
4:2	31, 71
5:2	31, 71
8:20–23	22
11:3–19	24

NEW TESTAMENT

Matthew
	xii
2:11	142
3:4	2
6:30	139
8:2	142
8:5–13	150
8:11	150
8:17	3
8:26	139
8:28–34	150
9:2–8	132
9:14–17	28
9:20–22	85
11:9–11	2
11:19b	87
13:10–17	26
13:31–32	22
13:34	18
14:13–21	145
14:20	21
14:22–33	146
14:31	139
14:34–36	146
15:1–20	146

15:1–6	146	9:33–37	29, 72
15:10–11	142	11:15–17	32
15:21–29	136–37	12:13–17	106
15:21–28	146	12:24	110
15:23	139	12:37	18
15:25	142	12:41–44	72
15:28	139	12:42	72
15:29–31	146	14:3–8	79
15:32–39	147	14:49	3
15:37	21	15:24	140
16:1–12	147		
16:8	139	**Luke**	
17:20	139	1	105
18:1–5	29, 72	1:5	106
22:15–22	106	1:8–20	102
22:20	110	1:26–38	102
22:25a	108	2	105
23:29–36	40	2:1, 3	106
24:38–44	32	2:2	106
26:6–12	79	2:25–32	102
28:9	142	2:36–38	41–42, 102
		2:38	41
Mark		3:1	106
1:15	113	4:18–19	150
1:21–28	153	4:18–19a	114
2:1–12	132	4:21	3
4:3–9	21	4:21b	114
5:1–13	150	5:1–11	29
5:22–24a	143	5:8	89
5:25–34	143	5:17–26	132
6:30–44	145	5:27–32	82
6:45–52	146	5:29–31	88
6:53–56	146	6:1–5	28
7:1–23	146	7:28–35	97
7:5–13	28	7:31–35	86–87
7:6–16	32	7:35	87
7:10–13	146	7:36–50	79, 80–81, 102, 104
7:18–19	142	7:39	40, 79, 92
7:24–31	136–37	7:41–43	96
7:24–30	51, 146	7:44	91, 96
7:30	153	7:47	92
7:31–37	146	7:50	92
8:1–10	147	7:50b	93
8:11–21	147	8:1–3	105
8:22–26	153	9:46–48	29, 72
9:14–29	153	10:25–28	99

Scripture Index

Luke (continued)

10:38–42	102, 104
13:29	21
14:12–14	88
15:11–32	92
16:1–13	57
16:19–31	157
18:1–8	104
19:1–10	88
20:1–8	112
20:7	112
20:20–27	106
20:20–26	112
20:25	108
20:27–44	99
20:28–31	111
20:35	113
20:36	113
20:39–40	110
20:41–44	115
20:45–21:6	74
20:45–47	102
21:1–4	72, 102
21:2	72
21:38	119
23:41–42	84
24:1–10	102
24:8	105
24:11	102

John

2:11, 23	133
4:54	133
5:1–18	132
5:14	121
5:14b	132
5:39–47	129
6:14	133
7	119–20, 121
7:16	8
7:36	119
7:44	119
7:45–52	126
7:52	121
7:53–8:11	123
8	121
8:3	119, 127
8:4	119
8:5	127
8:7, 59	121
8:11	121, 132
8:12–20	126
8:15	119–20
8:23–29	129
8:28	8
10:10	114, 159
10:16	150
12:1–8	79
12:1–5	80
12:37	133
12:38	3
12:49	8
13:1–17	82
14:10	8
20:30	133
20:31	121, 133, 159
21:25	119

Acts of the Apostles

6:1–6	102
6:1	109
11:27–28	40
13:1–3	40
13:1	2–3
15:32	40
18:24–26	102, 105
21:7–14	41
21:9	2–3, 40
21:10–11	40

Romans

3:2	76, 110
8:31–39	89
11:1–16	150

1 Corinthians

10:21	139
12:4–11	3
12:28	39

Scripture Index

Ephesians

2:19–22	40
3:5–6	40
4:11	39

James

3:17	87

Revelation

4:5	31, 72
9:3–11	31, 72
17:1–6	31

*Before You Were Born,
I Anointed You*